ROUTLEDGE LIBRARY EDITIONS:
ADULT EDUCATION

Volume 7

GRASSROOTS APPROACHES TO
COMBATTING POVERTY THROUGH
ADULT EDUCATION

GRASSROOTS APPROACHES TO COMBATTING POVERTY THROUGH ADULT EDUCATION

Supplement to Adult Education and Development No. 34/1990

Edited by
CHRIS DUKE

LONDON AND NEW YORK

First published 1990 by Deutscher Volkshochschul-Verband

2 Park Square, Milton Park, Abingdon, Oxfordshire OX14 4RN
52 Vanderbilt Avenue, New York, NY 10017

Routledge is an imprint of the Taylor & Francis Group, an informa business

First issued in paperback 2018

Copyright © 1990 Deutscher Volkshochschul-Verband www.dvv-international.de

All rights reserved. No part of this book may be reprinted or reproduced or utilised in any form or by any electronic, mechanical, or other means, now known or hereafter invented, including photocopying and recording, or in any information storage or retrieval system, without permission in writing from the publishers.

Notice:
Product or corporate names may be trademarks or registered trademarks, and are used only for identification and explanation without intent to infringe.

British Library Cataloguing in Publication Data
A catalogue record for this book is available from the British Library

ISBN: 978-1-138-32224-0 (Set)
ISBN: 978-1-138-34956-8 (Volume 7) (hbk)
ISBN: 978-1-138-36094-5 (Volume 7) (pbk)

Publisher's Note
The publisher has gone to great lengths to ensure the quality of this reprint but points out that some imperfections in the original copies may be apparent.

Disclaimer
The publisher has made every effort to trace copyright holders and would welcome correspondence from those they have been unable to trace.

Foreword

This is the first supplement to be published in conjunction with our journal ADULT EDUCATION AND DEVELOPMENT. It has always been a special feature to go beyond the regular publishing of a given set of themes and pages, adapting instead to changes in the needs of our readers and responding to their challenges.

We started off by incorporating all three languages, English, French and Spanish in one compendium. Since 1978 we have had three separate volumes. In 1982 we published a special edition which was dedicated to the late director of the German Adult Education Assocation, Helmuth Dolff, in recognition of his 25 years of devoted service to both German and international adult education; 50 adult educators from all over the world contributed. Issue No. 30 included, as an editorial review, selected reprints of the first 15 years of ADULT EDUCATION AND DEVELOPMENT. In 1988, well in advance of preparation for International Literacy Year, we published a special issue related to orality and literacy; more than 15,000 copies were distributed and requests are still coming in. The occasion of the Fourth World Assembly on adult education inspired us to focus the latest issue on adult education in Thailand.

Now we are publishing our first supplement. There are many good reasons for doing so, but two at least should be mentioned here: There seems to be a decline in the number of adult education monographs and books related to the development of adult education in Africa, Asia and Latin America being published by international publishers as well as by most of the countries in the region. On the other hand there seems to be an increase in important materials and manuscripts which are worth publishing but which do not seem to have a market from a commercial perspective. Terms of trade, adjustment policies, availability of foreign exchange etc. seem to have a direct impact on those adult educators who are in great need of relevant materials and who would be ready to pay for them, if their financial situation would allow them to do so. However, the trend is adverse if books cost a day's, week's or even a month's salary for adult educators working in Africa, Asia and Latin America.

This therefore is a start on a trial basis. We are publishing one of those interesting manuscripts received in the past, which is too voluminous for our regular journal and too important to not be widely circulated and read within the adult education movement. We are greatful to Chris Duke and his fellow researchers for allowing us to use this channel for communicating their findings on local and grass-roots adult education.

We have chosen a modest way of production and taken great care with respect to the distribution of the more than 10,000 copies. It is being sent out as a supplement to all the regular recipients of the English version of ADULT EDUCATION AND

DEVELOPMENT No. 34. The French and Spanish editorials carry a note on the availability of additional copies for those conversant language-wise.

At present we do not know how often we are going to publish supplements. It will depend on the feed-back, the availability of relevant manuscripts and the necessary funding. However, we shall try to continue this service to our readers and the adult education community at large, and try to be flexible and supportive even when times are not becoming easier.

Heribert Hinzen

CONTENTS

Preface 7

Chapter One

GLOBAL THINKING — LOCAL ACTION

Internationalism in Adult Education 9
Adult Education at the End of the Eighties 11
»National Development Strategies«: a Brief Review 16
Grassroots Approaches in the South 19
Notes and References 21

Chapter Two

WHITE HEALTH FOR BLACK AUSTRALIANS — A CAUTIONARY TALE

Introduction 23

Summary 24

Sandra Stacy

The General Context 25
The Institutional and Organisational Context 26
The Health Education Programme 27
Changing Objectives 33
Trying to Relate 34
Issues and Tensions 35
Evaluation and Appraisal 38
References 41
Appendix
Institute for Aboriginal Development: Basic Assumptions...
September 1972 41

Chapter Three

WOMEN WORKING TOGETHER — LEARNER-DETERMINED PRIORITIES IN THE TOTOTO-KILEMBA PROGRAMME

Introduction 43

3

Summary 44

Noreen M. Clark

Programme Content, Objectives and Learning Approach 45
Distinctive Features of the Approach 47
Evaluation and Appraisal 49
Issues and Analysis 54
Conclusions and Implications —
Why Are There So Few Programmes Like Tototo-Kilemba? 59

Chapter Four

DEVELOPING WOMEN'S INCOME-GENERATING SKILLS IN SWAZILAND

Introduction 62

Summary 63

Simanga Nxumalo

The General Context 65
Aims and Objectives 67
Programme Content and Other Features of the Project 70
Analysis of Achievements 75
Conclusions and Implications 79
Sources 82

Chapter Five

**ORGANISING WOMEN FOR ACTION —
SELF-EMPLOYED WOMEN'S ASSOCIATION (SEWA)**

Introduction 83

Summary 85

Anita Dighe

India's Self-Employed Women Workers 85
The Origins of SEWA 86
SEWA's Aims and Objectives 88
Major Areas of Activity 89
Some Distinctive Features of SEWA 100

Some Key Issues 102
Costs and Cost Effectiveness 105
Evaluation and Appraisal 105
Possibilities for Replication 110
References 111

Chapter Six

LEARNING AND ACTION IN RAJASTHAN —
THE WORK OF SEVA MANDIR

Introduction 113

Summary 114

Om and Ginny Shrivastava

Seva Mandir: Philosophy and Evolution 115
Features of the Project 120
Cost Effectiveness 125
Issues for Consideration 126
Evaluation and Appraisal 129
Conclusions and Implications 131
References 133
Appendix 1
Seva Mandir — Basic Data 133
Appendix 2
Women's Development in Chhani Village, by Rajkumari 135

Chapter Seven

FROM HEALTH CARE TO COMMUNITY DEVELOPMENT:
BROADENING THE BASE OF GONOSHASTHAYA KENDRA

Introduction 139

Summary 140

Rezaul Haque

The Origins of Gonoshasthaya Kendra (GK) 141
Structure and Functioning 143
General Staffing Policy 145
Training Programmes and Other Activities 145

Some Distinctive Features of Gonoshasthaya Kendra 155
Issues and Implications 158
The Achievements of Gonshasthaya Kendra 162
General Conclusions 166
Notes 168

Chapter Eight

ORGANISING AGRICULTURAL LABOURERS IN SOUTHERN INDIA: ASSOCIATION FOR THE RURAL POOR

Introduction 169

Summary 170

Felix N. Sugirtharaj

The Diversity of Micro-Projects 171
Problems of Organisation for Development from Below 172
Situation in the Project Area 174
The Project of the Association for the Rural Poor 176
Faith and Ideology: Values and Objectives 177
Politicisation: Strategies and Objectives 180
Results 186
Conclusion 193
Appendix
Agricultural Labourers Union — Tamilnadu: Demands 194

Chapter Nine

GRASSROOT CHANGES — AND SOME IMPLICATIONS

What Was Achieved? 196
By What Means? 203
Some Recurring Issues 208
What Are The Implications 212

Preface

The seven stories in this book are selected from about thirty studies, drafted in different parts of the world, of the relationship between adult education and development. All had a particular focus on the reduction of poverty. They were originally commissioned by the International Council for Adult Education (ICAE). The World Bank (IBRD) provided modest financial assistance. Field workers in different countries collected data in the early eighties according to a schedule prescribed by the coordinator, editor of this volume. This followed a process of inquiry and consultation with the widening network of those involved in this internationally arranged »commission of inquiry«.

An earlier set of seven studies was published by Croom Helm in 1985 under the title *Combatting Poverty Through Adult Education: National Development Strategies*. Those studies were all of relatively large-scale, national or regional adult education programmes. Six of the seven were led or controlled by governments of varying political persuasion, ranging from the uncompromisingly right-wing authoritarian through social democratic to Marxist-revolutionary. The final study was different. Although the project was also large-scale, and national in character, it was of a voluntary and non-governmental **movement**: the Sarvodaya Shramadana Movement in Sri Lanka.

Those involved in the ICAE project on adult education, development and the reduction of poverty took the separate studies to different stages of writing up. Each went some way beyond basic data collection. The original schedule for collecting data and drafting accounts was as follows:

- the general context of the adult education project
- the agency and the project aims and objectives
- costs and cost effectiveness
- distinctive features and methods
- issues and analysis (with suggested topics to consider)
- evaluation and appraisal (as adult education, and with respect to the reduction of poverty)
- conclusions and implications, including possibilities for replication elsewhere.

When these drafts had been prepared there followed a series of exchanges between field authors and coordinator/editor. Further data were collected. Wherever possible, the context and meaning was further elaborated and interpretation clarified. In some instances comment and advice from the World Bank, as a contracting party, was taken into consideration in revising early drafts. The published volume of studies of large-scale adult education projects used the basic framework of inquiry, while varying it to fit the unique circumstances of each study. It is of the nature of the »micro-studies« of the local-level voluntary efforts presented in this second volume that the initial common framework proved often to be too limiting. It was not entirely appropriate to the different circumstances of and the particular values informing the work of different groups and individuals. The discerning reader may still recognise the common framework underlying the generation of these accounts, but they display considerable diversity of final form. The names of the original field-worker authors remain with the different studies. Most have however been substantially rewritten. For this revision and final presentation the editor carries complete responsibility.

This book refers to and was developed as a companion volume to *National Development Strategies*. However, it is written and may be read as a free-standing volume. It adopts the slightly different perspective which a view from 1988, rather than from the beginning of this decade, allows and indeed compels.

Chapter One

Global Thinking — Local Action

Internationalism in Adult Education

Adult education, like so many other human activities, has witnessed a sharp increase in international discourse and international influences through the second half of the twentieth century. There is nothing remarkable about this. Much the same is true for instance of football, of drug-dealing, and of academic conferring, as also of political and financial transactions. What makes internationalism interesting, and important, in adult education, is its potential both for strengthening and for damaging local grassroots action. Good adult education tends to be very peculiar to its local environment, very context-specific. Internationalism, in the form of cultural or economic imperialism, and insensitive importation of alien models and methods, is likely to harm this work.

On the other hand, since adult education is so context-specific, so dependent on the various political and economic as well as social and cultural factors which are influenced, and maybe transformed, by international forces, it may gain in relevant knowledge, strength and energy from international linkages. This can be especially true where adult education is committed to social change and seeks to confront resistant public or private interests. Such is a common experience among nongovernmental workers in the South, in projects like those described in this book. It is by no means unknown, either, in the more comfy and affluent West. It is also likely to become commoner if adult educators in the West, or North, seek to sustain and recreate the social purpose which gave their work the status of a »movement« until recent times[1].

International comparative **study** in adult education has increased in the late twentieth century, as the growth of published materials bears witness[2]. International **action**, in the form of collaboration through exchanges, joint projects, planning and celebration alike, has also increased. From the modest First International Conference of Unesco in Elsinore, Denmark, in 1949, that Organisation came to host over eight hundred participants at the fourth such event in its own Paris headquarters in 1985. Meanwhile, as befits its status as the leading international nongovernmental organisation, the International Council for Adult Education (ICAE) has arranged a series of slightly smaller, but more convivial and much more rhetorically radical, international gatherings. Beginning, also fittingly, in Nyerere's Tanzania in 1976 where South African apartheid was strongly denounced, these migrated first to the headquarters of intergovernmental internationalism in adult education, Unesco, Paris, in 1982, to be inspired by the socialist Mitterand, and then on, now in the clothing of a World Assembly, to post-Galtieri Argentina in 1985, where the struggle of popular education against right-wing regimes in Latin America was feted and the Nicaraguan delegation cheered and sung to the echo.

Unesco's resources have been emasculated following its supposed politicisation against the interests of the West, and the withdrawal from membership of the United States and Britain by their conservative administrations. It has none the less continued to promote international comparative study, for instance through a meeting on »studies in common«, or conjoint study, midway through 1988[3]. This sought to foster new and more systematic joint study between adult educators in a number of agreed and practical priority areas. Meanwhile the international non-governmental sector has seen the formation, earlier this decade, of an International League for Social Commitment in Adult Education (ILSCAE), and more recently still of an International Institute for Policy, Research and Development in Adult Education (IIPRDAE). This, if less explicit about its values, none the less strongly shares the commitment which the League makes explicit, and which runs as a theme through the literature and work of the ICAE.

This book makes one further contribution to »socially purposive« or »committed« international comparative study in adult education. By contrast with its earlier companion volume on National Development Strategies, and echoing the distinction between Unesco and ICAE, its contents are essentially nongovernmental rather than to do with the programmes and resources of governments. Those whose stories are told here can however no more ignore the power and will of governments than can an international body like ICAE if it is to achieve the results it looks for. Nor can adult educators in general. One theme of this volume, therefore, is the modes of operation, and cooperation, which voluntary grassroots movements employ in their dealings with governments. Who sups with whom how often, and with how long a spoon? The issue, salient for ICAE working with governments and with IGOs like Unesco, precisely reappears at the most local level of these micro-studies, as does the fact and factor of internationalism itself.

Six of the seven accounts which follow are from Africa and South Asia: what is commonly called the underdeveloped or developing but now perhaps more frequently the Third World. The seventh account, first in published order, is from the »third world within the first world«. It tells the depressing story of the failure of a health education programme for a community of black Australians. »Underdeveloped«, and even the more hopeful »developing country«, has fallen into disfavour because of the implication that there is a natural and necessary path of progress from the lot of the impoverished Third World to the full or fuller development of the industrialised nations. The latter in turn have come to be described, with pointed irony, as over-developed, making the point that there is no attractive model or happy resting place to which poor nations can look and aspire.

A Note on Terms

»Third World« served for a while as convenient shorthand. In intent it contrasts the poor, relatively unindustrialised, countries with the richer, mixed economy and socialist, generally industrialised, blocs which dominate the world economically, militarily and therefore also politically. This collective term for the nations of Africa, Asia, the Caribbean, Latin America and the South Pacific, has in turn been criticised for its misleading connotations. It is misleading in respect of large and powerful, sometimes heavily industrialised, nations like Brazil, India and Nigeria, which yet indisputably suffer that syndrome of disadvantages to do with poverty, deprivation, disease, etc. which »Third World« connotes. It fails to discriminate between countries in these major regions, although aggregations like »Fourth World« and »NICs« (newly industrialised countries) seek to make such distinctions. Perhaps the simplest and strongest ground for objection is akin to that for extirpating sexist and racist terms and speech-forms: that it induces superior, and possibly also determinist, attitudes and thought patterns, which militate against genuine internationalism and beneficial change alike.

Recently, especially perhaps following the dissemination of the Brandt report[4], »the South« has acquired wider currency to refer to the poor countries and regions in question. This is alternatively contrasted with »the North«, meaning the older industrialised world, or »the West«, to refer more specifically to those countries and traditions from within which this book is composed. This is a something of an affront to geography, since Australia, the Southland, is for this purpose a part of the North and the West. In this book, none the less, the South and the West are used henceforth as shorthand, it being understood that each of the studies presented here is drawn from the South with the exception of the Aboriginal Australian. The concluding chapter, like this introduction, is however indirectly an eighth case study — of adult education and development in one post- industrial society of the West and North, Britain. This too is thus a contribution to South-North internationalism in adult education.

Adult Education at the End of the Eighties

»The Challenges of the 1990s«

Leirman and Kulich's *Adult Education and the Challenges of the 1990s*, published by Croom Helm in 1987, exemplifies the world view of socially committed adult education. Similar views, and a similar sense of priorities and urgency, inform the activities for instance of ICAE and of the International League for Social Commitment in Adult Education, referred to above. The 1986 international conference which produced this Croom Helm volume defined the challenges, in its title, as Peace, Development, Employment, Environment, and Technology. Leirman's opening chapter contrasts the »golden sixties« with the »iron eighties«. He writes of the »political and economic shockwaves of the late sixties and the early seventies« (p.7), and refers to the Club of Rome's *The Limits to Growth*, published in 1972. The 1980s are characterised by »multiple crisis, new social movements and the debate over alternatives« (p.11). Leirman asks »how the world and its several regions are to reach the goal of human and ecological equilibrium?«, and notes, following Gurr

(1985), that China has achieved a commitment to material equality and frugality, based on national planning and strong political control (pp.15- 16). The specific challenges addressed by different contributors to the volume consider problems implied in the conference title: global economic interdependence; labour and employment questions; the relations between the environment, the welfare of society and the economy; crises threatening the ecosystem; the absence of peace and the threats of war and violence; the need for intercultural understanding, or multiculturalism; and the issues of development and North-South relations highlighted earlier with the publication of the Brandt report, *North-South: a Programme for Survival*, in 1980.

Other sources of commentary and analysis present slightly different emphases, but the ingredients in the mixture comprising the »world problematique« are much the same. Interpretation varies too along a simple optimist-pessimist continuum. The role and impact of modern technology, especially communications technology, in particular tends to divide bullish modernists from doubters who may appear, or be labelled, Luddite. The debate about the implications of new technology for future employment levels well illustrates the rather crude polarisation between »optimists« and »pessimists« into which debate about the future can degenerate.

For those in adult education there is, and no doubt always will be, another continuum, or perhaps more commonly another dichotomy. This is between those for whom their work and its priorities derive from some perception and analysis of the state of society, its major needs and concerns, and those who find, and seek, no direct and practical connection. We might call this the difference between the political and the apolitical, although the former does not necessarily take the form of political party affiliation and conventional political action. Being in this sense political does not necessarily preclude »professional- technical« work in adult education. Boshier's 1980 *Towards a Learning Society* for instance, from the pen of a leading participation research empiricist, concluded with an analysis of the nature of post-industrial society which considers precisely the global and broadly ecological issues alluded to above, and relates these to future purposes of adult education. Boshier suggests a probable shift from the »radical learner-centredness« characterising contemporary adult education, a »luxury of affluence«, towards the social purposes of adult education, »the needs of collectivities« (pp.218-219). We return later to the question of »learner-centredness«, the luxury of individualism. It will however quickly be clear to the reader of this volume that, while learner-centredness may be a common methodological concern, parading usually under the banner of participation, it is social, or collective, priorities which inform the purposes of those whose work is described here.

From a British Perspective

Boshier's 1980 study concludes with several scenarios for the future. The last of these, dated 1990, is essentially optimistic at least in the professional sense: the

Vice-Chancellor of Sydney University is a former Director of Continuing Education! In the main, British adult education perhaps displays more pessimism than hope. If so, the reason may lie in the particular combination of contemporary British public affairs and the distinctive features of the British tradition of adult education which are peculiarly ill-attuned to the »iron eighties«. The prevailing political theory is that of the »New Right«. It is firmly entrenched in office, and there appears to be no prospect of a credible Opposition taking political power in the foreseeable future. British economic recovery and enhanced economic competitiveness in the international arena are the main policy priorities. They are sought by means of policies designed to relocate ownership and initiative in the private sector. Strong central leadership and interference notwithstanding, this implies dismantling much of the apparatus of State for managing the economy and the welfare of society, and specifically of the arrangements for the collectivity known as the Welfare State. The keywords are privatisation and enterprise.

The ecologically and socially concerned in Britain, those who belong broadly to the liberal tradition, perceive the emergence through the eighties of a selfish, uncaring, and increasingly unequal society. The yuppie is a symbol of the decade. Europe's largest multicultural event, the Notting Hill Carnival in London, is meeting embourgeoisement. Placards protest the arrival of the yuppies in Notting Hill. Privatised prosperity threatens the conviviality of the carnival. More generally, »self-help« and »community care« are seen as reducing public caring for the needy under a guise of restoring sturdy self-reliance. Britain's reluctance to impose controls on industry, and on automobiles, to protect the environment, is a source of embarrassment in the context of European Community cooperation. Job creation and training schemes are perceived cynically and with distrust, in a context of widening disparities in incomes and in wealth. A new social phenomenon is being named the underclass, those who do not participate in the rising prosperity of the home- and share-owning classes.

Britain may manifest the swing to the Right in politics more markedly than other countries in the West because it has had to make the most traumatic adjustments towards accepting its new post-colonial and post-industrial status. Its international (and British Commonwealth) identity, apropos aid and development in the South, and apartheid in South Africa, is no less embarrassing to those of liberal persuasion than is its record in environmental issues, and increasingly perhaps now in social matters such as labour law, within the European community. The Prime Minister's response has been to look to private charity as the responsible means to help the needy — a combination of public irresponsibility and an appeal to paternalism which leaves her critics speechless. Along with this goes an assertion of what among development economists has been called »trickle down theory«. The argument is that until the nation is economically strong and prosperous it cannot afford to alleviate the misery of the poor. Redistribution implies a general economic deterioration, so that all become progressively poorer. In a strong and wealthy nation the poorer too will eventually gain.

Neither charity nor trickle-down have worked generally in the poor countries of the world, and British liberals look in vain for evidence that they work for the poor of Britain. Rather they see an increasingly divided society: between the employed and the unemployed; between the inner cities and the suburbs and shires; between the North and the South within Britain and abroad. The exercise of the power of the State, even while its machinery and functions are being reduced, appears quite overtly to be in the interests of those who are prospering from its policies. The poll tax, the sale of council houses, changes wrought by the 1988 Education Act, as well as confrontation with the unions and the use of the police and other more direct expressions of power: each of these points to the intransigence of power, and the crucial importance of political will. Forty years on from the creation of the Welfare State, twenty years on from the optimistic and hedonistic sixties, Leirman's »iron eighties« are more familiar to British liberals even than to their counterparts elsewhere in the West. In the South fortunes have varied from country to country, but for the poor majority the sixties as a decade would have seemed none too golden and the eighties not perhaps obviously worse.

Charity and trickle-down look as shallow a delusion in the West as in the South. Political will, the power of the State, the alliance of dominant interest groups with this power: these are the more overt realities in Britain now, as they have been obvious in the South throughout these post-War years. The British post-War political consensus, it is often asserted, is now dead.

The Liberal Dilemma and Crisis

These global issues and problems, and their sharp and particular manifestation in Britain, pose a problem for the liberal tradition. At one level this is manifested in the disappearance of a distinct Liberal Party itself. At another it appears as the choice facing every group of social activists, whether for the Republican cause in Northern Ireland; for the protection of air, water and land from the pollutants of industry; for a land free of nuclear weapons; or for the rights and opportunities of blacks in the inner cities. In the liberal tradition the only cause over which adult educators may legitimately take to the streets and protest is the cause of adult education itself — for education as a good, or an end, in itself. Adult educators as citizens may join Greenpeace, camp at Greenham Common, protest with the blacks of Brixton, even perhaps support the IRA. According to the tenets of the liberal tradition, however, adult education must not subserve other ends: it implies »free, open-ended and critical analysis, observing the most rigorous methodological and democratic practices, with the aim of enabling adult students to find their own way to their own conclusions'«[5].

The comparative study of university adult education in England and the USA by Taylor et.al. which this passage introduces is but one example of the way socially committed adult educators in the West have sought to rescue and redefine a socially purposive liberal tradition. At the beginning of the decade Jane Thompson's edited volume *Adult Education for a Change* included several direct assaults on individualism, and imputed unwitting conservatism, which this tradition represented. Three years later the University of Leeds put together Crombie's and Harries-Jenkins' two essays on the future of British university adult education under the title *The Demise of the Liberal Tradition*, following it in 1988 with McIlroy and Spencer's *University Adult Education in Crisis*.

It is unsurprising that much of this analysis of the crisis of liberal adult education emanates from and concentrates upon universities. Traditionally opportunities and responsibility for reflective analysis have resided here. University adult educators have tended to articulate and speak for a broader adult education movement, even while the majority of workers in the field may always have been busy and unreflecting practitioners. The problem is that with this has gone a preoccupation with the forms of provision within a small and rather isolated pocket of university work, and also of adult education work. Discussion has been about the length of courses, the mix of subjects, and the social intake to programmes, with little reference to the national and global events which led Leirman to write of the »iron eighties«. Writers in the very special environments of extramural departments have thus tended in their professional adult educator lives to exclude from discussion both the crises confronting humankind, the predicament of the universities themselves, and the changes affecting the larger mass of adult education that takes place in other institutions and under other auspices.

Nor is the problem easily resolved by a broadening of perspective, whereby those in the scholarly and liberal tradition turn more attention, say, to the efforts of their colleagues in community and further education. The post-War liberal and social democratic consensus is clearly at an end. Commitment in the spirit of Voltaire to respecting all points of view may not in such circumstances be enough. At issue is not just more equitable access to the universities for working class students, for example, but the role of the universities themselves. The initiative of Government via what was the Manpower Services and then the Training Commission before its abolition, to inject »enterprise« into the curriculum of every student in higher education, illustrates this. If »enterprise« is an inadequate and misdirected programme for national well-being in a global village, then liberal adult education too is inadequate as a response. A natural response to such a diagnosis in Britain would be to recreate an adult education **movement** through explicit partnership with other social movements: movements perhaps of minority ethnic groups, of women, peace and ecological groups.

Such a move would be overtly partisan, although it might be partly masked by arguments about equity for economic efficiency: the waste of talent for economic growth that goes with under- educating women and blacks, for example. It would rapidly expose the special pleading which tends to characterise defence of the liberal tradition as socially committed, radical and purposeful, yet concerned only with open-ended critical inquiry.

The adult education projects described in this book display none of the hang-ups about extrinsic ends which have perplexed the intellectual tradition (rather than adult education work on the ground) in Britain. The stories which follow here are explicit about the values and purposes for which people work: the reduction of poverty, increase in economic independence and earning power, better health and lower infant mortality, reduced bullying and exploitation by landlords, moneylenders, police and bureaucrats.

In the South liberation appears as an alternative to liberalism. Liberation means mobilising people's wills, energies and purposes, often through a process combining direct material payoffs with conscientisation. Awareness is raised in a way which empowers the learner to challenge and sometimes redistribute power. Often the learner is a group or community rather than an individual. The stories in this book are introduced with reference to the British adult education tradition, in the belief that Britain, with its historic colonial ties with the countries concerned, has much to learn from the South as here represented. Insofar as the liberal tradition permeates adult education in other countries of the West the same will be true. This tradition has proved especially influential in British thought. The lessons from these local level, grassroots, »micro-projects« may none the less have meaning more generally in the West.

»National Development Strategies«: a Brief Review

The earlier companion volume to this book described six large-scale governmental programmes of adult education in the South, and the nongovernmental Sarvodaya Shramadana of Sri Lanka. Brazil's functional literacy programme, MOBRAL, succeeded in bringing literacy to many of the poorest in that country. It has since been disbanded, without regret on the part of those committed to social progress in Brazil, while the effects of uneven development, dispossession of land, harrassment, pauperisation and even murder continue to oppress the weak. The government programme in Kenya was also mainly concerned with literacy. Although it fell well short of its overall targets and timetable it was noticably successful in reaching women: so much so that this »lop-sided« development was seen as a problem! (Duke, 1985, p.65)

The saddest tale in that volume was of the Indian Adult Education Programme in Tamil Nadu. There a balanced programme of functional literacy intended also to create social awareness among the poor to help bring about social and cultural change came to be limited to literacy and functional skill acquisition. Conscientisation was quietly abandoned as too risky by officials away from the more committed, and possibly less vulnerable, federal centre. In Nicaragua, by contrast, political and popular will closely coincided in the triumphant days of Sandinista victory, and a centrally orchestrated but popularly driven Literacy Crusade was a remarkable success. Since the early eighties, however, the realities of power have continued to assert themselves. The socialist, complex and cumbersome Indian State has continued to peg away at adult education as one means to cultural, economic and social development. The Sandinista in Nicaragua have been bled, beleaguered, and partly diverted from social development ends by the geopolitical concerns of their powerful conservative neighbour to the North.

In Chile, the Educational Operative Units described by Gajardo which flourished under Allende, were virtually suppressed by Pinochet. Subsequently different manifestations of popular education there as elsewhere in South America have allowed the spirit of Freire to live on through new forms (the offspring sometimes disowning the father of conscientisation). In 1988 there appear to be signs of easing in a repressive regime which may allow a sceptical exiled opposition to strengthen the movement for social and political reform. Without a change of regime, however, State adult education is unlikely to be even the modest force for reform which it has been in India. In the Republic of Korea Saemaul Education provided a special case of controlled and quite authoritarian reform from above. National unity and anti-communism were wedded together with efforts to accelerate rural development and extend the »economic miracle« to the whole population. Possibly the tight control exercised by the South Korean Government effectively limited the reach of Saemaul Education. Certainly it did not »trickle down« to the most needy. Here as in the other non-revolutionary situations described, a large-scale government-led adult education programme was unable to effect significant change, which is inherently destabilising, although modest gains could be spread quite widely.

If wide reach but modest effect characterised most of the large-scale government-led programmes described in *National Development Strategies*, some other findings bear repeating as a prelude to the small-scale, non-governmental stories which follow. Several drew explicitly for strength or direction upon the internationalism of adult education described above, especially the lifelong learning concepts promoted inter alia by Unesco. The voluntary movement, Sarvodaya, in Sri Lanka, recovered from the crisis of terminated government support and came to rely instead on overseas funds. We will see the role of both international ideas and international aid in the lives of the small and vulnerable programmes described below — and the reservations at times expressed too about such reliance.

The spectrum of change from cautiously reformist to revolutionary-transformational is reflected among non-governmental programmes, but with the weight, predictably, towards the latter end. The large-scale studies imply some loss of energy and resources in bureaucratic systems, as well as very good value for money. The projects in this second volume are by their nature harder to cost accurately. They suggest even better value for money, especially because they mobilise so much unpaid and underpaid committed and volunteered effort. On the other hand the first volume makes clear that »government programmes and agencies of the right through to the far left are often able to mobilise quite massive community resources, especially the unpaid time and efforts of various kinds of volunteers«. (pp.222-223) Voluntary effort is by no means a monopoly of the non-governmental sector, although the quality of commitment and work may be generally superior.

Other themes from the first volume which recur here include the different strategies for training workers and extending the scope of provision. The Nicaraguan Crusade adopted a »cascade« approach. In this second volume induction into particular values, or selection of those with a shared commitment, features large in several stories. »Participation« is highly valued in many of the government programmes, albeit at times more honoured in the breach. Active participation, if only as a method to secure motivation and commitment, appears frequently too in this volume, but with the additional edge that most of the workers here looked for greater participation of the excluded poor in society generally. For this, participation in the class or learning group was a necessary, or essential, preparation. »Congruence« too, between precept and practice, is a common concern in several examples within each set of studies.

The earlier volume made reference to »a remaking of the middle classes«. It went on to suggest that »perception of and respect for indigenous knowledge appears a litmus test for the potency of adult education for development«.(p.230) In right-wing Korea, Marxist Nicaragua and Buddhist Sri Lanka alike there was displayed a concern and respect for indigenous skills and culture, and an awareness that the middle classes could learn from these, but stood in danger of destroying them, in their desire to help, introduce innovation, and improve living conditions from outside the local community. The paradox, inherent in the work of Paulo Freire, about middle class intervention as catalyst and change agent, is manifest in several of the studies in this volume. It is instructive to compare the ways this issue is recognised, addressed and handled, in the different local-level studies; and to compare these, also, with those examples in the first set of studies where the question is specifically addressed.

Different reviewers of *National Development Strategies* took up different aspects of that volume. Most naturally paid attention to the central themes of the relationship between adult education and poverty; and to the central conclusions about the limits to what adult education alone could achieve, the importance of the political and other context, and of political will, and the need to relate adult education to other development efforts and programmes rather than treat it in a sectoral manner.(6) One reviewer, writing in the South, called attention to the role of international links which could have been made more explicit in some of the accounts, especially the influence of international conferences. (Muchena, 1987, p.80). More generally, if less explicitly, the reviews look up the theme with which this introduction began: the role of internationalism, and the potential, or limitations, of transnational, especially South-North or North-South, learning.

Thus Alexander implies a lesson for adult education in the West in calling attention to »the importance of shared egalitarian values and purposes and the need for educators to engage in sound political and economic analysis rather than decline into timid addiction to fifth-rate and discredited 'behavioural objectives', 'basic needs' and neutral 'skills training' approaches« (Alexander, 1985, 348). Pearson, by contrast, writing in Australia in a comparative review of four books about adult education, found a preoccupation with concern with individuals versus the transformation of the whole society puzzling, since »these themes appear to address the concerns of western adult educators« rather than be of great moment to third world development. Calling for consideration of the issue of education and social control (an issue clearly addressed for example by Jane Thompson (ed.) in 1980 and again in her 1983 study), Pearson also cites Marriott's *Backstairs to a Degree* on the perpetuation of »disinterested« studies in the university extension movement, to this day — an aspect touched above in reference to the »liberal dilemma« (Pearson, 1987, pp.206-207). Margot Pearson's comments have considerable force in relation to what she calls third world development. In 1980 Boshier had referred to this individualism as a luxury of affluence which even the North might endure little longer; Fordham cites his Vice-Chancellor talking of »treats« for the already well educated (Fordham,198 , p.8).

However, internationalism is one theme of this book, as of reviews of its earlier companion. This being the case, and international influences being what they now are, we cannot put aside the collectivist-individualist tension as irrelevant, even to the South. Some support is provided to the view that the North, or West, can learn from such studies of the South (including confronting the tensions of liberalism and of highly valued individualism) by other reviews which turn to this question. Whitton, writing also in Australia but from an Ethnic Affairs perspective, finds lessons which are »valid anywhere in the world«, Third World but also for working class, non-English speaking background and Aboriginal Australians. The success stories narrated, he concludes »can teach us much about our own national priorities«. (Whitton, 1987, 49-50)

Finally, two British reviews coincide in their attention to one particular point of comparison, and of challenge for those working in the easier circumstances of countries like Britain. This concerns the attitude of adult educators to the power of the State, of those »who might prefer the purity and marginality of working 'outside the system' to the tensions and compromises which accompany working from within«. Fisher reflects on the various government-funded national initiatives over which British adult educators frequently agonise (such as taking money from the Manpower Services Commission). Fordham is clear: in the West we are too concerned with individual growth and individual interests to want to stress the collective and especially the broadly political aims of many of the world's adult education movements; »adult education in the West must now re-learn some of its social purposes from the South.« (Fordham, 1986, pp.21, 20)

Grassroots Approaches in the South

The accounts of adult education projects in Africa, Asia and Aboriginal Australia which follow have more than curiosity value, therefore, for adult educators in Britain and elsewhere in the West. Direct transplantation would be unlikely to work: from South to North any more than it has been successful with the introduction of exotica from North to South throughout the colonial and post-colonial periods. Even between economically and culturally similar societies, introducing models from other countries can be hazardous. On the other hand intelligent analysis, extrapolation and comparison can lead to healthy emulation on a selective, piecemeal, basis, and to less specific reorientation and reinvigoration of effort and sense of movement. Within the Asian region, for example, many of the exchanges among small groups of countries fostered by the Asian and Pacific Regional Office of Unesco in Bangkok have surely yielded specific, not always easily demonstrated, but valuable, results.

The seven studies are ordered approximately along a spectrum from the least to the most overtly political, and radical, in flavour and intent. All are local and small in scale, compared with the programmes described in the earlier volume. Although they range from the mainly technical to the transformational, they share to a surprising extent a common view of the world, of desirable values, and even of the role of adult education. All were drafted by active workers — participant researchers for the duration of this particular effort. The first tells a sad tale with considerable integrity. The second is much more cheerful, some might say almost too optimistic, while later accounts convey more or less forcefully the weight of oppression, the struggle for modest gains, the threat of harrassment if not of annihilation, which hang over activists working for real change through some form of adult education.

The Women's Network has been one of the most prominent and successful, and one of the most committed to change, of the ICAE's various networks and programme areas. The first four of these seven studies were prepared by women, and the fifth by a husband-wife team. Similarly, women feature almost exclusively as the intended learners in the first several studies and prominently too in the others. Women, it has been said, hold up more than half the sky. In the South they frequently carry a »double burden«: managing the household, including fetching and carrying water, firewood etc., often including growing crops or tending animals for partial self-sufficiency, with additional or sideline activities calculated to bring in a little cash income. In some cases the generation of cash income may enhance their standing and thereby reduce grotesque gender inequalities, as Haque for example makes explicit in the Bandladeshi study in chapter seven. The reader might ask, in particular, herself, at what price women must earn their status and relative independence in these circumstances — as indeed in the new era of »putting out« or home work which has spread, mainly among poor women, in the North.

After women, and obviously closely related, a second common theme through several studies is preventive health education. Three of the studies describe health education programmes as such, while health features among the »functional objectives« of others. Note however the non-exclusiveness that characterises these accounts. A clear and common theme is the inter- connectedness of life and learning, the artificiality of the divisions into which so frequently governmental programmes are segmented. Haque most explicitly tells how a focussed health programme spilled out into all areas of the life of poor villagers, but the same tendency may be discerned again and again. Literacy appears frequently as one item in the educative menu, but it does not tend to dominate as was the case with the larger-scale government programmes. Nor, with the exception of the Aboriginal story in chapter two, does lack of motivation appear as a major problem, although problems there certainly are — of resources, of staying power, sometimes of violent reaction to the threat of change on the part of powerful interests.

An intriguing and important common theme alluded to earlier is the place of middle class leadership; or, to put it a slightly different way, of non-indigenous leadership — the white nurse in Alice Springs from down south; the radical activist from Madras out in the border villages of Tamilnadu and Andra Pradesh; the educated doctor from Dhaka discomfited by the austerity and communality of Gonoshasthaya Kendra. They faced a common problem of learning to understand, live and work with the poor — learning how to empower them rather than further to disable them; how not to create merely temporary gain at the cost of a new, continuing, dependency. This led naturally into a common strategic consideration: how to replicate, or multiply, these intense, often highly successful, local efforts. Sugirtharaj pays particular attention to this in chapter eight. Stacy, by contrast, considers some of the problems of even a very small Institute become slightly larger. Here one can discern or deduce possible indirect, even national, gains from the experience, but in itself the project reached a dead end.

Finally, to state what is self-evident yet perhaps easily overlooked, none of these committed adult educators shows any sign of anguish about the proper means, ends or limits of education, about where »education« should end before »action« begins. Outcomes are suggested, and measured, long- and short-term, in less and more tangible areas. They are identified in terms of material gains as well as the probable delayed benefits of a more educated — that is to say confident, enabled, and activated — community. All whose work is described in this book however appear too busy to agonise over the liberal dilemma: a dilemma which in Britain has commonly resulted in paralysis.

Notes

1. See for instance Taylor et.al., 1985, on the United States and England.
2. See for example the *International Journal of Lifelong Education*, launched in 1982, and the Croom Helm Series in International Adult Education started in the mid-80s.
3. See the paper prepared by Duke on »Studies in Common« for the Unesco international meeting in Lille, June 1988.
4. Brandt Commission, 1980, *North-South: A Programme for Survival*.
5. From the introduction by Jo Campling to Taylor et.al., 1985.
6. Alexander, 1985, Christensen, 1986, Fisher, 1985, Fordham, 1986, Muchena, 1987, Pearson, 1987, Whitton, 1987.

References

Alexander, D.J., Review of *Combatting Poverty*, *Social Sciences*, 1985, 347-348.
Boshier, R., *Towards a Learning Society*, Learningpress, Vancouver, 1980.
Brandt Commission, *North-South: A Programme for Survival*, Pan, London, 1980.
Christensen, J.E., *Review of Combatting Poverty*, *Discourse*, 7,1, 1986 116-118.
Crombie, A.D. and Harries-Jenkins, G., *The Demise of the Liberal Tradition*, U. of Leeds DACE, 1983.
Duke, C. (ed), *Combatting Poverty Through Adult Education: National Development Strategies*, Croom Helm, 1985.
Duke, C., »Studies in Common by Member States on Particular Aspects of Adult Education«, Unesco, 1988. Revised for publication as »Research Studies in Common in Adult Education«.
Fisher, H., Review of *Combatting Poverty*, *Adult Education*, 58,3, 1985, 299-300.
Fordham, P., »West and South: the adult education dialogue«, *Adult Education*, 59,1, 1986, 6-11, 59,2, 1986, 98-104.
Fordham, P., Review of *Combatting Poverty*, *Studies in the Education of Adults*, 18, 1, 1986, 61-63.
Gurr, T.R., »On the political consequences of scarcity and economic decline«, *International Studies Quarterly*, 29, 51-75, 1985.
Leirman, W. and Kulich, J., (eds) *Adult Education and the Challenge of the 1990s*, Croom Helm, 1987.
McIlroy, J. and Spencer, B., *University Adult Education in Crisis*, U of Leeds DACE, 1988.
Marriott, S., *A Backstairs to a Degree*, U. of Leeds DACE, 1981.
Meadows, D.H. et.al., *The Limits to Growth: A Report for the Club of Rome's Project on the Predicament of Mankind*, Universe Books, New York, 1972.
Muchena, O.N., Review of *Combatting Poverty*, *J. of Social Development in Africa*, 2, 2, 1987, 79-80.
Pearson, M., »Adult Education — Another Field of Study of a Force for Change«, *Higher Education Research and Development*, 6, 2, 1987, 205-207.
Taylor, R., Rockhill, K. and Fieldhouse, R., *University Adult Education in England and the USA*, Croom Helm, 1985.
Thompson J. L. (ed.), *Adult Education for a Change*, Hutchinson, 1980.
Thompson J. L., *Learning for Liberation*, Croom Helm, 1983.
Whitton, R., Review of Combatting Poverty, *Australian J. of Adult Education*, 27, 2, 1987, 48-50.

Chapter Two

White Health for Black Australians — a Cautionary Tale

Introduction

Uniquely among the fourteen case studies in these two volumes, this one comes not from Africa, Asia or Latin America, the regions normally the focus of »development« studies, and known, controversially, as the »developing world«, the »Third World«, or »the South«. Instead it is from the »fourth World« within that wealthy southland, Australia. It concerns Aboriginal peoples, a few of the many indigenous groups in Australia as in other wealthy countries who, in their cultural deprivation as well as their socio-economic plight, may be judged even more alienated and dispossessed than the poor of the poorest nations. Not that cultural oppression and dispossession are a monopoly of industrialised nations; for there are few societies in which ethnic and cultural oppression, often of indigenous minorities, is absent.

Like other studies in this volume, this is a microcosm: a small, Church-backed, non-governmental organisation, and a programme touching barely 150 members of communities themselves a mere two thousand strong. It is however a microcosm rich in learning, a wry and regretful story but one as important as it may be bitterly unpalatable. Ironically it coincides closely with the initially optimistic, radical-egalitarian, »Whitlam years« in which a Labor Government committed to equity replaced a twenty- two year old conservative administration and addressed many social concerns, none more vigorously than the plight of the Aborigines. The case study makes passing reference to these changes, to the new policy commitment to self-determination and the attempt to turn white superintendents on Aboriginal reserves into community advisers. This apart the study is markedly apolitical, politically charged though Aboriginal affairs were at that time; Alice Springs, location of the study, was a main centre for the racist »rights for whites« backlash against the Aboriginal policies of the Whitlam Administration. The economic problems which have beset most countries since the mid-seventies have fed the backlash. If less dramatic, the charge of »throwing money at the problem« perpetuates a prejudicial and victim- blaming attitude towards Aborigines — a phrase, and an attitude, echoed for.instance in respect of Britain's deprived inner cities.

The study touches upon the almost inevitable »micro-politics« of the Institute, indicating the important role of individuals in this as in larger settings. More striking is the extent to which segmentation — looking after one's own programmes — is in evidence even in so small an organisation. This is a theme echoed, but in more positive key, in the second study in this volume.

Most striking however is the portrayal of a thoroughly well- disposed, »right-minded« project as culturally ill-attuned to its clientele and almost, for all the evident goodwill and sensitivity which informed its conception and development, neo-colonial. Sandra Stacy shows how all the right ideas were built into the approach — in terms of styles and methods of working, location and setting, choice of language, selection of participants, and so forth. Yet, in retrospect, the evaluation revealed an imposition of assumptions that meant the project was, by its own criteria, quite unsuccessful. It was new for its time and country, and there may well have been indirect gains, at least in the learning of white adult educators and others working with black, and other minority, communities and groups. The teaching employed what are called Socratic methods, and then incorporated some of the approaches and influences of Paulo Freire, whose translated writing was just then beginning to penetrate the English-speaking world. To recognise the depth of a cultural chasm such as was found here is the first step, if not to bridging it, then at least to not dragging into it those on the far side whom adult education is intended to help.

Summary

Pitjantjatjara people are traditionally oriented Aborigines living in the desert country of central Australia. Groups of up to four hundred dwell in village-type settlements or camps. There is a high incidence of infant mortality and morbidity caused by respiratory infection and diarrhoea complicated by malnutrition.

A health education was introduced by the Institute for Aboriginal Development in Alice Springs in 1971. It aimed to lower the incidence of disease among children by teaching their parents the basic principles of nutrition and hygiene, and encouraging them to find ways to apply these principles to their village or camp situations. Aborigines who indicated a wish to participate came to Alice Springs for a three week residential course. Courses were also held in the bush. Teaching was in the vernacular. A formal evaluation of the programme showed that those who had participated in the course could repeat accurately the facts taught, and perform appropriate tasks. There was however no indication that this knowledge was applied to their daily life. An attempt was made to discover why, despite apparently adequate communication, motivation and education, desired changes in behaviour did not occur. The health educator questioned the unwritten assumption on which the programme was based: that people would want to prevent illness, as defined by the western medical tradition, and deaths, among their children. It was found that this assumption was part of a world view not shared by these Aboriginal people. Traditionally oriented Aborigines do not view health as an alienable human right. They accept a high level of infant mortality and morbidity as part of their way of life, and were not motivated to lower the incidence of disease in their society. They chose to participate in the health education programme because they saw it as an opportunity to interact and establish relationships with other Australians. Relationships were an end in themselves. This is quite different from the view of the health educator who sees the establishment of relationships as a necessary step in achieving his or her goal of improved health.

The General Context

The Aboriginal people of Australia were hunters and gatherers until the coming of white men just over two hundred years ago. There are no longer any groups of fully nomadic Aborigines in Australia. All have been influenced more or less by contact with western society, but some are more traditional than others. Traditionally oriented Aborigines live in remote parts of Australia. They have access to western schools, medical services, shops and technology, but still live in family groups, speak their own languages, and perform the ceremonies that are part of their lives.

This programme was proposed by white people living in Alice Springs, the town in central Australia. The vast areas of surrounding countryside are arid zone or desert, and support a sparse population. The isolated industries are cattle production, mining and tourism. In the 1960s the Aboriginal people in this area lived in groups of between some 30 and 400 on cattle stations, missions and government settlements. Services were provided by various government departments and churches, mainly in the areas of education, health and welfare. There was no overall government policy and very little coordination of services. There appeared to be little change in the state of poverty experienced by the Aborigines and for some, particularly on the larger government settlements, the situation seemed to be getting worse. Those planning the Institute for Aboriginal Development in Alice Springs (hereafter the Institute) felt that any improvement depended not only on the availability of services but on Aboriginal development, a concept missing from existing programmes.

The aims of the proposed Institute (May 1969) were:
- »to recognise the Aboriginal as a person in his own right
- to equip him to understand and handle the pressures of rapid social change
- to enable the Aboriginal to make his unique contribution to the growth and development of his own people, and
- to fashion his place in contemporary Australian society«.

Among the many problems encountered by Aboriginal people in this area, priority was given to child care, communication, and accommodation. These were chosen since the concerned white people felt they were areas the proposed Institute could realistically tackle. Some of these activities had been carried out by the Uniting Church in Alice Springs, through its social work programme. Weekly classes in Pitjantjatjara were attended by white health workers, and camping facilities provided on church property for Aborigines from the bush who were visiting Alice Springs. It was planned that the Institute would take over and extend these activities. The Uniting Church supported the project financially until the Institute became an Incorporated Body and was able to receive government finance.

A decision was taken to concentrate initially on health education, or child care as it was called in the planning stages. This was stimulated by a climate of growing anxiety about Aboriginal infant mortality and morbidity. Information about the incidence of illness and death amongst Aboriginal children, ten times greater than in the white population, was being disseminated throughout Australia and beyond, and politicians were beginning to worry. The causes were respiratory disease and diarrhoea complicated by malnutrition. The cyclic pattern of early infection, hospital admission, discharge to the camp, reinfection and readmission, was known. The services allegedly available, which included detection and treatment of disease, immunisation programmes, infant feeding programmes, food subsidies and housing development, did not prevent children from becoming sick and often dying.

There were several Aboriginal language groups or tribes in Central Australia. The Pitjantjatjara, or Western Desert people, were chosen as the target population on the ground of being the least sophisticated and most disadvantaged. Furthermore, importance was placed on the vernacular and some whites immediately involved in the planning process spoke this language.

The Institutional and Organisational Context

The Institute was an independent free-standing activity controlled by a Board of 20 directors. Twelve were elected annually at a general meeting by people who had paid $2 to become members of the Institute. The remaining eight were nominated by Government Departments and the Uniting Church (four each).

The programme was seen as complementing work done by other agencies, and it was planned to develop it in cooperation with these agencies and with the Aboriginal people. There was cooperation between individuals at various levels of the Institute and those working in other programmes. Several members of the Board of Directors were involved with Aborigines through government or church programmes. Employees of the Institute cooperated in various ways with other white people working in similar professional or geographical areas. There was however no formal coordination with other agencies.

The Institute had a policy of involving Aboriginal people. At least six Board members were Aboriginal. Aboriginal labour was used to construct the Institute building and later Aboriginal people were employed in specific jobs and as apprentices. Aboriginal people were consulted at all stages of the health education programme, and their help enlisted in the production of teaching aids and in adapting traditional stories. As the Institute became established other programmes were begun (diagram 1). There was no policy to coordinate these programmes, and they developed as separate entities. The Health Education programme was conducted by a single health educator, and planned in conjunction with a subcommittee of three nominated by the Board. These people were Board members and one was also a member of staff. One member of the subcommittee was Aboriginal.

Diagram 1

Organisational Structure of the IAD December 1974

Board
Executive Committee
Administration

Health Education (health & community devt. health educator appt.d Jan. 71)	Language Laboratory (teacher linguist appt.d Nov. 72)	Hostel (manager appt.d Feb. 73)	Social Work (social workers appt.d Aug. 73)	Printing (printer appointed Feb. 74)

The Health Education Programme

General approach

The first document proposing an Institute was written in April 1969, and the Institute became incorporated under the Companies Act in February 1971. The first Health Education course commenced in May 1971 and the last was in September 1974. Evaluation was completed in June 1975.

The target population was Aboriginal people of the Pitjantjatjara tribe living within a distance of approximately 500 miles south and south-west of Alica Springs. Although the Pitjantjatjara communities were geographically isolated, the people moved freely and frequently between them. Individuals and families would visit for ceremonial or personal reasons. Groups of Aboriginal people from these communities came to Alice Springs for a three week residential course. Six to eight adults and several children attended each course, and groups came from nine of the ten Pitjantjatjara communities in the area. Courses were conducted with more than one group of people from each community during the four years the programme was operating.

The general approach of the Institute's Health Education programme was quite different from that of any other programmes for Aboriginal people at that time. In previous programmes educators tried to impose western ideas on Aboriginal people in a didactic way. The Institute planned to use the socratic, or two-way, method of teaching. This assumed that Aboriginal people already possessed information, feelings, interests and beliefs which profoundly influenced the learning process and must be taken into account before they could be modified. The Institute's Health Education programme was developed in consultation with Aboriginal people and the educator was encouraged to learn from them.

The most significant thing about the overall planning of the Institute was that it sought to be flexible. It was recognised that as the Europeans learned from the Aboriginal people the programme would need to change. The programme had formal and non-formal aspects. Through the course of »lessons« information was exchanged and ideas discussed. The informal part occurred during the continuing interaction of the health educator and the group members, while the group was residing at the Institute and when the health educator visited the Aboriginal communities.

Each formal course was planned after evaluation of the previous one. An overall course plan was written, and a teaching plan then developed for each lesson or discussion. Information gained from wider sources, such as changes in government policy, and discussions with Aboriginal and European specialists, were taken into account in planning. On two occasions anthropologists worked with the health educator for four weeks, planning a new approach to the teaching of the programme and later an evaluation of the whole programme. Changes also occurred in the informal aspects of the programme as those at the Institute sought to understand and accommodate the Aboriginal point of view, for instance over payment for the course.

Before the programme there was discussion and planning about how to evaluate it. Forms were devised using the accepted World Health Organisation indices of infant mortality and morbidity on which data could be recorded. Information collected in this way was eventually used in connection with government health records. It was planned to have control groups from communities which were not exposed to the programme, with which statistical information could be compared. It was also planned to observe any changes in behaviour that occurred after groups had participated in the programme.

Approaching Aboriginal Communities

The guidelines for who was to participate were worked out in consultation with the Aborigines involved. It was felt important that only those communities which expressed a desire to participate in the programme should do so. If such a desire was expressed then members of the community chose who was to attend the course. The health educator and others associated with the Institute, such as a Board member, visited each community and discussed the health education programme with them. Discussions focussed on changes that had occurred since the coming of the white man. Initially posters were developed to illustrate the difference between infant mortality and mobidity in the Aboriginal and white populations. The

Aboriginal people appeared interested in the pictures of malnourished and »healthy« children, and in the curved lines of weight/age graphs. However, it was learned that they did not relate these to infant mortality and morbidity, and the charts were not used after the first year.

The way of approaching each community varied for instance according to its organisation (some had village councils which were seen by white people as representing Aborigines); the gender of the negotiator (a male was more likely to meet first with groups of senior men and a female with groups of senior women); and the relationship the person from the Institute had with members of the community (they may have had previous contact with one family group).

Course Content

The subject matter was health education, but its definition changed during the course of the programme. Initially health was seen as the absence of disease, and education was seen as »providing instruction relating to improved child care in poor socio- economic environments«. The high incidence of disease, especially among Aboriginal children, was seen as related to poor hygiene practices and malnutrition. The prospectus written in 1970 stated that »a supervisor, with knowledge and skill in environmental health education, will teach mothers basic health concepts, nutrition, infant feeding, etc. at camp level (eg. mothers will be taught to do such things as to prepare bottles, and wash baby, using a camp fire and whatever minimal facilities she has to utilise back in her home situation).«

During the second year of the programme health was no longer seen as the absence of disease. The poor state of health among Aboriginal people was largely attributed to a breakdown in social patterns. The health, involving the well-being of individuals in relation to their whole environment, would be improved only if that total relationship was improved. The course was restructured to enable Aboriginal people to come together and find ways of attacking the general problems of their community, take responsibility for doing something about them, and obtain help necessary for their solution.

The content of the restructured course was based on developing concepts of lineal time, choice, responsibility and change. These were related to hygiene and nutrition in the community transition from nomadic to present camp life, and included explanations of European society and the external pressures which had been imposed on Aboriginal people. The emphasis had shifted from children and personalities to changing environments and technology. It was believed that a stable social structure would improve the condition of health, including infant mortality. Instruction of any sort was therefore omitted unless specifically asked for by the Aboriginal people. Family planning, with emphasis on spacing rather than stopping children, was included. The concept of deliberate choice to bring about desired situations, and relationships between money, food and community well-being over time — past, present and future — were discussed towards the end of the course. This was structured so that concepts, ideas and practices which were introduced as isolated phenomena were then presented as closely related parts of a whole. The overriding concept was community welfare, the well-being of the individual depending on the well-being of the community. Flexibility allowed specific needs of different communities to be met.

Teaching Methods

In Alice Springs the Aboriginal group and the health educator lived in a hexagonal building. The teaching was conducted in a central courtyard. Each day there was a morning medical clinic and a morning and afternoon teaching session. These were conducted with all participants sitting on the ground around a campfire. In the early childcare stage nutritional information was discussed. Posters indicating three food groups, good and poor food, developmental stages of children, and healthy and sick children, were used to illustrate the lessons. Hygiene lessons were based on the germ theory and germs and cross-infection were demonstrated using posters, flannel graphs and a microscope. After each lesson the group members were encouraged to draw their own pictures or copy the teaching aids. These drawings were made into a book which was taken home to show friends, and remind participants of the subjects they had discussed.

A small store was established in the Institute. This was used to teach about budgeting. Some members of each group went to the town shops each day to buy additional food. Teaching about food selection was discussed then. Instruction on food preparation, cooking, infant feeding and hygiene was given while the group members were preparing meals or cleaning up the courtyard. When the course became more oriented to community development, the format of discussions morning and afternoon was continued, and stories were introduced by Aboriginal people. Group members continued to make their own illustrations after each discussion. The acquisition of a bus allowed more mobility, and day trips were frequently taken to the bush and neighbouring communities.

The presentations allowed free group discussion, and the roles of teacher and pupil were frequently reversed, both during discussions in Alice Springs and when groups took the health educator into the bush. It was hoped that by teaching the white educator the Aboriginal people would regain pride in their own knowledge and traditional social structure. It was also hoped that the educator would learn more appropriate ways of encouraging the Aboriginal people to develop a stable social structure. In the early part of the programme, when the emphasis was on child care, the teaching methods were based on widely accepted principles of teaching and learning, as concisely stated in World Health Organisation Technical Report Series No.89 Expert Committee on Health Education of the Public, First Report, 1954. When the programme changed to emphasise community development some of the teaching methods described by Paulo Freire were included, using Freire's Cultural Action for Freedom, first published by the Harvard Education Review in 1970 and later by Penguin Books in 1972.

Follow-up

The white people planning the programme hoped that participants would return to their communities, practise what they had learned, and pass on the information to others in the community. It was recognised that to do this the Aboriginal people would have to have the authority within their community. It was at first thought that grandmothers had this authority in the area of child-rearing, and the first groups consisted of grandmothers and mothers with their children. It then seemed that in some communities fathers had this authority, and they were included in the groups. Later, when the courses focussed on community development rather than child care, senior men and women as well as younger mothers and fathers attended the courses. Some anecdotal feedback from Aborigines and Europeans on the settlements, missions and cattle-stations from which the groups came indicated that some ideas discussed during the course were passed on to others in the community, but not, the evaluation showed, to the extent that the Institute had hoped. The health educator made numerous plans for regular follow-up work, but apart from some irregular field trips and discussions with Aborigines and Europeans in the communities, follow-up did not occur.

Costs

As the Institute expanded, costs were not itemised out separately to identify the proportion that should have been charged to this programme. In the following estimation of costs, the years in which the Institute and the programme were being established are identified separately, indicating donations and voluntary work involved. An annual average cost is estimated for the following three years.

1970 building constructed at cost of $ 11,000 given by the Presbyterian Church; land given by Methodist Church; administrative officer salaries given by the Congregational Church; voluntary work by building supervisor.

1971 programme commenced: $ 5,000 donated from church organisations plus $ 250 fees from course participants; expenditure of $ 600 for health educator's salary (equivalent to missionary's salary) and total operating costs of $ 5,000; voluntary work by administrative officer and for transport and field work.

1972-74 estimated annual operating costs: $ 13,450 (health educator's salary equivalent to Commonwealth Senior Sister $ 5,200; direct health programme operating costs for food, equipment etc. $ 1,250; vehicle costs $ 500; interstate travel $ 500; proportion of IAS administrative salaries $ 4,000 and general operating costs $ 2,000).

Many white people, mainly from education, anthropology and medicine, gave much time helping with the planning, ongoing assessment, and final evaluation of the programme. These included people living in or visiting Alice Springs, and others in government departments, universities and other institutions around Australia. One trained nurse helped in a voluntary capacity with clinical work while groups were in Alice Springs. Indigenous leaders cooperated in discussions and some attended courses; but they did not, as had been hoped by white people, carry on the teaching in the communities. Those employed by the Institute gave much unpaid time and frequently bore some direct cost, for instance personally financing field trips.

Changing Objectives

While the programme was broadly in health education the objectives changed over the years. The initial objective was »to provide at least part of the answer to the most urgent need in the field of Aboriginal health; that of excessively high infant mortality, by giving informed instruction relating to improved child care in poor socio-economic environments«. The principles behind this objective lay in the western medical/disease model. This is illustrated by table 1.

In February 1972 the aims of the course were restated to be:
(i) create a concept of health (as opposed to one of life which includes sickness) by helping women to gain knowledge and understanding of food, germs and family planning;
(ii) help mothers develop a favourable attitude towards health and to place value on it by helping them to:
— develop an appreciation of their responsibility towards themselves and their families
— become motivated over a need for change
— gain confidence to initiate change;
(iii) improve the mother's psychomotor skills within the resources available in their camp environment, in areas of childcare, diet, hygiene, budgeting and disease. These aims also reflected ideas about the principles of teaching and learning brought to the programme by a new staff member with qualifications from the discipline of education. The underlying, and unstated, philosophy remained the same.

In November 1973 the objectives changed. The stated aims were now to:
(i) help Aborigines to rebuild their communities by fostering their self-confidence and encouraging them to take responsibility;
(ii) help the groups think about their traditional society, values and patterns of interaction and the purposes they served;
(iii) feed new information about European society to the group using a non-authoritarian approach;
(iv) encourage the group to see how changes are influencing them and how, using

their own social structures, they can respond to the environment to meet their present needs.

Table 1

Problems Associated with Respiratory Infection and Diarrhoea in Aboriginal Infants*

The Problems	Causes of These Problems	Some Institute Answers
overcrowding	high birth rate. static communities. inadequate housing.	family planning. explain effects. motivate need.
poor hygiene	poor understanding of infectious disease and disease transference. cultural pressures to maintain status quo. inadequate facilities.	extensive teaching and demonstration. teach older people too. motivate need.
malnutrition	poor understanding of dietary needs, health as a concept, normal growth, etc. low purchasing power and poor understanding of money values, wages, budgeting, etc.	infant welfare. budgeting.

(* IAD unpublished document, 1971)

The changes in course aims came about as the white organisers searched for answers to questions that rose as the programme developed. Some of these related directly to the content of the course, e.g. the difficulty Aborigines appeared to have in understanding the nutritional values of European food. The course was restructured according to accepted education principles in an attempt to make the teaching about food more relevant. However the problems remained. Other questions concerned the motivation of the group to learn, continuing problems about payment for the course, and the social pressures exerted on members of the groups when they returned home. The search for answers to these questions resulted in a redefinition of the problems and needs of the Aboriginal people, and aims of the course were altered to meet these redefined needs. The overall aim of the programme remained that of health education, but broadening the definition of health, and changing the basic assumptions about the cause of poor health in Aboriginal communities resulted in a programme shift towards community development. The reduction of poverty, while not a stated aim of the programme, was implicit in the community development purpose.

Trying to Relate

From the initial planning and through the three and a half years it was implemented until the beginning of formal evaluation of the programme, the white educators attempted to take account of traditional Aboriginal beliefs and customs, and of the contemporary conditions in which Aborigines were living. The programme was started because both Aborigines and whites were distressed when children became sick or died. The latter assumed that the Aboriginal people would therefore be motivated to do something about this problem. This assumption was later questioned.

Many Aborigines were consulted about the programme, in a genuine effort to find out what they wanted, and how they wanted it done. In retrospect, however, it was found that many of those consulted were not traditional leaders, and had little or no authority to speak on behalf of their groups. The white people had thought they were leaders. Furthermore these consultations usually took the form of white people presenting ideas about the programmes to Aborigines and asking for opinions about the ideas. The Aboriginal people usually agreed with the ideas. This form of consultation was later questioned.

The building and facilities in Alice Springs were designed to make Aboriginal people feel at ease, and to simulate their home environment. The hexagonal building was designed following a C- shaped symbol used by Aborigines to denote shelter and security. The sleeping areas were furnished only with mattresses and hooks on the walls since Aboriginal families slept in close proximity and beds prevented this. Cooking was done with simple equipment on a camp fire in the courtyard. As well as using facilities similar to those in a camp situation, it was known that the people believed a fire prevented unwanted spirits coming near the area.

The choice of participants was made by the communities. It was felt by the whites that the Aboriginal people would best know who would benefit from the course, and who had the authority to pass on the teaching when they returned to the community. Furthermore, because of traditional kinship taboos some Aborigines could not associate with others; only Aborigines knew fully about these things.

Teaching was in Pitjantjatjara. A two-way, socratic method of teaching-learning was adopted. The educator spent time with Aboriginal groups in the bush where she became the learner. In Alice Springs information about white society was introduced in a non-authoritarian way, during discussions and daily activities. If the Aboriginal group expressed a desire to do something special, attempts were made to do it. For example one group asked to visit a community of Aborigines from a different language group. Such a visit was included in all future courses. Aboriginal concepts were used as a base for introducing information about white society. For example it was learned that Pitjantjatjara people had one word for meat, kuka, and one word for everything else, mai. It was thought that information about different food values would be more easily understood if these two food groups were used, rather than introducing three or more food groups. The fact that Aborigines had traditionally eaten botk kuka and mai was a starting point for talking about a balanced diet. Each group was asked about their traditional foods as a basis for the discussion. It was learned that Aboriginal people did not relate pictures of isolated food items with eating the food or becoming healthy, so posters showing just food items were replaced by pictures of people eating food. These were drawn by Aboriginal people.

In the latter part of the programme, when ideas of community development were introduced, a series of stories was developed in conjunction with Aborigines and illustrated by them. These followed the pattern of traditional stories and used everyday situations to introduce the concepts of linear time, choice, responsibility and change. Story-telling was a traditional method of teaching. The stories stimulated discussion. The groups would discuss the old times and the changes that had occurred since the coming of the white man. The educator would encourage them to verbalise the implications of this, and to decide if anything could be done by them. For example, one result of the change from nomadic to static living conditions and the introduction of clothes, utensils and packaged foods was that such a thing as rubbish occurred. The implications and actions related to this were discussed.

Those involved in the programme believed they were basing the teaching on Aboriginal concepts and that the new knowledge would be integrated with traditional beliefs. It can be seen in retrospect that they were in fact trying to select isolated fragments of Aboriginal belief and fit them into a white framework. From the beginning the course was to be flexible to allow changes to occur as the educators learned more about Aboriginal culture. It was expected to learn better ways of introducing information. It was not foreseen that the Aboriginal people would see the programme completely differently, and would be happy for it to discontinue.

Issues and Tensions

During the planning stages, and when the health education programme first started, there was no ambiguity. The aim, to do something practical to lower infant mortality and morbidity rates, was accepted by all, and the method was also agreed upon. At this stage those involved included members of the Board, and a very active executive committee, a secretary, an administrative officer and a health educator. Executive committee members were enthusiastically involved with the health education programme. They were working with Aborigines and on field trips to the communities they discussed the programme. For the first twelve months most of the liaison with communities was by members of the Executive. (The health educator did not have a vehicle at this time.)

As other sections of the Institute developed — social work, language laboratory, hostel and printing — staff members became increasingly involved in their own work and support for the health education and the health educator diminished. Changes in the health education programme were worked out between members of the sub-committee, and proposals accepted by the Institute Board before being implemented. However, conflict developed between those who thought the programme should teach mothers how to care for their children (the initial aim) and those who emphasised community development (the later aims). When the educator suggested that courses be suspended and the work evaluated there was little support from the Institute staff, and strong opposition from some Board members. Opinion remained divided but the Board approved the evaluation. Some members of staff attempted to have the evaluation stopped but the Board, again by a small margin, voted that it should continue.

Problems also arose between a social worker and the second health educator. The social worker had been working for some years with Pitjantjatjara people developing health education material, teaching the language and providing accommodation to Aboriginal people in Alice Springs. He was very active in the creation of the Institute, a member of the Board and of the health education sub-committee, and later joined the Institute staff. The second health educator arrived when the first one resigned twelve months after the programme commenced. A personality clash developed. The social worker felt that the educator was too interested in theory and should spend more time teaching. The educator criticised the social worker for failing to see the increasing contradictions between what the programme claimed to be doing and what appeared to be happening, or not happening.

Occasionally there were also problems over the division of responsibility within the Institute. These were usually resolved by referring to the organisation chart and by discussion. Occasionally the Board Chairman acted as arbitrator. The health educator experienced problems over lack of liaison between other staff members and herself, mainly in the area of planning and follow-up of health education courses. They concerned discussion with members of the isolated communities, both Aboriginal and white. She felt that careful planning and follow-up work was necessary, and as all Institute staff visited the communities they could help with this. Probably no other member of staff shared this view, and attempts to have regular staff meetings to discuss what everyone was doing were unsuccessful.

When the health education programme began, the few people involved worked as a team and the concept of management was barely applicable. As other sections of the Institute developed and more staff were employed the laissez-faire approach continued and organisational problems arose. Some concerned the potential overlapping of work areas, such as health education and social work. Others were over practical matters such as use of vehicles and telephones, and emptying of rubbish. A high degree of flexibility was considered advantageous by those running their different programmes, but it resulted in fragmentation of the work being done. This was partly resolved by a restructuring of the Institute after the health education programme closed.

In the broad political arena the health education programme was encouraged by such bodies as the Federal Government, major churches, and the Freedom From Hunger organisation. These bodies, all based in the South of Australia, were eager to support a programme which was seen as using a new and different approach to education. Locally there was initially some resistance from some people in the Health Department, but this was largely resolved by personal contact. Some white people working in the Pitjantjatjara communities saw the programme as an unnecessary intrusion. This was resolved by building up personal trust, planning the programmes with them, and cooperating in their programmes where this was possible. The problem started to re- emerge towards the end of the programme because the health educator did not have time to maintain the relationships that had been established, or to build new ones with the newly arrived white people.

Changes taking place at this time within other organisations, and within Aboriginal communities, need to be considered. A change in government policy resulted in large amounts of money being given to Aboriginal communities. Aboriginal groups were being encouraged to organise themselves into cooperatives and to take responsibility for running their own local affairs. The whites involved were to be helpers rather than organisers. Missions and settlements had hitherto been run by superintendents; these people were now called community advisers. The word self- determination was used to define overall policy.

When the health education programme changed its emphasis from instructing mothers how to care for children to community development, it was a leader in this field. Two years later there was a lot of talk about community development, and many people thought the best way to encourage this was by working with communities on a day to day basis in their own environment. Although the health education programme still had health as its overall aim, the link between this and the objectives stated later was rather tenuous. Certainly the educator encouraged the groups to discuss health-related problems when they were discussing change; but Aborigines were also to be encouraged to define their own problems, and it became increasingly obvious that improving health was not among these. Whites in other agencies were still concerned about Aboriginal health and were prepared to cooperate with the programme on this basis. They were however less inclined to be interested in the community development aspect. Some, including the health educator, questioned the concept of an isolated three week course in Alice Springs attended by just a few members of a community.

Evaluation and Appraisal

Towards the end of 1974 the programme was formally evaluated, and an attempt made both to describe what was happening and to explain why this was. Change was sought in the areas of nutrition and hygiene, so the results of the evaluation would be in these terms. There were other areas where change could have occurred, but as investigation was not directed towards these it was not expected to find out information about them.

Answers to the »what« questions were sought by examining medical records and observing people's behaviour. These widely accepted criteria had been the ones planned when the programme was initiated. For the statistical evaluation, information was collected on the number of births, and of hospital admissions and deaths in children under five years, occurring in the Pitjantjatjara communities involved in the health education programe. The data covered a period commencing twelve months before the first course and extending to November 1974. Similar data on births, hospital admissions and deaths were obtained for five Aboriginal communities of similar total size not involved in the health education programme; these were Walpari and Aranta communities, Pitjantjatjara communities not being available for comparison. Data on achievement of child growth were also used in one community from which members attended four health education courses. The analysis of information on infant deaths showed a downward trend over this four and a half year period which was statistically significant. This trend was however evident prior to participation in the health course in many communities. Analysis of data on hospital admissions and child growth showed no statistically significant change.

While examining the changes in nutrition and hygiene practices an attempt was made not only to observe behaviour directly but also to discover what knowledge the Aboriginal people had retained. It was found that knowledge about European food and hygiene practices initially given as information and discussed in later courses was retained by the participants. When asked to do so people could repeat accurately such things as the nutritional needs of infants or the most appropriate means of rubbish disposal. They were also able to perform actions necessary to apply this knowledge; but there was no evidence that they did this in their day to day lives. Therefore the desired changes had not occurred.

Other widely accepted criteria involving correlation of various aspects of specified data may have provided an explanation of why there was no change. However, it was decided not to look for explanations in this area, for several reasons, including limited time and resources, difficulty of isolating variables, and concern that the collection of these data might cause disruption to the lives of the Aboriginal people. But the main reason was that during the three and a half years that the programme had been running, the health educator had been learning from the Aboriginal people how they viewed the world, what values and priorities they held, and how they interpreted specific situations. The reasons why there had been no change were thought to lie in this area.

An anthropological approach was therefore adopted in an attempt to explain why the desired changes had not occurred. This did not seek explanations within a framework determined by those organising the programme, nor did it look for »facts« which were seen to be relevant in terms of pre-selected criteria. Rather it sought for explanations by discovering how those involved saw the world, and the meanings they gave to their actions. The anthropological approach assumed that people had different ways of viewing the world, and that the actions people took were influenced by the meanings they gave to situations in which they found themselves.

Data were collected from anthropological literature and Institute records. Interviews were held with anthropologists who worked with Aboriginal groups, and with some Aboriginal people. Following the collection of these data, an anthropologist, an Aborigine and the health educator planned ways to ascertain how those who participated in the programmes saw the Institute and health teaching, and how they related this to their understanding of the world. The health educator carried this out, and held discussions, formal and informal, with Aborigines who had attended the courses and with some from the same communities who had not. Photographs and teaching aids relating to the courses were used as a focus for the discussions. Specific data collected in this way were analysed in association with the data collected during the years the programme had been operating, and with general anthropological data. The results provided an explanation why the desired changes had not occurred.

The ways in which Aboriginal people viewed health and illness were examined. This led to a questioning of the taken-for- granted assumption on which the programme was based: that Aboriginal people would want to prevent illness (as defined by the western medical tradition) among their children. It was assumed that because Aboriginal people showed concern when their children became seriously ill or died, they would wish to do something to alleviate this concern. This assumption was found to be part of the way of thinking of the white health workers. It was not shared by the Aborigines. These traditionally oriented people did not view health as an inalienable human right; they accepted a high level of infant morbidity and mortality as part of their way of life. They accepted this in much the same way that those in modern societies who place a high value on modern technology accept high levels of vehicular deaths and other environmentally caused disease.

The health educator then sought to explain why these groups chose to participate in the programme by finding out how they saw it. It appeared that the Aboriginal people saw relationships, that is interactions with other people, as the most important thing. They wanted to do things which enabled them to interact with other people. They chose to participate in the programme because they saw it as an opportunity to interact and establish relations with other Australians. The relationships were an end in themselves. This was quite different from the view of the health educator, who saw establishing relationships as a necessary step in achieving her goal of improved health.

Understanding how Aboriginal people viewed relationships enabled another problem to be identified. As the health educator worked with Aboriginal people she found herself in two roles, a relationship role and a teaching role. These tended to be mutually exclusive. As the relationships developed the ability to function as a teacher decreased. When working with traditionally oriented groups, to be able to understand them it is necessary to work in the context of relationships. The nature of these relationships is such that it precludes the teaching role. Once the relationships are formed the teaching becomes irrelevant to the Aboriginal people because their ultimate goal has been achieved: the nature of the relationship which develops in response to the need to interact in a manner meaningful to the community is such that it tends to prevent the community worker from filling the role which is the reason for his or her presence in the community.

One hundred and forty six adults participated in the programme out of a total of approximately 2,180 in their communities. In terms of what it set out to do the programme was a failure. The health education programme aimed to tackle one of the symptoms of poverty, the high incidence of infant illness and death. This was not achieved. For the first two years the emphasis was on giving »informed instruction«, and for the remaining two years on »community development«. The emphasis changed because as those involved learned more about Aboriginal society they came to believe that giving »informed instruction« in the narrow field of child care was inappropriate. The »community development« approach, by trying to help Aboriginal groups to cope with a period of rapid social change, was shifting towards tackling one of the causes of poor quality of life. In retrospect this approach may have been more appropriate, but the aim was too ambitious for the facilities and means which the programme had at its disposal.

The programme was innovative. It was the first organised attempt to teach Aborigines at camp level using the vernacular, and it was one of the first to attempt to use the principles of community development. It received wide publicity, and it would be reasonable to assume that this influenced the development of other programmes. It is however impossible to tell if, or to what extent, the health education programme influenced subsequent changes in the Pitjantjatjara communities, for instance the desire to control their own medical services. There has been no significant change in the overall health patterns since the programme ceased.

The programme also gave Aboriginal people the opportunity to teach whites. It appeared that those who participated felt free to use the resource of the programme in their own way. They used such things as transport, accommodation, food, acute medical care, and interpreting, to help meet needs identified by them. Furthermore they were able to form relationships and interact with white staff in their own way.

The programme was designed to learn from Aborigines as well as to teach them. It was not however expected that those implementing it would learn that the Aborigines did not want the programme at all. The reasons for the »failure« of the programme have been widely publicised, and it is reasonable to assume that they have contributed to a growing awareness among some white people of the way that Aboriginal people view the world.

The programme developed and was conducted at a particular moment in history. It is unlikely that the attitudes of politicians, the general white community and the Aborigines that existed at that time would be repeated. In this way the programme was unique. On the other hand the aims of the programme, the methods used, and the problems experienced, were not unique. The value of the programme lay in the willingness to learn from Aboriginal people and their experiences, and in its flexibility to adapt to the inevitable changes.

References

Freire, P., *Cultural Action for Freedom*, Penguin, 1972
Stacy, M., »Institute for Aboriginal Development: Health Education«, report submitted to the Institute Board, September 1975.
W.H.O., Expert Committee on Health Education of the Pacific, *First Report*, WHO Technical Report Series No. 89, 1954.

Appendix

Institute for Aboriginal Development: Basic Assumptions in Relation to Health and Community Development Amongst Central Australian Aborigines, September 1972.
1. Health is not merely an absence of disease. It must involve the well-being of individuals in relation to their whole environment.
2. The poor state of health among Aboriginals in largely due to the breakdown of social patterns which has resulted from the influence of one lifestyle upon another.
   The relationship which Aborigines had with their environment, including food and water supplied, and with each other, especially their children, has been seriously disrupted.
3. Aboriginal tribal life was a close integration of beliefs, laws, interpersonal relationships and daily living. The whole lifestyle was effectively adapted to the environment.
   European society is based on small isolated family units, individual specialisation of roles, and a cash economy which are largely foreign to Aboriginal ways.
   Aborigines now live in static communities with at least some contact with Europeans. An understanding of the needs and aspirations of Aboriginal people is the only real basis to providing assistance. If there is inadequate consultation with Aboriginal groups administrators unconsciously tend to impose European ways which are inappropriate and confusing.
4. Worthwhile social changes can only develop from the needs and desires of members of the community. It follows that efforts to impose change from outside the community will certainly be ineffective and may arouse antagonism.
5. The Institute course is designed primarily:
   (a) to assist Aboriginal people to see more clearly the nature of the problems arising from their present situation (especially in regard to health),

- (b) by an exchange of ideas between an educator and groups of Aboriginal parents and children to discuss ways in which their needs can best be met, and
- (c) to foster the Aborigines' confidence in themselves as parents and members of a community and in their ability to recognise and to resolve problems arising out of a changing pattern of life.
6. Control of, and responsibility for, Aboriginal communities will ultimately be taken over by the Aborigines themselves. The aim of the Institute's programmes is to assist them to do so.

Chapter Three

Women Working Together — Learner-determined Priorities in the Tototo Kilemba Programme

Introduction

This second case study, like the Australian one, is also concerned with women and mainly, formally, with health. It is on a similarly small scale: six villages in a coastal part of rural Kenya. It is however markedly more optimistic a story — essentially a success in five out of six villages. It resembles the first study in another respect, and one which makes both accounts still somewhat unusual among small-scale voluntary efforts: it too was quite carefully and formally evaluated, though in this case in an on-going or formative way which, Noreen Clark asserts, proved of considerable value to those involved as they worked. (The Aboriginal project undoubtedly displayed the effects of reflection along the way, in its shifting objectives towards »community development«, but evaluation was a matter of controversy and marked the end of the project as such.)

The most striking difference is that in the National Christian Council of Kenya-World Education Inc. (NCCK-WEI) Tototo Kilemba project, the learning objectives and intended outcomes were not determined or assumed by health professionals at the outset and imposed, in however sensitive and well-intentioned a way, on the learners. Health and hygiene teaching and benefits grew out of the different groups' self-chosen learning projects, along with and mingled with other community, group and individual interests. Learners identified priorities with the help of their coordinators and thus set, and were committed to, the agenda. Along with functionality, keywords would include process, participation and thus motivation; the exercise of choice, resulting in commitment to action, and thus mobilisation. Along with these went a marked increase in confidence and thence in participation in the community generally. Another theme which comes through the project description and is drawn out in the analysis was the integration between different areas of need and interest which in modern society and administration are normally separated into different departments, often in a non-cooperating or even competitive way — a theme which echoes one of Stacy's observations within the microcosm of the Alice Springs Institute.

The evaluation showed clear gains in a number of areas, especially »community« and economic, but also in terms of health and nutrition. The importance of community choice and voluntary commitment is sharply delineated by the failure of the project in the sixth village where, it was later realised, the coordinator was imposed rather than really chosen. and the project too then seen as an outside imposition.

Stacy's account touched upon the importance of politics and personalities within small-scale organisations. This is echoed by Clark, who also suggests, in her conclusions, that politics in a more conventional and larger-scale sense may provide a main explanation as to why the Tototo Kilemba kind of approach is so rare. Significant mobilisation of groups and communities is likely to unleash energies and efforts that must inevitably alter the economic (and so political) status quo. This is made worse by the narrow and often exclusivist attitudes of different development professionals and their departments which are inclined to promote their own objectives and targets rather than listen and respond to what the poor, but wise, might believe matters most.

Another challenging concluding point is Noreen Clark's suggestion that approaches such as that described here are uncommon simply because we have difficulty in conceiving how such individualised approaches can be replicated on a mass scale. Small may be beautiful, but faced with the alarming scale of development needs and problems, we may be tempted to resort to mass production approaches which appear more efficient. If however this removes the capacity to heed and respond to felt needs in unique local circumstances — surely the key to success in the Tototo Kilemba story — then the result will simply resemble the sixth village on a larger scale. How to replicate and multiply without in the process massifying, imposing and rendering ineffectual is a challenge indeed.

To revert to the note of optimism on which this introduction commenced, Clark does suggest that there tends to be a natural coincidence of interest between accepted development goals and the goals participants set themselves; such at any rate was a starting point for this project, »although the order of priorities... might differ from the order of development priorities set nationally«. This essentially apolitical note is sharply discordant with the tone of some later studies in this book.

Summary

Professionally planned education programmes are often ineffectual since they do not engage the learners' felt needs. NCCK, via its Tototo Home Industries division and World Education Inc. jointly ran a project for rural women in Kenya, 1978-80, with careful ongoing evaluation of the results by a variety of means. 180 women in six rural communities were involved, and 130 of these took part in the learning programme. Coordinators were to be selected by participating groups and trained for the tasks involved. The central focus was on establishing a group's capability for continuous learning.

Findings from the evaluation showed practical success according to several key criteria for application of learning. These included a fourfold increase in participation in **harambee**, or community self-help, and significant changes in diet. On other health indices there were no measurable changes, although perceptions of level of health did alter. Income generating activity showed perceptible gains.

Community trust in coordinators reflected the extent to which they were genuinely chosen. When one was in effect imposed on the group the project was unsuccessful. Another factor in success was genuinely identifying and responding to members' interests and priorities, rather than imposing an agenda — a process of identifying and solving problems. Groups learned how to limit membership to a manageable size, while assisting new groups into being.

This indirect, need-based approach to health education proved far more effective than a professionally created programme imposed from outside. Development goals were thus reached by focussing on learners' priorities. The fact that this approach is so uncommon may be explained by fear of real economic change, compartmentalisation of services and competition between them, and the **apparent** contradiction between mass and individualised approaches.

Noreen M. Clark

Programme Content, Objectives and Learning Approach

Introduction

From the viewpoint of a rural person in any of the world's developing countries, much of the education made available to them seems irrelevant. One reason is that programmes are generally developed by those who, because of the discipline-specific nature of their ministries and agencies, focus on one development topic: health, nutrition, or literacy, for example. This approach assumes that the topic has the same priority for villagers as it has for the ministry or agency. In addition, development topics are frequently treated in the abstract in educational programmes, as if each were a category of events and behaviours separable from ongoing concerns and to be given special attention. Emphasis is placed in programmes on what professionals deem to be most important to learn, and little effort is made to integrate learning with the events of daily life. Few people, educators and villagers included, would disagree that good health for example is an important goal. However, people often disagree on how to reach the goal, and on how important it is in relation to other priorities.

The rural person often rejects practices espoused in education programmes because they do not appear beneficial or important in the light of other things considered more crucial to personal or family well-being. Many programmes proceed solely on the basis of professional and technical judgements of what will result in community development. Intentionally or unintentionally, they overlook the more personal and familial reasons why someone will become involved in development efforts. Despite the resulting attrition and failure to reach even modest goals, education planners continue to mount widespread programmes that are categorical and didactic; programmes which tend to reflect the concerns of the planner as opposed to the priorities and values of the participant.

Project Aims and Objectives

From 1978 to 1980 the National Christian Council of Kenya (NCCK) and World Education Inc. (WEI), two private voluntary agencies, implemented and evaluated a nonformal education programme for women in rural Kenya. NCCK-WEI entered into the project with the intention of responding to objectives set by learners themselves. It seems highly likely that project participants would, for the most part, select learning objectives associated with improving their social and economic lot. It was also assumed that the goals participants set for themselves would be consistent with and would complement accepted development goals related to health, nutrition and community improvement, although the order of priorities would vary from community to community and might differ from the order of development priorities set nationally. The project hypothesised that learning which addressed one's immediate objectives, reinforced one's sense of competence, and developed skills through collaborative activity, would benefit both individuals and community. These benefits would include: increased self-confidence; greater participation in community life; improved health and nutrition practices; new sources of community goods and services.

The division of NCCK implementing the project was Tototo Home Industries, a handicraft marketing organisation in the coastal area of Kenya. The director of Tototo, who agreed to become director of the NCCK-WEI project, was interested in developing the educational arm of her organisation. She recognised, as many do, that while handicraft production was immediately accessible, particularly to rural women because of their indigenous skills, it can rarely generate the level of income needed to bring significant change to the woman and her family. In most areas, the market for crafts is limited. In addition, if women are to enter more fully the economic systems of their communities, they need to acquire skills of a more technical nature. In developing its educational arm, Tototo received assistance from WEI consultants and staff, in the form of initial training for Tototo personnel and for the coordinators selected by each village group agreeing to participate in the project. The training was to enable them to engage project participants using the Tototo Kilemba learning approach. In addition, as the great majority of rural women do not read and write, the approach was to be unfettered by any requirement that participants be literate.

NCCK and WEI agreed to evaluate the project closely, both the learning processes and their impact. World Education Inc. provided training and assistance in conducting the comprehensive evaluation in collaboration with the Institute of Development Studies of the University of Nairobi. Ongoing evaluation was deemed of critical importance to all concerned. Representatives of NCCK wanted information for decision-making about their programmes. Representatives of WEI and the University wanted to understand better nonformal development approaches, their efficacy and outcomes. Credibility and mutual trust began with the co-sponsors. Each had something to contribute and each had something to gain from participation in the project. This pattern guided and pervaded all project activities from the central organisations to the community level.

The Participants. The project involved 180 women living in six small rural villages in the coastal region of Kenya, who were members of women's groups or clubs. Of these, 130 participated in the learning programme which included being interviewed at the outset and at the completion of the programme. The other 50 women were interviewed but did not participate in the learning activities. In only one village were there differences between participants and non-participants on demographic items collected in interviews, and these were not significant.

The typical project participant was a twenty to thirty year old mother of three children who had never attended school, or who had left in the very early years. She neither read nor wrote, but spoke both her own language and Kiswahili. She was Muslim and was more likely to be the only wife than a co-wife of a Muslim man. She was engaged in one or two activities to earn income and worked at these individually rather than in a group with others. Her major activity was farming subsistence crops, from which she earned no income. To earn money she made handicrafts or sold products from the cash crops her family grew. These activities earned her less than one hundred shillings (£13.00) a month, and the amount was likely to be less than 50 shillings a month.

Distinctive Features of the Approach

The Education. The learning programme was supervised by staff members with headquarters in Mombasa who were assigned villages to assist. The education was implemented in each village by a coordinator selected by the group of participating women. Each coordinator could read and write. Each was paid a small amount by the project, equivalent to that earned by others in the village performing similar services. The education comprised a series of learning group activities over a twelve month period. Coordinators were trained to use similar materials as discussion starters, to engage group members in dialogue and problem-solving, to draw on members' experience and abilities, to introduce related health and nutrition information, and to provide or help learners obtain needed resources and technical assistance. The intention of the training was to enable central staff and coordinators to become:
- skilled in community organisation and experienced in facilitating group processes
- able to create and use innovative learner-centred materials and methods that

acknowledged learning as a dynamic exchange between educators and learners
- able to create on-going dialogue and discussion in a group to raise the critical awareness of the learners about themselves and their communities and to assist learners in deciding on courses of action that would improve individual and community life
- able to practise a form of technical assistance that encouraged group members to mobilise their own resources and recruit needed outside material or expertise (as opposed to choosing and doing things **for** the group)
- able to help group members recognise the health implications of the things they selected to be able to view assisting the group to self-sufficiency as their primary goal.

Staff and coordinators were trained to carry out the following:
- involve participants in discussion of personal and community priorities
- assist them to select from among these an attainable goal
- assist them to organise themselves and to plan specific tasks to reach the goal in small achievable phases
- assist them to recognise or acquire skills and resources needed, and to complete the tasks
- assist them to assess progress and set new goals.

The process used to move women towards these goals was the same in each village, even though the specific goals of each group differed. In briefest outline:
- existing groups of women agreed to participate in the programme and chose a coordinator from the group to receive training.
- Women convened to consider what they would like to achieve, working together. In effect they considered the questions »what are the problems we confront? what would we like to learn that might help resolve them?«
- Using materials designed according to group objectives and problems, the coordinator, who received training, assisted the group through dialogue and discussion to analyse what members wanted and needed to learn in order to achieve their goals, and helped them plan and carry out steps to meet the goals they set. The materials (tapes, serialised posters, flexi-plans, hand-made drawings) did not require literacy skills. During group meetings and other activities coordinators and programme staff helped participants to see relationships between their priorities and practices conducive to development concerning health, nutrition, agriculture, etc. These practices were frequently discussed and analysed in the same way as were other steps the group took to achieve their specific objectives. Introduction of these ideas, however, was secondary to focus on the groups' goals.
- Plans involved recruiting experts initially from within the group and village and, when unavailable, from outside to teach needed skills. They also involved raising the capital needed to implement projects. In some villages in Kenya this included making handicrafts for sale. In all, it included canvassing official and voluntary agencies to locate appropriate assistance.

The focus of this process was on establishing a group's capability to engage in continuous learning. This included moving to new learning objectives when previous ones had been met.

Evaluation and Appraisal

Data Collection. As the Tototo-Kilemba programme was exploratory and involved a complex series of activities, data were needed to help us understand what happened and why. We therefore collected both quantitative and qualitative information. There were five phases in the evaluation plan:
- an extensive interview with each of 100 participants, and observations of conditions in each village at the initiation of the programme. Included in the questionnaire were items related to basic health and nutrition practices.
- Formal and informal interviews were again conducted with participants and programme staff at midpoint, with questionnaires focussed on the learning approach itself.
- Endpoint data were collected using interview and observation schedules comparable with those at baseline.
- Ongoing collection of data documenting project events was instituted at the outset including: weekly logs kept by each village coordinator; monthly observations of groups by supervisory staff; quarterly reports by the programme director; compilation of external events in each village by staff (that is, those events not initiated by the programme which might influence participants).
- An endpoint evaluation seminar involved experts from outside the programme, and their assistance was obtained in analysing the data collected during the life of the project.

The bulk of evaluation procedures were carried out by the programme staff as part of their regular responsibilities. Efforts were made to maintain objectivity. For example, for interviews with participants, staff members were sent to villages where they were not employed, so that learners would be candid in their responses.

The evaluation system, as it drew from all staff and participants, proved very valuable for ongoing decision-making about the programme. It assisted regular communication between field and central staff. Supervisory personnel were able to pinpoint and often circumvent problems. Data were used to determine inservice needs, and examples from logs and observations were often used in teaching. Endpoint data shared with staff and participants affirmed their individual and collective achievements. This motivated the majority to continue and expand on their work. The evaluation seminar enabled staff to see things in the data which they might otherwise have overlooked. It also served to disseminate information to others who could themselves benefit from new ideas and subsequently assist the programme in various ways.

Data Analysis

Data were tabulated and analysed initially by programme consultants. Data collected in the pre- and post-programme interviews were compiled and analysed by machine, using the Statistical Package for the Social Sciences. Change scores for pre-post responses to each questionnaire item were computed, and Pearson correlates and McNemar Chi Square used to determine the statistical significance of pre-post changes. Differences between responses of participants and non-participants were also computed, again using Chi Square to identify if differences were statistically significant.

Findings

Data compiled after eight months and again after sixteen months of programme operations suggested that the basic project premises were accurate. In five of the six coastal area villages the combined elements of the approach were successfully implemented.

In one village women chose to build a blocks-and-mortar nursery school for their children. Accredited nursey education is the first step towards formal schooling in the country. In four communities women chose to establish businesses. These included building coops for broilers and layers, then beginning egg and poultry farming, and constructing and operating a bakery — the first of its kind in the area. While no project chosen was specifically related to health, evaluation results indicate that each project had major consequences related to the improvement of environmental sanitation, nutrition, and health. There were also other outcomes in the five villages deemed important to community development and improving the situation of rural women. For example, after sixteen months there was significantly more participation in harambee [Kiswahili for community self-help, a principle widely practised in Kenya], and more members who held office in community councils, committees or organisations. The expressed confidence of women in all five villages to earn income, attain their own goals, and participate in harambee, increased fourfold. Five groups were able to raise significant amounts of capital to invest in their projects. The majority of participants engaged in significantly more collective effort towards earning income.

Overall, parrticipants reported significant changes in diet, primarily that they ate more chicken and eggs. Other health changes related to immunisation and sanitation were evident in individual villages according to the type of learning project selected. For example, in the two villages where women elected to begin egg and poultry selling, group coordinators used feeding and care of healthy chicks as an analogy for disease prevention and proper diet for families. From this women moved to sharing on a regular basis a number of eggs and chickens for family use in lieu of part of their earnings. In another group, where a bakery was constructed and operated, the women, as required by law for such a commercial venture, installed sanitary latrines. They also developed a design for a system for catching and storing rainwater (the water in the area was frequently fouled), and each of the 53 bakers was immunised for typhoid strains A and B.

(a) Changes Pre to Post Among Participants

Several changes in behaviour were documented in pre-post scores of participants in activities related to the project hypotheses (all findings significant at the $<.05$ level unless otherwise noted).

(i) Health and Nutrition. Wherever possible learning group coordinators encouraged members to eat protein-rich foods, a practice suggested in national nutrition policy. Indeed the poultry and egg businesses in two villages created new access to these foods for people in the areas. Participants were more likely to report that they ate chicken twice or more a week after the programme than before. There was a marginal trend for children to eat eggs at least twice a week or more after the programme than before. There were no changes related to eating other protein-rich foods: fish, meat, legumes.

There were no statistically significant changes in the population as a whole related to other health behaviours: owning a latrine and boiling drinking water. There were gains in different villages on some specific health practices such as installation of latrines, securing immunisations, purchasing safe water, in order to comply with requirements to operate a particular business. No population-wide change emerged however regarding any other one health practice. Neither were there significant differences in the population on individual health knowledge items, which included a list of healthy things to eat and healthy practices. The participants scored very high, 95-98% correct, on these knowledge items in the baselines survey and again scored very high at endpoint.

After the programme, participants were as likely to rate their state of health »fair« as »good«, whereas before the programme their modal rating was »good«. Participants experienced several events that probably influenced them to move their ratings downward. Some had physical examinations because of their learning group activities; some had exposure to healthy role models for the first time, in the persons of field staff; and most discussed aspects of illness in group meetings. These events would naturally cause some participants to revise their definitions of health and become more critical of their own health status.

(ii) Community Participation. Participants reported a higher degree of participation in community life after the programme. Their participation increased in relation to harambee (village self-help); that is, they contributed more time, money, or labour to community activities, and more participants came to hold leadership positions in village councils or organisations.

(iii) Income Activities. As would be expected, given the learning group activities which participants chose, there were significantly more income-earning activities on a group rather than individual basis after the programme. Members were more likely to raise poultry and less likely to engage in subsistence farming. They were also much more likely to report that their own salary was the main source of their income as opposed to reporting no income, spouses's salary, or digging (subsistence farming). In one sense these reports may mean that participants came to see themselves as »earning people«. They were also more likely to have opened bank accounts after the programme.

(iv) Confidence. One of the indicators on which the most dramatic change was seen was global confidence. The expressed confidence of participants increased fourfold. This comprised confidence to earn income, to attain one's goals, and to participate in harambee.

(b) Participants Compared to Nonparticipants

Comparing participants with nonparticipants is a somewhat risky business. The major reason is that in small, closely-knit villages like those on the Kenyan coast, the effects of the programme can touch everyone in the village; in a sense there is no such thing as a nonparticipant. The comparison is made even more complex because there are no pre-programme data for nonparticipants; therefore, it is not known where they were in terms of views and practices prior to the programme. Nonetheless, comparing the data that were available gives hints and clues as to where the programme may have been particularly effective and least effective.

(i) Health and Nutrition. At the time of final evaluation, participants in general were not more likely to eat eggs or chicken (using the measure two or three times a week) than were nonparticipants. An increase is seen in the consumption of chicken and eggs among participants, and participants were much more likely than nonparticipants to raise poultry by endpoint. Nonparticipants either ate more chicken and eggs to begin with, or more likely they also increased their consumption by endpoint, since the learning activities established new sources of eggs and chicken available to everyone in the village.

On the other hand, participants were much more likely to report that their children ate eggs two or more times a week than were nonparticipants. It is highly probable that discussion of nutrition and child health in the group meetings encouraged participants to feed eggs to their children. There was no difference between participants and nonparticipants on other health or nutrition items.

(ii) Community Involvement. At the time of final evaluation, participants held more village offices and contributed more time, money or labour to community projects than did nonparticipants, and significantly increased their community participation pre to post. Nonparticipants may also have increased their community involvement, yet it remained significantly below the level of that of participants; only one scored above zero on the community participation index.

(iii) Income Earning. Participants engaged in significantly more income-earning on a group basis at end point than did nonparticipants. They were also much more likely to have opened a bank account. No differences were found between the two groups on other money-related items such as giving or receiving credit or loans.

(iv) Confidence. Participants' confidence in themselves to produce income, reach their objectives and contribute to community life increased greatly. The difference between the level of confidence of participants and nonparticipants at the time of the final evaluation was significant, with the former exhibiting much higher levels.

(c) Effect on Individual Income of Group Projects

Participants earned and had potential to earn yet more significant sums for their efforts (Figure 1). Using the standard Kenyan income as a measure, individuals could realise 11 to 20% of an annual income from 24 to 60 days per annum worked. »Global success« as rank-ordered in Figure 1 refers to the rating of groups by project administrators. Success equals the administrators' combined scoring of the extent to which a group met its own objectives and development objectives.

Figure I

Groups by Rank of Global Sucess	Number of Members	Number of Days Work Per annum Per Member	Return* to Member per Annum at Endpoint Evaluation	Projected Return* to Member if 20 to 50% Increase in Production	Projected Return to Member as Percent of Average Kenyan Income*** Per Annum	Projected Business Net Profit Per Annum
(1) Barkery	53	60	264**	528	20	27,984
(2) Poultry A	25	12	267**	550	21	13,750
(3) Poultry B	28	12	456	912	34	25,536
(4) Nursery School	20	--	—	—	—	—
(5) Firewood	11	24	220	280	11	3,080

* In Shilling. US – 1.00 = KSh 7 (approximate average of the rate which fluctuated in 1979).
** his group had reinvested all earnings till endpoint and this figure represent the return when earnings were distributed.
*** Average income KSh 2660 (1979) World Bank; World Development Report 1980.

Issues and Analysis

Credibility, Contacts, and Constituency

Credibility and mutual trust between teachers and learners, development workers and community residents are widely acknowledged as fundamental to successful development. Yet it is surprising how they are in practice mishandled. No doubt a chief reason for the success of Tototo-Kilemba, and the NCCK-WEI project, was the constant attention paid to these elements. As the first step, the director of Tototo-Kilemba and the fieldwork supervisor, an NCCK social worker specially assigned to the project, began making contact in villages of the coastal area to find groups willing to collaborate in the project. Both women knew the areas well, both had strong connections with a variety of private and official service agencies, and both were respected and admired in their communities. Neither was hesitant about leaving her office to visit the village. Both considered the interests and concerns of rural women important and worthy, and recognised that the only way to discover how to assist people is to be with them and learn from them.

The intention of these leaders, following project principles, was to find existing groups in six villages that would want to participate. The leaders looked for natural groupings of women who were not organised for purposes of the project but who, for reasons of their own, chose to be together. Attempts were also made to find groups that differed in size, in distance from a town, and in their lengths of association. These were points of interest to project evaluators as both factors might influence participation and success. Initially the villages to visit were selected because the director and fieldwork supervisor knew that a group existed there. Soon they determined that women's groups could be found in most coastal villages, although the degree of their formal organisation differed greatly. Visits were made to over 15 potential village groups, each visit coordinated through village elders. Project purposes were explained to them, then contact made with leaders and a few members of the women's groups. In most cases project staff were invited to return to address a group meeting. The six village groups were then selected from those interested in collaboration. Members were invited to select a person, based on any criteria the group deemed important, to send for training to become a group coordinator. The project had no requirements for the trainee, and the group was to use whatever selection process was appropriate to its village. The trainee was to come with the full confidence of the group. A major project tenet was that each group would use its collective wisdom and experience to make decisions and resolve problems. Coordinators would be trained in ways to help the members do this. During the life of the project coordinators would be paid a small sum, an amount equivalent to what a group itself might be able to pay the coordinator after the end of the project, should they wish her to continue the work. Each coordinator would be the group's representative and each would have the group members as her constituents.

It became evident to programme staff some time after the training that two people sent to be trained did not have the full confidence of their groups. After careful and discreet inquiry it was found that in both cases the coordinators had been thrust on the membership. In one case a village official had decided for a group. In the other case a member had demanded that her daughter be selected as she was the member with formal schooling. The group was told that this criterion had been established by the programme planners. It had not. It was also clear after programme evaluation that these two groups were less successful in setting and meeting group objectives, and in moving to new group endeavours. We learned from this that the process of selecting the group's representative is fundamental and critical to success. The process used by a group, eg. election by the membership, appointment of one who fits certain criteria, or like methods, must not only reflect what is culturally appropriate to an area (for example in some places the Chief might be expected officially to appoint all individuals representing a village constituency) but must ensure as well that the representative is deemed acceptable by all members of the group. The time initially invested in this is time well spent. We found a direct connection between group members' confidence in the one who assists them to learn and eventual group success. Although there are no foolproof ways to ensure this, it is possible to build into a programme designed to reach rural people steps, time, and the assistance needed to help groups select representatives who are viewed as serving the interests of the full membership.

The Growth and Development of Groups

There is a significant difference between a programme conceived to fit the interests of an existing group of learners and a programme where the content is predetermined and learners must be recruited or otherwise enticed to attend. Programmes of the former kind, of which Tototo-Kilemba was one, have the advantage of being self-propelling, of having momentum and energy generated by a collection of individuals who already share similar goals and perceive them as important. Programmes of the latter kind reflect goals of the planners who must themselves expend most of the energy persuading individuals to accept the predetermined goals as important. Such programmes are mounted with little regard to motivation theory, and despite growing evidence that they are ineffective, given the costs.

The aim of Tototo-Kilemba was to help women identify and organise themselves around their own learning projects. In this process, as one would expect, individuals showed more or less interest in different particular learning group projects at different points in time. Rather than resist this tendency programme staff accommodated to it. In one group for example some members wanted to learn to make handicrafts as a means to earn capital to invest in their group project, while others preferred not to raise money in this fashion. In another group where poultry-keeping was a main activity, some members wanted to learn bee-keeping as an additional source of income and others did not. Small learning clusters therefore formed within the larger group as a result of particular interests and goals.

In conventional programmes reference is sometimes made to the failure of women to show interest in the activities. This assumes that women should be interested in the programme because planners are. Their failure (to attend, participate, learn) is viewed as the learners' failure. In the case of Tototo-Kilemba, the planners took the view that it is programmes that fail, not people. Special attention was paid to providing learning opportunities in configurations (time, place, topic, pace) suited to learners as opposed to planners. The programme was also carefully organised to provide experience of small successes which might lead to larger ones. The process of working towards group goals was broken down into a series of manageable problem-solving steps: identification and analysis of specific problems; discussion and decision-making; planning appropriate steps; and assigning tasks and taking action. In one village for example a group decided to build and operate a bakery for the purpose of generating income. Through discussion in the learning sessions the group analysed and made decisions about a series of tasks they had identified as necessary in order to have a successful business. These included obtaining capital and materials for the building and ovens, and purchasing raw materials and other equipment; finding markets; obtaining a licence; learning how to bake bread in quantity; keeping records of raw materials and sales; and organising into work groups actually to produce the bread.

Emphasis on identifying and analysing potential problems before they arose meant that in most cases the group was aware of the consequences of possible decisions before making them. The coordinator often used simple pictures or stories to help the group focus on problems and options. The group, therefore, was able to make choices with a high probability of success. By repeatedly engaging in this problem-solving process group members were not only able to acquire the specific skills needed to run a successful bakery but, perhaps more important, to learn the skills of planning, analysing, and organising action, which have broader applications to other situations in their family and community lives. The members' subsequent decision to add a tea and bread concession to the bakery building is evidence that they indeed applied this process to the accomplishment of other goals.

In one village however, no projects or group efforts were forthcoming. Several factors surfaced during the evaluation indicating that the programme criteria did not take hold within the project period. For example the group members had not come together for their own purposes but had been organised by an official agency and presented to Tototo as an existing group. The members had little in common and little credibility with one another. The choice of the coordinator was imposed on the group by one member. Even after the training the coordinator was not very well able to assist the members to analyse their situation and take appropriate steps. In this area, using our evaluation standards, the programme had failed after sixteen months.

Participants in the five other groups, however, experienced success: success in learning, in contributing to a group, in seeing a project realised, in earning money. This generated confidence and enthusiasm, and increased the momentum. In the most successful groups two factors associated with group growth and development became evident. One was increased solidarity, as evidenced in stabilised membership, attendance at meetings, and completion of tasks. Another was a tendency for size of membership to increase. This latter factor had to be handled carefully by members and their coordinators. Two very practical views prevailed in most groups: it is somewhat unfair for new members to join when a project is under way and successful, as newcomers reap the benefit of others' hard work; and a bigger group is not necessarily a better group, since it is more difficult to manage and coordinate. It is also more difficult to generate out of a small business sufficient economic rewards (either goods or money) for each individual when membership is too large. These views led groups to set up guidelines for changing participation and membership. In one, for example, newcomers were allowed to participate in projects growing from the individual endeavour, but proceeds from the original effort were earmarked for the founding members. In another group women imposed a ceiling on the size of membership. In the process, however, they elected to explain the reason to others in the village in order to diminish potential bad feelings. They also provided assistance in organising into a new group those neighbours who wanted to join. This took the form of advice based on the group's experience, material resources, and human resources in the form of the coordinator and a few group members who volunteered to train some of their neighbours to assume leadership in the new group.

Maintenance of group relationships such as those just discussed was fundamental to success. Indeed, data collected in a continuous process over the life of the programme illustrated that groups spent almost equal amounts of time on three major areas: (a) group development — keeping the membership informed, motivated and feeling confident; (b) organising — drawing up work schedules and making assignments related to learning and carrying out project tasks; (c) acquiring technical skills and knowledge related to the groups' projects (such as poultry-keeping, handicrafts, gardening, baking, record-keeping, and sanitation). Ignoring any of these led to diminished success: creating the opportunity to gain and apply new skills is as important as learning the components of the skill itself.

Where do Health, Nutrition and Other Development Issues Fit?

A most reasonable concern of professionals involved in health, nutrition, family planning and other development domains is as to where the specifics of these issues fit into such a learner- determined programme. The fear that rural women will not select health, for example, as a priority interest is an understandable fear: in our experience they will not. This is not however unique to rural women in developing countries. The efforts of most individuals, regardless of status or nation, are concerned primarily with economics, maintenance, and quality of family life. People come to view and adopt certain practices and behaviours because they are consistent with these efforts.

The premise of Tototo-Kilemba project planners was that the educational task is to help rural women see a connection between their own goals and healthful practices. This assumes that there is an eventual fit between the learning choices of women in small villages and the goals of development. It assumes that the momentum and energy generated by women pursuing their own interests will cause a spillover of interest to learn about health, nutrition, and so on. The results of the evaluation bear out this premise.

Women participating in the programme were not resistant to new practices that made sense in the light of personal and group goals that they were trying to reach. No health or nutrition practice discussed was to be introduced in the abstract, unconnected from the immediate interest of the women, or touted as beneficial for reasons understandable only to the programme planners. In the most successful groups, topics were introduced in connection with a need. For example discussions on sanitation and cleanliness were essential for those in the bakery group, as they affected the marketability of their products. Nor did the programme set as a criterion of success that all women adopt all practices in standardised fashion. It was acknowledged that each participant would make decisions based on her own needs and priorities. A most revealing example is the woman whose children, house and self were dangerously unwashed but who changed this situation radically when it was pointed out that these conditions made the handicrafts she produced too dirty to sell. She subsequently has little trouble seeing the connection between cleanliness and her own well-being.

Women in the programme changed their health and nutrition behaviour not because they were told to, or given extensive lessons on food groups, or recited a litany of do's and don'ts. They changed primarily because they had new access to needed resources, and because they saw a connection between a new practice and their own interests. To paraphrase Achola Pala Okeyo (*A Preliminary Survey of the Avenues for and Constraints on Women in the Development Process in Kenya*, Institute of Development Studies, University of Nairobi, 1975, p.26), women join good programmes, absorb relevant information, and adopt useful practices because they use their intelligence to determine that the advantages of doing so outweigh the disadvantages.

This project has illustrated that development goals were reached by focussing education on learners' priorities. These priorities were generally selected (by learners) from among the social and economic concerns that pervade daily life. Take the development goal of improving health practices, as an example. No choice of learners in Kenya was specific to health, yet there were important health implications in every group project. Consider each separately.

Look first at the objective of building a nursery school. Aside from ensuring that a child will have the opportunity to enter the formal schooling process, a nursery school is also an entry point for health services for children, such as immunisation and screening for problems such as malnutrition and infectious disease. In addition, in order to qualify under local regulations. nursery schools in Kenya must provide access for children to sanitary facilities, and adhere to other public health ordinances. As in most developing countries, lack of sanitary facilities is a major source of disease and infection in Kenya. A nursery school can also provide the impetus for organising parents around aspects of infant and child care. For most parents, particularly mothers, children are a primary reason for considering and adopting effective health practices.

Next, consider the bakery business. The income earned and saved by the bakers from the sale of bread, in general, goes towards basic needs of the family — housing, clothing, food, schooling — all of which have direct bearing on family health. In addition, to be approved as a commercial entity, installation of sanitary facilities for use by the bakers was required by law. Similarly the bakers, all 53 members of the women's group, were screened by the provincial medical officer. Fouled water had long been a problem in the area, and to ensure an available and safe source the women began to explore ways to capture and store large amounts of rain water, which would be the first large-scale system in the village. A poultry project was in the initial planning stages as the group wanted to add cakes to items for sale and must therefore have eggs. The cakes would be higher in protein than the bread. The bread has not replaced the traditional staple, ugali, which is taken at the afternoon and evening meal, but is taken in the morning with tea. The bread is considered of higher quality than that sold in the nearest towns, and costs the same.

Consider the poultry business to raise layers. Protein deficiency is a major problem in Kenya, and the National Institute of Nutrition has called for an increase in the consumption of protein-rich foods including chicken and eggs. For economic reasons and because of traditional taboos, many rural Kenyans do not eat eggs. When they are acquired it is frequently considered more advantageous to sell them.

When group members first began their poultry business they too did not use eggs themselves: first, because the eggs would fetch money, and second, because the women were not accustomed to using them in cooking. In the process of preparing the eggs for market a few eggs are generally broken. First the women determined to share the broken eggs among themselves. This developed into a policy that when each took her turn tending the birds, partial payment was two or three eggs for family use. In addition, just prior to each time the layers were sold off, the women allowed themselves to take a bird or two for family use. There is little doubt that a new dietary pattern has emerged among group members and their families.

Conclusions and Implications:
Why Are There So Few Programmes Like Tototo-Kilemba?

There are undoubtedly many reasons for the scarcity of programmes of the Tototo-Kilemba type around the world. Three stand out in particular: (a) resistance to altering the economic status quo or acknowledging it as the major cause of development problems; (b) the categorical organisation of development problems; (c) the difficulty in visualising mass machinery for delivering unique, specialised programmes at the community level.

One reason why some continue to focus only on categorical education (exclusive to topics such as health, nutrition or agriculture) and to avoid education for economic change, is that the latter implies a shift in control over resources. Planners with the former focus seem to conceive of poor men and women as competitors for the same limited supply of opportunities, and to see the basic problem as lack of information rather than lack of resources. A more accurate view is that economic opportunities and resources must be more equitably distributed to the poor if health and nutrition are to improve.

A second factor keeping the incidence of integrated programmes such as Tototo-Kilemba low is the unilateral and sometimes competitive division of development services in many countries. At the time of this project Kenya had a policy of integrating services at the village level, which was the task of the Ministry of Community Development. In other places the circumstances may not be so conducive to learner-determined projects. The key in such programmes is for people to learn how to recruit needed experts and resources from the range of available extension services provided by health, agriculture, community development and so on. This is necessary since each department or division has a categorical interest, and is generally not prepared, either structurally or with resources, to assist beyond its own departmental brief. Health people must deliver health services and not agricultural. People's lives are however more integrated. Health services and information are needed only at certain times for particular reasons. As a result, health workers frequently come to deliver their information and service in ways and at times that are inappropriate for villagers. The Tototo-Kilemba staff worked closely with agency service providers, assisting them to see the approaches and the timing most helpful to groups for reaching their goals. Subsequently, credit for success was widely shared with all extension workers who contributed expertise. In effect women learned to use the expertise of the professionals, and the professionals learned how to share their expertise.

A final reason why programmes of this kind are not much in evidence is closely linked to the categorical division of services. It is difficult for many planners and policy-makers to visualise machinery for reaching a mass audience while at the same time addressing small-scale interests and priorities. The conventional way in development education has been to standardise, to try to reach everyone with the same content, to persuade them with the same curriculum and configuration of services and resources. Possibly we have been standardising the wrong things. If one accepts the premises underlying Tototo-Kilemba it is evident that a process for implementing learner-determined education can be replicated on a wide scale while the content of learning is left open for rural people to select. Such a way of organising education helps to bridge the gap between national development priorities and those of rural people. It also greatly increases the opportunity for villagers to exert influence on those who constitute the delivery systems. Equally important, it capitalises on the energy, momentum and collective wisdom of existing groups of men and women, actualising their potential for national development.

To conclude, the project premises appear to be borne out:
(a) rural learners in the project areas were motivated to learn what they themselves deemed important, and these things had both implicit and direct outcomes corresponding with generally accepted development goals;
(b) it was possible systematically to organise and deliver education so that unique needs and goals of learners in different areas could be addressed — that is, to design education that was both situation-specific and that reached large numbers of people.

The factors which proved most important in organising this kind of education were:
(a) identifying and working with self-initiated groups who select a coordinator according to their own criteria;
(b) having coordinators sufficiently trained to be able to facilitate group discussion and problem-solving, and to help groups to see connections between practices essential to community development and their own goals and priorities;
(c) persuading cooperating official and voluntary agencies to match their service and technical assistance to what people request and are ready to receive, rather than focussing on what providers want to deliver.

Chapter Four

Developing Women's Income-generating Skills in Swaziland

Introduction

Simanga Nxumalo reports in this account on the early stages of another project for women, in a very small country, and one very dependent politically and economically, compared with both Kenya and Australia. Again the project is by and for women, but this time with the stress heavily upon the acquisition of skills and knowledge for income-generation, and with an interesting consideration of the introduction of appropriate technology in this context. Integration — the links between educational and other development activity — again proves significant. Here the emphasis is particularly on the link with borrowing facilities. The Revolving Fund concept echoes the essentially similar system which Penmas was testing in Indonesia at about this time, and which featured in another of the studies commissioned for this ICAE inquiry, but not included among this volume of published papers. The Penmas approach included functional literacy within income-generating development projects, where the link apparently provided motivation for acquiring literacy skills also. In the next study in this volume Dighe shows how literacy became valued and sought at certain points in an evolving project and set of needs-led activities, but was not introduced by the organisers at the outset.

Dighe's study echoes Nxumalo's in respect of borrowing facilities. These proved crucial for women in and around Ahmedabad to break the hold of money-lenders. Note the difference between the intended duration of financial support systems. For Nxumalo they are clearly but temporary. Dighe in the next chapter shows how while SEWA sought to bend existing institutions to serve the needs of poor self-employed women, it was also quite willing to create its own long-term financial and other institutions to serve their special needs. There is a question here for adult educators, in Britain for instance in these days of Economic Development Units and Enterprise, as to how far »education« might or should be extended into, in this instance, practical economic and financial activities, and beyond study, simulation and reflection. It was a very practical question when the German Adult Education Association (DVV) was supporting the Indonesian Revolving Fund approach: it was easy to see the desirability and legitimacy of supporting the training elements in such an integrative approach; less clear whether legitimacy as well as desirability attached to creating a Fund to buy sewing machines for productive purposes subsequently, from funds allocated from the German Government for »adult education«. Unless such problems can be resolved, the thoroughly practical, pragmatic, development- and production- oriented approaches described in these chapters by Clark, Nxumalo and Dighe may be frustrated.

Nxumalo's snapshot leaves several questions unanswered. This was part of a large national project, with three ministries involved, but the full picture, including the effective per capita cost in this particular segment, and the contribution of various international aid agencies, governmental and intergovernmental, is not quite clear. Much of the money went on technical aid personnel who feature little in this story, other than in a negative sense apropos the marketing expert. There are some echoes of Clark's and also Stacy's accounts in terms of (lack of) consultation over choice of projects for income-generation. Compare the very explicit needs- and demand- led approach in the SEWA story below, which accords with Clark's explicit philosophy.

Looking at this case study in a broader political context, it does appear a sensible and basically successful socio-economic strategy so long as the larger issues of relations with South Africa must be assumed to continue essentially unaltered. In a very poor, dependent, country and economy the men will continue to migrate for work and the women to be left with a multiple responsibility and burden. The larger problems of economic dependency are obviously beyond the scope of such a project. Indeed the »problem of South Africa« and of the black neighbouring enclave and frontline states has so far defied all world attempts at solution and even, it appears, amelioration. In this context the approach to local community development and to equipping women better to cope appears entirely positive. The local production and sale of school uniforms in place of purchase from South Africa is heartening; but one must remember that the materials and markets for much of the production described here continued to be South African.

If Stacy's story can be characterised as pessimist-realist, and Clark's as confidently optimistic in (for the particular group) less difficult socio-political circumstances, Nxumalo's analysis provides a well-balanced account of an adult education development project and the limitations of education as a force for change on its own. She notes that the project, as is so common, failed to reach its particular »target group«: the poorest women and families in the region. Echoing Clark in her stress upon the importance of consultation and participation, as well as functional relevance, if a project is to reach those for whom it is intended, she does none the less find the project, with these significant reservations, a success.

Summary

In 1975 a group of community development officers and adult educators approached the Government of Swaziland to propose a project to develop women's income-generating skills. Consultation between the Government and the United Nations on ways of complementing government efforts to improve levels of living and welfare in rural areas led to a start late in 1977. This was the first project since independence to attempt rural development in an integrated and multidisciplinary fashion. Emphasis from the outset was upon strengthening capabilities for income-generation among rural women and their families. These were identified as the principal project beneficiaries.

The project was located in Entfonjeni in Northern Swaziland, one of the least developed areas of the country but one with great potential. The Ministry of Agriculture and Cooperatives was responsible for integrated rural development through its Rural Development Area Programme so the project was placed under its Community Development Division for purposes of government budgeting, staffing and administration. Some decentralisation was envisaged for the future, eg. to a project responsibility centre.

The interdisciplinary nature of the project allowed the Centre to offer subjects such as agricultural extension and health education; but the main thrust was towards vocational skills. Rural women received training in textile and fashion design, sewing school uniforms, batik and macrame work, tie and dye. A Village Technology Unit provided training and technical advice on improved devices and procedures for production, processing and storage of various farm products, homestead sanitation and portable water storage. Some of these devices have been widely accepted because they respond to expressed demands of the community, but problems remained to be overcome.

The project supported graduates of the Centre through a Revolving Loan Fund. The Fund quickly assisted 15 women to own sewing and knitting machines, and through the loans women were able to provide schools in their respective areas with school uniforms and jerseys. The cooperative sales shop Sukumani Bomake (meaning literally »stand up mothers!«)located 30 km south of Entfonjeni in Pigg's Peak on a major national road, provided a facility for former project participants to display their various consumer goods and handicrafts, appealing to both domestic and tourist demand. Quality was quite high, and prices reasonable.

The first project activity was a community nursery, strategically located opposite the community clinic and adjacent to the Training Workshop. Some of the rural women took their children to the nursery school. The Ministry of Education provided facilities and staff for the school.

The ultimate aim of the project was to develop rural areas by developing and involving women in national development. The intention was to reach the poorest in the community but these did not fully participate. The project therefore sought ways to reach the grassroots. It aimed explicitly at reducing poverty. It was hoped that successful implementation would change the lifestyle of rural people in a tangible way. On the whole it did prove successful in terms of income-generation in rural areas, though not among the poorest of the poor.

The General Context

Swaziland, the smallest country in Africa after Gambia, has an area of 6,754 square miles It is situated in the southeast of the continent, with a subtropical climate, and is landlocked, bounded by the Republic of South Africa to the south, north and west, and by Mozambique on the east. There are four geographical regions, Highveld, Middleveld, Lowveld, and Lumbombo. Drainage is by perennial rivers. Most of the rain occurs in the summer, and once a decade the rains are deficient. The Middleveld, the most densely populated area, is the location of the commercial and industrial town of Manzini. The capital, Mbabane, is in the Highveld. The population is over 80% rural. Over 75% are illiterate. A British protectorate until Independence in 1968, Swaziland has two official languages, Siswati and English Its population of over half a million has a majority of women and an annual growth rate of about 3 per cent

The Swazi people are a cohesive nation with common language, culture and customs. The king (the longest reigning monarch in the world) and Swazi National Council support a modern constitutional government with a bicameral parliament. This new system of government follows the Swazi tradition. The position of the chiefs is very strong. Even in modern administration their traditional role is recognised and respected. Projects need the support and blessing of the chiefs of the area. The framework of relationships and the type of coordination must be well defined and supported for any project to make an effective contribution.

The economy is diversified: agriculture and manufacturing account for 35 and 15% respectively, mining for just under 10 per cent. Swaziland has the world's largest manmade forest and ranks fifth in asbestos production. Subsistence farming is however the mainstay for many people, though its contribution to GDP is modest. Data on income distribution are hard to come by but it is evidently skewed; the traditional subsistence sector receives little benefit from economic growth.

Emergence of a cash economy has led to high migration of males to the towns in search of wage employment. The aim is to get wages to improve agricultural output. What in fact happens is that the income earned is insufficient to support both the man and his family. The absence of men from the rural areas exacerbates problems of agricultural production, overburdening the women who may plant late and so produce a small harvest. In addition a significant proportion of men who migrate to urban areas seek wage employment in mines in the Republic of South Africa. Official recruiting organisations which issue contracts to migrant workers account for 8,000 a year but an estimated 30,000 Swazi men migrate to seek employment in the mines and other fields of activity in the Republic, by their own private means. The large-scale migration has adverse effects on the family structure, often causing quasi-seasonal family living and imposing on women the obligation to tend crops and maintain home.

The Status of Women

Women have a very significant role in the economy. Male migration leaves women dominant in agricultural production. Typically the traditional woman would be responsible for tending domestic animals and performing domestic chores. On the farm she assumes the tasks of planting, weeding, harvesting and storing crops. The tasks of ploughing, felling trees to clear the land, and maintenance and building of houses, were male responsibilities, but with male migration women have had to assume these responsibilities as well. Although the function has changed with the combined responsibilities of both sexes, however, the woman's traditional position remains unchanged. There is for instance no improvement in access to and control over the resources required to fulfil these responsibilities. Access to credit remains a problem, a result of lack of security to obtain a loan, and because of the prerequisite, for a loan, of a collateral agreement of the husband or other male relative. Wages from absent males are irregular and quite insufficient to allow investment in alternative activities.

The women of rural Swaziland therefore lead a very hard life. although they have come far since precolonial and colonial times. Even though a number are now educated and moving into different sectors of government and business, the prematurely aged woman trudging up hill bent double under a load of firewood, or with an earthenware pot on her head and a toddler on her back is still a common sight. Nevertheless women have always made a contribution to income-generating activities. Women selling their produce from rural areas is a common sight even in urban settings.

In the commercial sector a large number of traders in the established markets of Swaziland are women. One of the biggest markets is the country, Mahlanya Rural Market, was constructed by newly literate women through community organisation and action. The Ministry of Commerce, Industry, Mines and Tourism estimated that more than 2,000 women engaged in marketing, usually of consumer goods in small shops. In the traditional rural sector the principal activity of women is handicrafts. These range from simple fabrication of garments and baskets for home use to sophisticated fine headwork which is increasingly in demand in the modern sector, both for sale in the Republic of South Africa and for export elsewhere.

The Project

Swaziland's Second National Development Plan emphasised rural development. The rural areas, where most people live, and which depend mainly on traditional agriculture to provide a livelihood, command high priority. Physical development of the rural areas through improving and expanding infrastructure facilities, creating job opportunities, establishing rural-based organisations, and modernising the agricultural sector: these are means through which the rural areas may contribute to economic growth, self-reliance, and social justice. The role of rural families, and women in particular, in this process has been identified as a major concern, being the backbone of the agrarian economy. Improved national and local capabilities, training and advisory services in income-generating activities among rural women and their families, should enhance their roles as contributors to national development. In 1975, therefore, a group of community development officers and adult educators approached the Government of Swaziland about introducing income-generating skills for women in rural areas. By improving conditions here it was hoped to reduce migration to urban areas. Consultations began between the Government and the United Nations on ways of complementing government efforts to improve levels of living and welfare in rural areas. The project, »the development of income-generating skills for women«, began in late 1977. Although it was inter-ministerial, it was placed under the Ministry of Agriculture and Cooperatives, to facilitiate government budgeting, staffing and project administration. The project was financed by the United Nations, the Government of the Netherlands, and the Government of Swaziland, and located at Entfonjeni in the most rural northern part of the country.

It was intended to deal with rural development in an integrated and multidisciplinary manner, with immediate emphasis on strengthening capabilities for income-generation among rural women and their families. Later the target group expanded to include school leavers of all ages and both sexes, as well as the unemployed in rural areas. The principal thrust was promotion, training and advisory services in income-generating activities.

Community leaders were consulted during the first stages of the project to familiarise them with the objectives and solicit their support. The local chiefs were thus enlisted and all available means of indigenous communication in the area used whenever possible, including public meetings arranged by the chiefs to persuade people to take part. Inducements to participate when the project was first introduced included payment of expenses to cover the cost of the course, provision of free material, free places and a small per diem. The project, intended mainly for the poorest of the poor, was strategically placed next to the Rural Development area of the Ministry of Agriculture and Cooperatives.

Aims and Objectives

The Meaning of Poverty

According to Todaro the concept of absolute poverty has been used to estimate the magnitude of world poverty. In 1969 about 35% of the world's people were attempting to subsist at barely minimal levels of living. Some countries are characterised by high per capita income without necessarily eliminating poverty; thus Kuwait's per capita income in 1969 was second only to that of the U.S.A. Development is not synonymous with rising per capita income. Care should be taken if this is used as a rough measure of development.

Poverty is relative. Its measurement presents technical, social and political problems. Although standards and costs of living vary from country to country, poverty can be defined by the number of people living below an imaginary international poverty line. In Swaziland's Third National Development Plan »it is government policy and its foremost policy to ensure an equitable distribution of the fruits of development among all Swazi people. This policy demands that priority be given to measures which will improve the well-being of people in rural communities where 80% of the people live.«

Countries are neither poor nor rich. It is the individuals who are well-fed or hungry, sick or well, literate or illiterate. One criterion which may be used to determine level of poverty is the standard of living and the level of basic needs and standard of household consumption. This includes: shelter and food — on the basis of a 1962 Nutrition Survey in Swaziland 65% of the families in rural areas were not reaching the minimum required nutrition levels; access to essential services such as safe drinking water (ie. a fully equipped borehole or a well at a reasonable distance serving not more than 300 people). Available figures suggest that about 65% of the people of Swaziland lack adequate water facilities, only the urban areas being reasonably served. A poverty-stricken area is characterised by poor health facilities, malnutrition, high infant mortality, and poor educational facilities. It is not easy to say whether these characteristics are causes or effects of poverty, or both.

Adult Education and Reduction of Poverty

Reduction of poverty should lead eventually to its elimination. According to the Third National Development Plan the Government of Swaziland would promote social justice by spreading economic opportunities and social services more widely. It was intended to increase clinic coverage so that by 1983 75% of the population would be living within 8 km of basic health facilities, and to increase the quality and distribution of preventive health services. Adult education is taken to mean any educational activity designed for adults to bring about change in knowledge, skills or attitudes. Marx called the person the most productive force of all, believed firmly in the classical tradition, and regarded education as a means of combatting the alienation of man from economic activity. One function of education is to help improve the quality of human beings as productive agents. It should lead to improved knowledge, improved health and skills, better organisation and management of one's life. According to Alfred Marshall the most valuable form of capital is that invested in human beings. Over a century ago H. Mann preached that »education prevents being poor«. Today the Government of Swaziland seeks education as a powerful device for achieving social change: »the future development of the country's natural and human resources depends largely upon the quantity and quality of their education. Every effort will be made to create a system that gives the desired result.«

Philip Coombs identified four broad areas in which education can be crucial in reducing poverty:

occupational education — designed to develop particular knowledge and skills associated with various economic activities and useful in making a living;

community improvement education — designed to strengthen local and national institutions and processes through instruction in such matters as co-operative community projects;

general or basic education — covering literacy, numeracy and understanding one's environment;

family improvement education — designed primarily to impart knowledge, skills and attitudes useful in improving the quality of family life, in such subjects as health and nutrition, child care, family planning.

Project Objectives

The long-range project objective was to maximise women's contribution to national development by increasing their capacity to perform better their tasks in the home and family, in domestic agriculture, and in the wage employment and income-generating sector. Income-generating must relate to the environment or context: that is, to the socio-economic and political climate in which projects are introduced. They must increase participants' income, but should also lead to changes in their social position. The social impact should include an improved social image, improved bargaining power. Politically the project should enable women to get into the mainstream of development. The project should not make worse the existing sexual inequality.

Specific Objectives were as follows.

To provide promotion, training and advisory services in income- generating activities among poor rural women and their families, including school dropouts, with special emphasis on technical and managerial training in handicrafts, needle, leather and macrame crafts, textile and fashion designs, and tie-dye textile work. This relates directly to the reduction of poverty through imparting practical knowledge and skills.

To gather marketing intelligence and establish a marketing pool to sell the finished products of women's groups and associations. A cooperative sales shop, Sukumani Bomaka, in Pigg's Peak, provided an outlet. Inadequate knowledge of the market and lack of management skills had been identified as the weakest aspects of women's projects. Very often organisers and participants are unaware of the nature of the market, and whether products will compete successfully with those already being produced. This objective pertains to increasing knowledge and changing attitudes. Rural women need adequate information about the dynamic nature of the market, which might help them decide whether to upgrade, modify or redirect local practices, or replace them altogether.

To establish a day care centre at the Entfonjeni location and day care centres in the Northern Area. This would release women from looking after children, enabling them to participate fully in learning income-generating skills; it would also alleviate the shortage of pre-school facilities in the area. Poor performance in primary schools is caused among other things by pupils' socio-economic and educational background. The dropout rate is alarming, particularly higher up the educational pyramid. In Swaziland, of 100 pupils in Grade 1 in 1974 for instance, 70 reached standard one and only 22 completed standard five. One third of Swazi pupils leave school without achieving literacy even in Siswati. Here an educational objective also has indirect implications for changing economic standards; it is about satisfying basic needs such as health, and increasing income.

To provide training for a core of governmental and nongovernmental leaders through fellowships and practical training, creating a much improved base for future women's programmes. The core group should carry out other community development projects, in the pilot area or in other parts of the country.

Programme Content and Other Features of the Project

Training needs and programme content were determined by means of staff assessment and consultation with local women and their families on consumption needs and production possibilities. Income-generating activities were concerned largely with small- scale import substitution of selected categories of consumer goods. There were also limited efforts at promotion of exports.

The interest and will of project participants determined the extent to which the input (training in income-generating activities) contributed to improved levels of living and general welfare. An equally important factor was the extent to which the project responded to specific requests of participants. Continuous encouragement was particularly important, given that the target group included young school leavers who had been ruthlessly discarded by the formal school system. These young people commonly develop personality traits such as lack of confidence and a fatalistic approach to life.

A medium-sized training workshop was opened as Entfonjeni early in l979, and provided with electricity and running water. The greater part of the building was devoted to a training area where sewing, knitting and other training equipment were kept, and training supplies stored. There was also some office space for project personnel.

Located next to the workshop was a combined Appropriate (or Village) Technology Workshop and Demonstration Unit. Founded in 1979, the Unit identified and promoted improved domestic practices. Seminars and workshops in 1979 for both senior headquarters staff and local staff considered the need for and applications of appropriate technology in Swaziland. The Unit conducted demonstration devices for improved grain and water storage, latrines, water waste disposal system, production of improved building material, a solar system drier, fridge and stove. Altogether 28 items were made, using local material. Since most homesteads in the rural areas lack the capital to buy building materials such as cement, chicken wire and pipe fittings, the centre sold the finished items at a price which the homesteads could afford.

These items were modified to suit the requirements of the rural population. For example the grain and water storage had to be improved several times. A padlock had to be fitted because of the prevalence of witchcraft in the area. Several people, many of them relatives of the author, expressed fear of poisoning if the tank were left outside and unlocked. The Appropriate Technology Unit certainly created awareness and enthusiasm in the area. It also took advantage of local skills. For instance the portable water storage unit resembled in many ways the traditional earthenware pots made of clay. The Unit improved upon the idea. It also helped improve facilities of the project training workshop. Requests for demonstrations and training came from residents in the area; in a way the Unit served the nation rather than just the local area.

A vegetable garden was cultivated close to the training workshop, to demonstrate to women and their families practical applications of dry-land farming techniques for growing types of food important to improve family nutrition.

The first construction put up by the women was the community nursery. It was to motivate them to take part in the programme, and to take care of the children while the parents were learning. Strategically located adjacent to the centre and opposite a rural clinic, it demonstrated the integrated nature of the project. The Ministry of Education trained teachers here, and community-based nursery schools were developed in cooperation with the Ministry of Education.

The cooperative sales shop at Pigg's Peak provided a facility to display and sell various consumer goods and handicrafts produced by people trained under the project. It appealed to both tourist and domestic demands. Quality was quite high but the management still planned to set up a bureau of standards. Staff were housed with all modern amenities on a main road at Pigg's Peak rather than at Entfonjeri, because of limited domestic water supplies at the latter.

No entry qualifications were required. Some active women participants attended regular literacy classes in the area, but enrolment in literacy classes was not a prerequisite. Because of the mixed level of participants — school dropouts, illiterates, some with no previous experience of dress-making, using a sewing machine or knitting needle — training to a commercial standard took a long time. The training period varied from three to six months, depending on participants' background, motivation, the training approaches used, and so on.

At any one time the limited resources of technical staff and training equipment allowed only about twenty women to participate in a course of training. Because of homestead responsibilities participants could not be trained on a full-time basis, so their period of training took up to a year or even longer.

Most of the instructors came from the local community; some were recruited from other parts of the country. Training was conducted in an environment apropriate to the education of adults, and a participatory approach was often preferred. The experts realised that, experts though they were in the skills they taught, they could also learn a lot from their students. In fact local community members were often invited to teach certain skills popular in the area.

The Project Manager, herself an adult education practitioner, habitually sent instructors to attend adult education workshops in Swaziland or abroad. Four local women assumed instructional duties at the Entfonjeni training workshop and were part-time Diploma of Adult Education students at the Division of Extra- Mural Services of the University of Swaziland. They were thus equipping themselves effectively to impart skills to adults.

The women were involved in producing school uniforms, jersey knitting, woven sisal handicrafts, crochet work, tie-dye fabric design, block screen printing, macrame work, batik, design and manufacture of shirts and dresses, patchwork and household linen manufacture, traditional doll-making, and shoe-making. Sisal weaving accounted for about one third of all project products. It is time-consuming and the women were searching for a more efficient and profitable area, especially as the sisal in Northern Swaziland is inferior to that from other parts of the country. Needle crafts accounted for about one third of production. This had important implications for both import substitution and export promotion.

Training was mainly in technical skills in needle crafts and textile design. Bulk purchases were often necessary to cater for the large numbers of trainees. Needle craft training covered five basic styles of school uniforms and eight different styles of shirts and dresses. Each item required approximately three metres of cloth; uniform training therefore required a minimum of 15 metres, while 24 metres were required for training for shirts and dresses. Most participants required to make about four examples of each style before reaching a commercial standard. Each thus needed some 156 metres of cloth.

Training in needle craft was limited by the number of sewing machines available, so concurrent training was organised in batik and tie-dye fabric design, and in the manufacture of patchwork, placemats, aprons and hotpads out of traditional Swazi cloth.

Consumption of training materials was high: six months' training for a group of twenty in needle crafts and textile design required some 1,560 metres of cloth. Pigg's Peak, the nearest town, is very small, and local demand was insufficient to justify a shop for wholesale purchases of various types of cloth required for training. Consequently wholesale purchasing was done in Nelspruit some 130 km away in South Africa, or in Manzini 110 km to the south-east. Purchases must therefore be on a scale sufficient for weeks of training demand. Bulk purchasing also served an educational purpose: participants were taught to plan, to compare product quality, and to negotiate. The Project Manager occasionally travelled with participants so that they were exposed to different wholesalers in the Republic of South Africa, often an educative experience.

Maintaining good human relations should be a major characteristic of projects of this nature. Fortunately project staff were well endowed for this; they also exhibited a high degree of initiative in responding to requests for technical advice. In the light of the response to batik training and the rapid progress participants made in developing their skills, for example, DANIDA was requested to assist by making available the services of an expert in batik design to conduct an advanced level seminar. The workshop was a success, and the textbook written by the expert used as a basic reference by the Project Manager.

Training constituted the core of all project efforts but its success and the effectiveness of the project lay in the potential it offered to rural people for cash employment. In her final report the previous Project Manager observed that intended beneficiaries would not consider their training valid unless it resulted in an immediate cash return. The women's initiative in starting the cooperative retail shop Sukumani Bomaki therefore tended to confirm the appropriateness of current training efforts to the needs of residents in the area. Project support to the shop essentially took the form of assistance in training staff in basic management and bookkeeping skills.

Project staff acted as facilitators among women who had attained a commercial skill level. A good example was school uniforms and jerseys. Traditionally schools in the Entfonjeni area purchased these items from manufacturers in South Africa. The geographical and economic position of Swaziland makes it completely dependent on its powerful neighbour for all sorts of commodities, even the most basic such as soap and rice. It was a commendable breakthrough that once an initial group of needlecraft trainees had attained a sufficient skill level, project staff began consulting with parents' associations about their willingness to purchase a local product of better quality at a lower price than that from South Africa. Parents' associations of twelve area schools then asked their principals to purchase uniforms and jerseys from the cooperative producers' group formed by project participants. There were 50 schools in the area, so due to limited production capability, additional demands for uniforms and jerseys were going unfulfilled.

Rural women and families in the Entfonjeni area were poor; the average annual family cash income was less than US$ 600. They were not able to use conventional credit sources to finance modest investment in fixed assets required for various income- generating activities, or to provide a source of working capital to support their group. Consider for example the cost of a sewing machine: between three and five months' average family income. Some knitting and sewing machines were made available on a cost-recovery basis. This was the beginning to stimulating the creation of viable producer groups, an initiative which would also help to establish a credit rating for project participants, so that conventional credit mechanisms could be used for subsequent credit needs.

Revolving Loan Fund

The Fund was introduced in June 1980 and assisted fifteen women to become owners of sewing and knitting machines to a total value of E3,885.84. This approximated the total amount allocated for equipment loans. Over 60% was outstanding in April 1981. Out of the Revolving Loan Fund a number of women were provided with loans for the purchase of other equipment and raw materials. Through this loan women were able to provide schools in their respective areas with uniforms and jerseys, and to sell other products, both to neighbours and through the market outlet shop at Pigg's Peak.

Loan terms were kept simple to meet special circumstances; for instance the loans were interest-free. The work involved in collecting outstanding debts was underestimated initially. Experience showed that this required a lot of effort and time. Documents were introduced for the effective management of the Revolving Loan Fund, among them loan application and loan agreement forms.

Loans were made for the purchase of material for school uniforms, jerseys, tie and dyes, textile printing, batik, and for other income-generating products. Working capital loans were also provided to male artisans who had been trained, for appropriate technology purposes. The Raw Material loans were of very short duration and usually meant to be repaid in total at an agreed due date. The majority were provided in kind from the revolving stock of raw materials kept for this purpose. During the 1980-81 financial year E6,979.85 worth of various types of materials was sold to about 300 women producers, partly on a loan basis and partly for cash. This comprised 60% of the total sales for the period.

The Fund helped to supply three schools with uniform, while women's groups supplied for 23 schools during the 1980 school year. As a result of the failure of some women to provide schools with uniform, the Revolving Loan Fund got directly involved. The Fund protected them from losing their markets in following school years. It was also involved in buying sisal products from about 100 women's groups. Since the biggest market for sisal products was in South Africa producers could not wait between accumulating the minimum economic level of sisal products to warrant transportation to South Africa, and the subsequent receipt of their money from the buyer. Hence the Fund gave a sort of commodity loan by providing cash for every product made and delivered to the stores for onward transmittal to the buyer. In any loan activity bad debts are inevitable: they can be minimised by using certain measures. At the beginning credit rating procedures were not well established, and loans were granted on a »start somewhere« basis. Monitoring of progress, and loan collection follow-up, were not adequate, partly because of lack of personnel to do the job. However, most beneficiaries successfully completed repayment, or continued to repay on schedule.

Financing

No adequate figures were available for costs. It appears that the following amounts were expended on the project (UNDP figures in US dollars, Government figures in Emalangeni (E); the Lilangeni is roughly at par with the US dollar).

1975-77	UN: $ 263,469	Government: E101,980*	Total: 365,449
1978	169,312	22,030	191,342
1979	303,288	47,780	351,068
1980	232,868	44,780	277,648
1981	74,431	49,430	123,861
1982(est.)	194,494	137,600	332,094

* E85,000 for buildings

The total of $ 268,925 listed for 1981-82 as UN appears to have been divided between UNDP ($ 40,000) and the Government of The Netherlands ($ 228,925). Itemisation suggests that most of the Government of Swaziland money after 1977 was spent on project personnel. Project personnel were also the main cost in the UN budget (including volunteers) with smaller amounts for training equipment, travel and consumables. Figures for the Revolving Fund in and leading to the first half of 1980 suggest an operation of a few thousand dollars in all: grants in cash of $ 8,300 and in kind of $ 5,000, with sales and incidental income in a half year of E11,837 yielding a net surplus after expenditure of E589.

Analysis of Achievements

The project made remarkable progress. The immediate objectives were quickly being met. Suitable areas of training for women in income-generating activities were identified and others investigated. There was no formal advertisement in the media for new recruits to join. The Project's activities spread by word of mouth, in particular by extension officers of the Rural Development Area. The demand for the project was so great that staff recruitment could not catch up. Staff were overworked in trying to cope. The progress was made through the interest and enthusiasm of rural women who were very anxious to improve their standard of living and to pay school fees for their children. Education was not free in Swaziland, and even universal primary education was expected to be achieved only in 1985. Many of the women who had been trained then worked at home but came to the project for business training and coordination with their group, and to accept orders and purchase cloth.

The project contributed to reducing poverty through imparting vocational skills. A large number of those who took part became financially self-sufficient. Many of the women who had been trained then worked and became conscious that they had special talents which could help them improve their standard of living. Looking at the activities one sees a good programme, and also an outstanding contribution to nation-building.

More specifically, about 180 trainees were being trained in the following subjects: batik, patchwork, spinning, weaving, tie- dye, block-screen printing, knitting. The skilled graduates had become independent producers and had formed the cooperative producers' group in Entfonjeni and Pigg's Peak. The cooperative shop functioned as an outlet for products, although a more prominent site was being sought especially to increase sales to tourists. The marketing aspect of the project was still in its infancy, and more research required before a marketing policy could be formulated. The marketing expert seemed to have operated in a vacuum. His activities and those of other UN experts were not coordinated, nor synchronised with the activities of the local or national instructors. Communication was bad and there were apparently personality clashes.

The *Village Technology Unit* progressed well. The Project Manager and two artisans attended a solar conference in Atlanta in 1979. Twenty-eight items had been devised using local materials; they were continually being modified to suit the requirements of the rural population. There were many visitors to the demonstration area from Swaziland and other countries. The local rural people showed great interest in many of the devices. Two local artisans were successfully trained in carpentry by the UN volunteer carpenter.

Demonstration Units should be close to rural communities, not necessarily in the wilderness or in semi-urban towns but in strategic places. The units should vary between low and higher technology according to the felt needs of the area. The devices should, so far as possible, adhere to local conditions and answer to them, for instance social acceptability, cultural patterns, religion and beliefs. For instance the solar food-dryer all too closely resembled graves in the Northern area, suggesting a need for redesign to an oval or even round shape. Equipment should take into account the level of technical knowledge prevailing in the countryside, which is not static. The equipment must be efficient, durable, and able to perform a high volume output. The centre had taken this into consideration. The danger with Appropriate Technology, though, is the makeshift and clumsy appearance. There is a need to consider making the items more attractive. Some of the equipment produced by the centre was just too big for rural kitchens (emadladla). The stove, for instance, was modelled along the lines of modern kitchens, and was simply too big and clumsy, out of tune with the habits of the community. Most women in rural areas were not used to standing when they cook; they either bend from the waist or, preferably, sit down. The stove needed to be made and remade; the centre was considering a new design suited to traditional round-bottomed earthenware pots.

There was a question whether appropriate technology should spearhead social change or facilitate it. This will differ from country to country, but for change to occur many variables need to be in play. Just as education cannot be a panacea for all the social ills of the country, appropriate technology will contribute to social development when the whole superstructure is in motion. There is however no doubt that the Unit created awareness and enthusiasm in the area. People discussed it in their homesteads, showing that it had affected or was likely to affect their lives. It was certainly playing a role in motivating the community to seek solutions to problems within their sphere and means to influence.

Project staff should however take advantage of meetings, for example meetings called by local chiefs for demonstrations of appropriate technology. Also extension staff need to attend more leadership training seminars, communication skills workshops, etc., so that they can plan demonstrations which will emphasise useful and practical things which local people can comprehend, feel, touch, see and be able to make. Appropriate technology implies a major attitude change, and this seldom happens in isolation. To change one's way of doing things can be traumatic. Chiefs' meetings should be used to the utmost. For one thing, community members can see that the chief favours the idea. Even more important, especially for attitude change, is group cohesion and conformity. Members belong to groups and most will find it difficult to depart from group norms. It helps, therefore, to aim at groups in changing attitudes.

The extension officer should also learn to learn from the community before teaching anything. A person who is suddenly told to use a solar dryer for preserving greens, instead of the method her forefathers used, will certainly abhor the intrusion unless the »change agent« shows a genuine idea to learn before teaching. When an extension officer comes along with an innovation, rural folk ask themselves why they should take up the idea. The officer must enter into a dialogue with the people so that together they can solve their problems. The package approach of doing things for the people should give way to a truly participatory approach where no party feels the weight of the other.

The knitting, school uniform and textile design group did extremely well. The machine knitting group increased its number to ten during 1980. They had many orders from schools and became financially independent even though they still had a loan to repay for the first materials they used. The group teacher was able to handle the accounts, and with a book-keeper did monthly stock-taking. At first the bulk of accounting work was done by two of them, but the others were learning rapidly. All needed help in building their confidence and in using their initiative to expand their group.

The school uniform group had six very competent trained workers, with four more in training. Some of these women had had up to three years of secondary education, and even some technical training; others were illiterate. The trainees needed more practice in the use of patterns and the finer art of commercial production before being good enough to join the other group. Their training was slowed down by their mixed educational background, and also because of shortage of staff; business education and store management had taken up much of the teacher's time. With a storekeeper/book-keeper employed it was hoped that these workers would improve quite quickly and complete their training.

The *tie and dye group* were all able to produce work of commercial standard, but still needed advanced training in both dyeing and fashion design and pattern construction. One trainee graduated and joined the project staff to assist in training the others. There was a local market for this product. The dress-making and tie-dye staff undertook a study tour in these skills in September 1979 in Kenya, Ghana and Sierra Leone.

The *batik group* was small, and three of them left the training for reasons that were not clear; their work was good, and sold well. The demand was too high for the remaining group to meet. More trainees were since taken on. The group had just started producing lampshades and duvet covers as well as hangings; there seemed to be a commercial interest in these things.

The *Swazi cloth and toy-makers* became fully occupied with other activities. The group deserted toy-making because the market was small and there was a market for the patchwork and household made in traditional Swazi cloth which they now concentrated on. Sisal work continued but it was hoped that the group would shortly become more independent. They delivered their products to the workshop but were still dependent on the project and large-scale buying of the sisal bales, and for its transport.

Mohair spinning was started because of an overseas market. The activity was shaky but the project staff still embarked on it. The most likely economic viability lay in hand-spun, hand-woven goods produced at home and marketed cooperatively as high quality goods for the upper income bracket. *Agricultural activities* were mainly at the demonstration and training stage. Four women sold pigs which they reared at home, at a profit of 20 emalangeni per pig. They were happy with this profit margin, and others were expected to expand the group.

Business management was the most difficult area — not only to train the women, but also to assist them to manage bank accounts, stock-taking, and general book-keeping. Efforts were being made to improve marketing, and a brochure was produced on this. These women received training from the Ministry of Industry, Mines and Commerce as well, but did not seem to have benefitted from the expertise of the market expert. *Supplying* of raw materials and dyes was a major problem. Cloth for school uniform needed four to six months to order; dyes ordered in April had still not arrived in August.

The new *nursery school* was started during the reporting year (1981), and the new building for the Entfonjeni nursey school was opened in September 1979. A nursery school teacher since returned from Israel where she studied for nine months. It was expected that after discussions with the Ministry of Education and the parents' committee she might be asked to give practical training to the other nursery school teachers. UN would then help to subsidise her salary.

Conclusions and Implications

This assessment of project performance and results is based on discussions with project staff and graduates at the centre, and on project documents. Even though rural women and their families had become a focus of government concern through the Integrated Women in Development project, there was still no government policy on women. This absence of policy was conspicuous. Projects like the Entfonjeni will succeed only if there is support from above. If the initiative of progressive women is thwarted by shortage of funds and staff then clearly therapeutic relief in the face of rural neglect will solve little.

Project staff in promotion, training and advisory services in income-generating activities and village technology are however highly valued by the Government. These efforts are significant for the ways they build upon latent potentialities of rural women and assist in opening new opportunities for them. Promoting self-reliance and strengthening local capabilities are important to the continuing development of Swazi women. They in turn can contribute to the development of their rural areas. Rural women's motivation and involvement has been substantial because of the focus on activities with immediate development impact. The project demonstrated key non-formal educational characteristics — short-term, participative, and flexible.

Project efforts need to be extended to other Districts of the country. Special emphasis was placed on the Chiselweni (South), Manzini (Central) and Lubombo (East) of Swaziland, but limited staff and financial resources led to lower output. Counterpart and national posts were required. The incumbents were only on secondment. This created insecurity of tenure: of the 16 national staff only 6 were being paid by the Government. Project expansion required consolidating the Entfonjeni experience, developing local technical staff, and an adequate resource base of training facilities. In this regard the importance of continued UN support cannot be over-emphasised.

Training remained the core project concern, concentrating on technical and managerial training in topics which would further strengthen and improve the development potential of rural women and their families. The value of well planned tools is stressed: these helped broaden the horizons of potential local trainers, facilitating exchange of relevant knowledge and experience among poor countries. Enhanced income-generation is concerned especially with expanding the range of goods and services provided by indigenous entrepreneurs, as a means of creating additional non- farm employment opportunities and promoting a greater sense of self-reliance. Fundamental to an effective project is the decision as to what products and services are to be promoted, and what kind of technical and managerial training provided. Such decisions need to reflect the production possibilities which exist in rural areas, and market conditions.

Two sets of endogenous factors and one exogenous factor will influence product selection. One of the former concerns relationships between enterprise, market and resource base. The first of these relationships concerns the extent to which an enterprise may be developed from a resource occurring locally. An example from Entfonjeni might be enterprises using the timber which is abundant in the area. The enterprise also needs a market. In the case of wood products the domestic market may be national rather than local. The other such factor relates to development of an enterprise in response to specific demand; for example at Entfonjeni development of cooperative production teams to manufacture school uniforms and jerseys. An exogenous constraint in rural Swaziland is the Customs Union Agreement to which the country belongs. Although this contains an infant industry proviso it has effectively discouraged many industries from getting off the ground.

In terms of the purpose of increasing women's participation, and that of their families, in national development, the emphasis on cooperative arrangements seems to have been successful. Families in rural Swaziland are very poor. They face great difficulty in securing finances to purchase fixed assets and obtain working capital to undertake income-generation. They are trapped in a vicious cycle when attempting to use conventional banking resources. The project has been invaluable in providing loans. The Revolving Loan Fund is short-term in nature. It is used only to meet initial capital requirements for training project beneficiaries, not capital requirements on a recurring basis. To do the latter would be to create conditions for dependency. It is important that the Fund serves only as a bridge, facilitating access to conventional financial resources, not as an alternative to them.

Some problems stemmed from lack of material and equipment; others from the fact that the project failed to attract the participation of those for whom it was specially meant. Although the intention was to reach the poorest of the poor, these people did not take part. People in rural areas commonly prefer their long-established ways of doing things. Some women ignored the centres since they felt that they could not make any significant contribution to their lives. This indifferent group has been described as apathetic, fatalistic, resigned, content with their lot. Instead of labelling them ignorant and unsophisticated, adult educators should seek other means to encourage them into development projects. Through the direction of the Project Manager, herself an adult educator, the centre went on to explore ways of attracting the people for whom the project was originally meant, encouraging rural people to suggest the skills they would like to learn. The chief of the area acted in this case as an opinion leader.

In other ways the project progressed satisfactorily. Staff reported that some 500 people learned skills in the centre since the project started in 1977. They acquired skills and became self-employed, with a cooperative shop as an outlet for their products, also a day-care centre with Ministry of Education help in teacher training, and a number of children of pre-school age enjoying kindergarten facilities. Project learning was utilised. The project contributed to reducing poverty by imparting vocational skills. A number of women became financially self- sufficient. Apart from the batik women who left there was very little wasted training, indicating that the women found value in the project.

The Revolving Fund contributed to this. However, for training to be completed and more women to be trained, additional inputs would be required. These should increase teaching capability and provide more space for training and production, also finance for providing the raw materials. There was also the need to integrate project activities and ensure a smooth flow of information. Machinery for marketing and distributing women's products was needed through a central marketing outlet. The Ministry of Agriculture under which the project fell had the necessary facilities and should assist in this respect.

So the project did contribute to reducing poverty for a few people in the area. The intention was to raise the standard of living. This was however made difficult by lack of basic data on the real needs of the different categories of women in the area. The rural poor are not a homogeneous group. Many variables affect their behaviour. The poorest of them, for whom the project was intended, did not participate effectively. Only a small section of this real target group took advantage of it. First, the project was introduced by a group of community development officers. It did not come from the community. One reason for non-participation was that women did not want to invest energy in a project the benefits of which would take time to mature. The intended beneficiaries did not take part in project selection. There was no survey of women's activities; of what the typical rural woman's day was like, what income- generating skills were popular in the area, and so on. There was very little participatory research at the beginning. To develop skills that respond to social change women need to participate fully throughout, from project selection to evaluation. Thus will they develop leadership skills. Although the project was a success, in that those who took part earned income, politically it has not given women much awareness of their problems.

Overall, the project still had great potential, providing participants could be fully involved in all stages of project development. This must include illiterate and »ignorant« women whose experience could enrich the learning and the project. Also instructors required instruction to be innovative, imaginative and creative.

Education will not solve all the development problems of poor countries. Programmes can help to bring about development and reduce poverty, so long as the other variables crucial to development are introduced at the same time. Education of the Freirean kind can make people aware of their potential and the role they should play in society. It will not on its own give land to the landless, remove racism and sexism, eliminate unemployment and inequality. Adult education programmes will therefore only be effective if the socio-economic and political context in which they are embedded is receptive to the forces of change. A country that does not want to develop critical consciousness among its citizens will halt any educational programme of the Freirean type, tending to introduce instead programmes that are merely therapeutic.

In summary, the project succeeded in imparting vocational skills to the few women who took part. It was unsuccessful in reaching the real target group. It was a success in that the methods used were learner-centred, experiential, peer-taught, flexible and informal. It failed to involve the community during both the planning and the project selection stages. There is room for innovation, imagination and creativity. Apart from helping women achieve economic independence the project should also have improved participants' social situation. Its enhanced usefulness would depend on correcting this. The project was however quickly introduced into the other three Districts of the country.

Sources

Government of Swaziland *Third National Development Plan 1978-1983*
ILO *Reducing Dependence. A Strategy for Productive Employment and Development in Swaziland*, ILO Addis Ababa 1977
Streeton Paul *Frontiers of Development Studies*, MacMillan London 1979
Todaro M. *Economic Development in the Third World*. Longman New York 1977

Chapter Five

Organising Women for Action — Self-Employed Women's Association (SEWA)

Introduction

This is the first of three studies of adult education by Indian non-governmental organisations in this volume. Each displays more political »edge« than the first three studies. *National Development Strategies*, the earlier volume of »poverty and adult education« case studies, also includes an Indian study: Ramaskrishnan's account of the National Adult Education Programme (NAEP) which, in describing a governmental initiative, interestingly echoes the »political« themes of Dighe's and the other voluntary programmes described here. Ramakrishnan's analysis of the backing off from conscientization in the NAEP makes interesting reading alongside this basically optimistic account of the early years of SEWA, and the sharp-edged studies by the Shrivastavas and especially Sugirtharaj. *National Development Strategies* also contains an account of the Sri Lankan Sarvodaya Shramadana movement which, like SEWA, reflects a strong Gandhian influence, and which is national rather than local, in that much smaller country.

SEWA itself is larger in membership and scale, if not strictly speaking in geographical spread, than the projects described here so far. By 1981 its membership had reached 13,000 women in the large city of Ahmedabad and the nearby rural areas. Like Stacy and Clark, Dighe describes a women's programme which included health among its multiple areas of activity. But she also describes a women's movement, and one which at the end of this period broke away from its male-dominated trade union parentage. It is a movement dedicated to social as well as economic change for and with perhaps the most depressed and exploited sector of the Indian population and workforce — self-employed women in a variety of occupations. Both within India and outside, the present decade has seen a widening consciousness of the continuing gross abuse and exploitation of many Indian women (middle class women sometimes included), despite the remarkable strides in »development« which India has made in many respects. Anita Dighe has remained active in the front line of the battle for women's rights and writes of these issues, through the story of SEWA, with a particular authority.

SEWA has come to be quite well known outside India during the eighties. Its 1970s origins and the reflections which Dighe provides upon its formative years and developmental processes are therefore the more interesting. Note the issues of institutionalisation of mission, flexibility of response, and diversification of programmes, which are echoed in the later chapters by Haque and the Shrivastavas.

SEWA, then, is the fourth study in this book of adult education for women with an overt development objective — again written by a woman who was central to the work and who analyses the impact on the lives of the women participants. It enjoyed a higher profile than the Australian and Kenyan projects, and by 1981 had been taken up in different ways at State and even Union levels, as Dighe shows. Dighe echoes Clark's emphasis on active participation, creating self-confidence and building on the experience of success. She reveals a delicate balance between confrontation with authority and other interests inimical to the working women's »upliftment«, and willingness to work with, and so to modify and redirect the efforts of those with economic and political power. The balance between confrontation and cooperation — while avoiding cooptation — is one of the most important, and tricky, for reform-minded adult education activists wishing to achieve real and lasting change. It is as important and difficult a practical matter in Britain today as it was in India when SEWA was formed.

Another matter of contemporary interest to the British reader of the late eighties is that of evaluation: performance indicators or measures of efficiency and output. Dighe addresses the problem of identifying true costs in the voluntary-based, permeative and multifaceted operation which SEWA rapidly became; and the equally difficult task of identifying and measuring the true benefits to participants of such an operation. The gains are not, indeed, restricted to participant members, as Clark points out in addressing the same problem of evaluation and »controls« in the Kenyan villages. If they are in any sense successful such programmes almost inevitably spill over and alter the »environment«, the broader socio-politico-economic context of the work. And they may well influence, encourage and mobilise others who are not formally speaking a part of the SEWA movement at all. This said, Dighe does succeed in presenting certain measurable outcomes as well as indicating sometimes more important non- quantifiable areas of significant change.

The study has many other aspects of very contemporary relevance to British as well as Third World adult educators. The stress on self-reliance, commitment and mutual support within hard-nosed financial parameters surely resonates with adult educators looking at the challenge of the »enterprise economy« and the partial dismantling of the British welfare state. Then there is the use of data collection as a means both of communication and of consciousness-raising among different groups of women. And the strategy of working with and through existing cultural forms while seeking to effect something of a cultural revolution in economic and gender relations. Finally — an issue we return to at the end of this volume — there is the intriguing if subdued theme that may be discerned running as a thread through Dighe's study: the role of committed middle class animators and mobilisers of the most exploited and underprivileged. The same theme may be found in Miller's Nicaraguan study in the previous volume of »poverty and adult education« studies, as also in Sugirtharaj's chapter in this volume. It is perhaps too easy in Britain, with its tradition of (middle class) philanthropic charity, to misperceive, possibly to envy and thence to despise, such work. The relationship presents real problems, as Dighe hints. It also involves genuine reciprocal learning. And it calls for considerable moral and indeed physical courage in the circumstances described in this and some of the later studies in this volume.

Summary

The Self-Employed Women's Association (SEWA) was established in Ahmedabad in 1972. By 1981 it had 13,000 members and became independent of its parent body. It sought to serve especially self-employed and non-unionised poor women first in the city and then in the surrounding rural area. It involved in turn many trade groups, first overcoming resistance to their unionisation to provide legal protection. Obstacles were encountered in government as well as threatened commercial quarters. SEWA addressed women's multiple pressing needs: for capital, for skills, for confidence, for an end to harassment in the workplace and at home, and generally for reduction of powerlessness.

SEWA's aims are described as »economic regeneration and social upliftment«. It was flexible and responsive to needs. Main areas of activity have been: the SEWA Union (for pay and conditions); the Cooperative Bank (founded in 1974, to remove dependence on the money-lenders and to provide various services including enhancing skills and confidence in economic matters); the Women's Trust (started in 1975 with basic social security aims including especially support during maternity and early widowhood); defending the rights of the self-employed (notably through a successful sit-in); the Economic Wing (providing skills in design, production and marketing); and the Rural Wing, which was formed in 1977.

Key issues include the following: the Gandhian ideology; techniques of mobilisation, including the use of surveys and the training of local leaders; responsiveness to new needs through a flexible, evolving structure; techniques of organising, raising consciousness and building confidence; working with and through traditional cultural and communication forms. Some outcomes were tangible and quantifiable, such as membership numbers, figures for savings, loans and repayments, reduced numbers of deaths at childbirth. Others, including some of the most important, were intangible and qualitative. Some economic gains, and gains in women's confidence and standing, could be indicated or measured only approximately. Many lessons from SEWA are generalisable at least within the Indian situation, and by 1981 part of the experience was being drawn on internationally as well as elsewhere within India.

India's Self-Employed Women Workers

Jasodaben, a vegetable vendor, borrows Rs.50/- ($ US1 = Rs.8.60 NP. approx.) from a private money-lender early in the morning, buys and vends vegetables, grosses Rs.60/- during the day and returns Rs.55/- to the moneylender at the end of the day. Next day she borrows from the moneylender again. This goes on day after day.

Saihabanu, a garment worker, gets work from a private trader to stitch rags of waste cloth from textile mills into quilt-covers. She is paid 60 NP [naya paise] per quilt-cover for which she has to use her own sewing machine and thread. The private trader sells the quilt-covers at any price from Rs.7/- to Rs.15/- a piece.

Jiviben, a petty trader, has been allotted some space to sell in a residential colony in Ahmedabad. A male trader forcibly occupies her place and pushes her to sit near a garbage heap. No-one in the residential colony comes to Jiviben's rescue. The police refuse to interfere on the grounds that it is an »internal« matter.

These are not isolated cases. Rather, they typify the everyday life conditions of thousands and thousands of women workers who constitute the »invisible« workers of the city of Ahmedabad — and of India. These women face three major problems: much of their work is unrecognised; their earnings are meagre; and they have limited control over their income and working environment. With limited opportunities in the wage sector, they are forced to work in their self-created niche of employment. Many work as vendors, hawkers, artisans, and casual wage-earners. They rarely own any capital or tools of production; have no links with organised industry and services; and certainly no access to modern technology or facilities. They are vulnerable to all the exploitative forces in the environment that viciously govern and control their lives. Such women constitute the vast majority of self-employed workers normally characterised as the »unorganised« sector of the economy: six per cent of working women are in the organised sector and services; the remaining 94% are left to fend for themselves. [UN statistics released at the Mid-Decade Conference on Women, Copenhagen, 1980]

The Origins of SEWA

It was in order to cater to the needs of such poor working women in the unorganised sector that the Self-Employed Women's Association (SEWA) was registered as a trade union in the city of Ahmedabad, Gujerat, in 1972. By February 1981 the membership of SEWA had risen to 13,000 workers in twenty different trade groups scattered in the 40 square km. area of Ahmedabad city and some of its neighbouring rural areas. Originating with the Textile Labour Association (TLA), in May 1981 SEWA dissociated from this parent body which was a bastion of male-dominated leadership. Thus it came into its own as a solely women's organisation working for the cause of women.

Ahmedabad, population 2.5 million, a well-known textile centre of Western India, had a labour force of some 150,000 in its 62 textile mills. Of these 130,000 belonged to an old trade union, the Gandhi Majoor Mahajan or Textile Labour Association

(TLA), formed by Mahatma Gandhi in 1917. As part of Gandhiji's constructive programme a women's wing was created in the Textile Labour Association in l954 specifically to assist women belonging to the households of mill-workers. One of its first activities was to set up four sewing classes in the city's labour areas. A survey conducted in 1970 to probe into complaints of women tailors showed that their employment was irregular and wages exploitative. It revealed to the organisers of the women's wing that there was a vast multitude of labour force untouched by unionisation and unprotected by legislation. One morning in 1971, forty women head-loaders from the cloth market of the city entered the offices of the women's wing of the TLA. They did not belong to the families of mill-workers but were aware of the advantages of unionisation. Hence their demand to the organisers of the women's wing: »you do so much for workers and families, why can't you do something for us?«. The TLA women's wing decided to look into the head-loaders' complaint.

Then followed requests from used garment-workers, women hand-cart pullers, and women who traded steel utensils for used garments. The problems faced by each group were similar: meagre earnings, exploitation by money-lenders and traders, lack of credit facilities. About this time the organisers decided to call a public meeting, which was attended by about 100 women workers, one of whom suggested that they form an association of their own. Thus was SEWA born in December 1971, and officially registered as a trade union in April 1972. It was the initiative taken by the organisers of the women's wing in response to an appeal from unorganised working women for help that led to its establishment. (The acronym means »service« in several Indian languages.)

SEWA initially encountered resistance to registration as a trade union. The Indian Labour Law on the registration of trade unions does not recognise the legitimacy of a trade union of workers who do not work for an identifiable employer, thereby identifying a specific employer-employee relationship. SEWA challenged this narrow connotation, arguing that a trade union could be formed for the betterment of the workers through freedom from exploitation, assurance of regular work and access to opportunities for occupational mobility. It should not be conceived merely in terms of the power of the employees to organise strikes against the employer. Only after protracted representations in the Labour Commission and the State Labour Department was SEWA finally registered under the Indian Trade Unions Act, 1926, as a trade union of self-employed women workers.

Working with various trade groups, the organisers learned that three main problems affect working women's lives: lack of capital, harassment by municipal authorities and the police department; and poverty-induced family problems. A survey of the socio-economic conditions of women engaged as head-loaders, handcart-pullers, garment-makers, vegetable-fruit vendors, used garment dealers, junk-smiths, milk producers, etc., revealed a profile of exploitation, economic distress, overwork and ill health. Almost all the women were illiterate; they lived in slums, and had an average of four children each.

The organisers sought membership for SEWA by calling meetings with women members and offering them support. As time went on it became apparent that what attracted women was the prospect of augmenting their income through improvement of working conditions. Various other trade groups also approached the organisers — milk-maids, junk collectors, block printers, carpenters, basket weavers, bidi (indigenous cigarette) workers, papad (tortilla- like crisp wafer) workers, etc. All flocked to the SEWA meetings. However, their active involvement in the Union followed only after the leaders from among each trade group had agreed to join. The SEWA organisers normally established working relations with a trade group only after enough women in a particular trade were convinced of the need for joining SEWA after long and patient discussion.

SEWA's Aims and Objectives

The main aim for SEWA has been »economic regeneration and social upliftment« of self-employed and other working women of the poorest sections of Ahmedabad and surrounding areas. This goal appears broad and somewhat ambiguous. But therein lay the strength of the organisation: rather than specifying clear parameters, the organisation allowed for growth in new directions. On the basis of the needs and problems expressed by its members, SEWA expanded its operations to experiment with possible solutions to them. »Economic regeneration« is normally understood as increasing the productive potential and capability of the self- employed women workers to earn a better livelihood, maximising their entrepreneurial or service potential. At the same time, through its own physical and financial resources, SEWA guides women workers to achieve optimal returns from their labour.

»Social upliftment« has had a wider connotation: from raising a woman's status by fostering a better self-image, to securing her participation in society. The basic aim is to cultivate a feeling of self-confidence among women and to liberate them from the socially induced self-perception of being weak and helpless members of society. SEWA seeks to be an institution with which women can identify and to which they can turn to redress grievances and secure justice in matters relating to their occupation or their relationship with authority, or with regard to family affairs.

Its relevance to adult education relates to the fact that SEWA does not view women in their traditional roles as mothers and craft workers. An adult education programme intended to provide vocational training for women invariably becomes a handicraft training programme, with its emphasis on embroidery, sewing, knitting and craft work. The productive role of the women in society is more often that not ignored. SEWA on the other hand, has uniquely recognised this productive role, as this chapter shows. It has encouraged the confidence of women in themselves, has viewed them as participants in the planning and implementation of its varied activities, and has created the means for action as well as for improvement in their lives.

Major Areas of Activity

SEWA activities have grown in response to specific needs and problems expressed by its members. Following its formation, its first service was the supply of credit, converted in 1974 into a full-fledged banking service and followed by the establishment of the legal aid service, social security scheme, day-care centres and training centres.

The SEWA Union

Membership of SEWA is open to any working woman above the age of 15 years who resides in the State of Gujerat. She may be self- employed in a craft or trade, or engaged in an occupation as a casual wage-earner. Each member pays an annual subscription of Rs.3/- in monthly instalments of 25 paise. SEWA has continually laid stress on persuading its members to pay their union dues; default of payment for a continuous period of six months can lead to suspension of membership. But it has also encouraged its members, despite their low earning capacities, to save small amounts which have been used to employ women workers who do the field work. Gandhian ideology of initiating and sustaining a self-financed movement has permeated the thinking and the functioning of SEWA.

Members are grouped according to trades and geographical locations so that each group has 60-65 members. A leader is elected or appointed by the members to head each group. A total of 153 group leaders collectively constitute the Representatives' Council. The 25-member apex body of the SEWA union, the Executive Committee, comprises SEWA organisers and representatives of the trade groups.

The basic activity of the union is concerned primarily with representing workers' interests with respect to earnings and conditions of work. A SEWA Union field worker carries out intensive investigation to identify problems, then makes representation to the authorities concerned on behalf of the workers. There are thus two kinds of Union activities: resolution of individual grievances, and collective representation of the wider body of members as trade groups. Each SEWA organiser visits her area of operation, contacts the group leader of each trade group, and through her collects and records all the occupation-related complaints of her members. These complaints can relate to harassment by the police, »challan« [prosecution] by municipal authorities, misbehaviour by husbands, family members, etc. The organiser thereafter visits the members affected and makes a first-hand appraisal of the problem. In most cases she attempts to find a solution on the spot by discussing the matter with those concerned. Where complaints require more thorough investigation and/or representation to senior officials, the field worker informs the woman who heads the grievance cell, a full-time SEWA worker who pursues all compliants unresolved at the level of the field worker. She in turn lodges the complaint with the officials of the department concerned, calls on them and sees the matter through until a satisfactory solution is reached. »On an average, 300 letters of complaint are issued by the SEWA Union every month to the police department, municipal corporation, labour commissioner's office and so on. Frequent representations are made at Gandhi Nagar, the seat of the Gujerat Government, in behalf of the workers.« (Devaki Jain et.al., *Women's Quest for Power*, Vikas Pub. House, Ghaziabad, 1980, p.31). Other problems of a more personal nature such as pregnancy, childbirth, illness and beating by husbands are either taken up on a person-to-person basis or referred to Mahila SEWA Sahakari Trust for further action (see below).

The demand for fair and higher wages for women engaged in various trade groups invariably leads to confrontation with businessmen, traders and the middlemen. »The struggle for higher wages has met with success in some trade groups such as garment workers, head-loaders, papad sellers, cotton-pod shellers, agricultural workers, incense stick makers but continues in other groups. This struggle soon led to a realisation that only an integrated set of services would help the various trade groups to become self-sustaining and in control of their struggle, thus paving the way for SEWA's entry into developmental activities for its members.« (»Organising self-employed women: the SEWA experiment«, SEWA, Ahmedabad, 1981)

The Mahila SEWA Sahakari Bank (SEWA Women's Cooperative Bank)

One of members' commonest and most serious problems was lack of capital, and so indebtedness to the money-lender. The self-employed women had no personal security and, but for the money-lender, no source for obtaining credit. They had not approached or been offered loans by the commercial banks. The only solution was to find cheaper sources of credit. A scheme of the nationalised banks had been in operation to provide loans to small entrepreneurs, but the banks did not know how to reach the poorest self-employed; and the women, for their part, did not know how to avail themselves of these services. SEWA decided to act as an intermediary between the banks and the women. Initially however there were problems. The banks lacked the technical knowhow and trained personnel to serve the poor, and complained about »lack of collateral and the inability of bank staff to deal with illiterate women unfamiliar with banking procedures« [Ela R. Bhatt »Organising the self-employed women workers (an experiment)«, paper presented at Regional Consultation on Strategies for Women's Development, Colombo, 1979].

Even when the first step of providing credit facilities to self-employed women was taken they faced a number of practical problems. »The problem of bridging the gap between women in filthy clothes, accompanied by noisy children, and the bank staff used to educated middle class clients, still remained. The women's heavy schedule did not permit them to keep banking hours. If the banks refused to accept payment at the time of the day when women were free to come, then the money got spent. Very often they deposited the loan money with the very wholesaler or money-lender from whose clutches SEWA was trying to rescue them.« [Bhatt, op.cit.]

It was evident that providing cash from the banks did not solve the problem. The women urgently needed not only a credit facility but also an institutional framework for various kinds of services. At a meeting of SEWA members and group leaders in December 1973 various banking problems were discussed and a spontaneous suggestion made by members to the organisers: »Behn [Sister], let us have a bank of our own! We can do it. We are poor but there are so many of us.« SEWA members decided to contribute Rs.10/- each towards the share capital; in a short time they collected a sum of Rs.40,020/-. Thus the Mahila (Women's) SEWA Cooperative Bank was established, despite stiff opposition from the banking system. The main objection was that a bank for poor, illiterate, self-employed women would be a disastrous proposition. »How can women who cannot even sign their name have a bank account?«, the bank officials asked. When it was realised that the members of the executive committee of the bank were required to sign the registration papers, all eleven members, in a singular display of determination, sat up through the night to learn how to sign their names without error. The Bank was officially inaugurated on 25 May l974.

SEWA Bank has been a bank with a difference, deviating from the general pattern of cooperative banks. A multi-service organisation, designed to serve the needs of poor self-employed women, it has formulated schemes which ease access to those services that ensure the loans taken are used productively:
(i) by providing credit facilities and raw materials at a fair price to further the productive and income-generating activities of the self-employed;
(ii) by undertaking redesign of tools and equipment used by women to alleviate physical strain and ensure maximum productivity. The Bank commissioned design studies for an efficient cart for hand-cart pullers and a collapsible umbrella to protect women vendors from the sun. Likewise experiments were conducted with new designs for various products, to enhance their appeal to a wider market. The bank also explores new markets and advises members on the marketing of their goods.
(iii) The bank provides technical help in the storage and processing of commodities;
(iv) it encourages thrift among members and motivates them to save by providing safe custody of their savings;
(v) it also trains women in the banking habit and imbues them with the confidence that they can handle and deal with money just as well as men. The husbands and sons are also taught to encourage women to operate their own accounts, so that the idea of economic independence begins to gain ground among women.

(a) Functioning of the Bank

From 1974 to 1976 SEWA Bank concentrated on encouraging self-employed women to bank with it, acting as an intermediary to enable depositors to get loans from the nationalised banks. In 1976 the bank started advancing loans from its own funds, and since then it has developed into a viable financial unit. In December 1980 SEWA Bank had about 13,000 depositors and over 7,000 shareholders, with a working capital of over Rs.3,300,000/-Table I shows its growth since 1974.

Table 1
Growth of the SEWA Bank (l974-75 — 1979-80)

year	shareholders	share capital (Rs)	Accounts	Working capital
l974-75	7,132	71,320	6,116	332,231
l975-76	6,513	74,990	10,383	1,060,431
1976-77	6,824	77,970	10,913	1,198,872
l977-78	6,910	80,100	11,451	1,448,586
1978-79	6,980	80,800	12,123	2,743,564
l979-80	7,216	82,080	12,789	3,324,844

(Source: *Banking with Poor Women*, SEWA, 1981)

The governing body, the Board of Directors, represents nine major trade groups from SEWA's membership. It meets monthly and takes all the Bank's major decisions. »Illiteracy of the members has rarely come in the way of taking decisions and finding solutions«. [*Banking with Poor Women*, SEWA, p.4] Any woman can open an account with the SEWA Bank. All members of SEWA Union are depositors with the Bank. As the majority of account-holders are illiterate the Bank introduced a unique system of identification: »every account holder has an identification card which has a photograph showing her holding a slate with her account number written on it. This photograph is also pasted on her pass book. Her name and account number are thus associated with her signature, as is the usual banking custom« [ibid. p.13].

(b) SEWA Bank's Credit Service

In the initial period 9,000 members were advanced credit amounting to nearly Rs.5,000,000/- from the nationalised banks. In 1976 SEWA Bank started advancing loans to its depositors from its own funds and gradually ceased arranging credit with the nationalised banks. Applications for loans are made by members either direct or through field staff. The Bank staff does the scrutiny and processes loans. These are available only for economic activity, not for personal use or for expenses to meet social occasions. The applicant's income-generating ability, financial status, soundness of working conditions and ability to repay are carefully scrutinised and then put to the Board for approval. Table 2 shows the amount of money advanced by the Bank, and repayments.

Table 2
Advances and Repayment of Funds by SEWA Bank

Year	no. of women	advances (Rs/-)	repayments (Rs/-)
1976-77	78	37,253	17,910
1977-78	173	69,295	39,822
1978-79	113	79,875	49,249
1979-80	145	150,985	83,825
total	509	337,408	190,805

(Source: *Banking with Poor Women*, SEWA, 1981)

Every year repayments were made amounting to about 50% of the funds advanced. At an interest rate of 12%, loans had to be repaid in twenty monthly instalments. Both Union and Bank accorded high priority to the recovery of loan instalments, not only because the success of the scheme depended largely on regular repayment to commercial banks, but also to make members realise that the financial assistance received was not charity but credit, based on trust. In the words of one SEWA publication »a member who pays instalments regularly on her own has reached a state of responsibility and self-respect, the very first step towards helping herself out of distress. We are striving to achieve this in every member.« The performance of the SEWA Bank in repayment of loans has been generally good, compared with that of a commercial bank: there have however been cases of defaulters, mostly women unable to pay on time due to domestic circumstances, basically heavy economic pressures on already half-starved families. These may arise out of: frequent illness in the family; unsteady employment of the husband; frequent pregnancies leading to loss of work; social customs that necessitate expenditure; unplanned expenses to the family during religious festivals.

Mahila (Women's) SEWA Trust

The conflict between work and motherhood is perhaps most trying in the weeks immediately before and after childbirth. Most poor families depend on the women's income for survival. Thus a major decision for a woman at the time of childbirth is whether to give up work to care for the child, depriving the family of a crucial source of income, or to continue to work right up to the time of birth and during the neo-natal period, thus exposing the child and herself to various health hazards. Due to extreme economic exigency the women generally have no alternative but to continue working, so jeopardising their own health and that of the new-born babies. SEWA organisers found this problem particularly pressing among self-employed women. A survey of 500 women in 1975 revealed that within two years

20 had died — fifteen due to complications relating to childbirth. Attempts to persuade the Life Insurance Corporation of India to provide maternity and death insurance cover to its members were unsuccessful. Consequently SEWA decided to develop its own social security scheme.

Its trade union background always helped SEWA to compare the plight of the self-employed with that of industrial workers. Women in the organised sector are entitled by law to paid leave and cash benefits after maternity, whereas the large numbers of self-employed women workers are not. SEWA's main concern was why these women, who comprise the largest proportion of the urban and rural poor and contribute to the economic development of the nation, should be deprived of maternity benefits. Why should such women suffer a higher mortality rate due to motherhood?

In the absence of public maternity protection for the self-employed the Mahila SEWA Trust was instituted in 1975 to provide minimal social security to its members. Members of SEWA donated one day's earnings to the Trust, which was by and large inspired by the Gandhian principle of self-reliance. The SEWA Trust created three social security schemes and several other supporting programmes. Funds were mostly self-generated, though the Trust also received donations from some philanthropic institutions and charitable trusts. The Trust was presided over by a board of trustees, mainly SEWA members and group leaders. A Trust Secretary, who was also manager of the SEWA Bank, operated the funds. Its field work was conducted by the SEWA organisers.

(a) Maternity Benefit Scheme

The Maternity Benefit Scheme was designed to improve the health of both mother and child, and to compensate the woman for loss of income during the period immediately before and after childbirth. Any member who was five or six months pregnant could register for the programme by paying Rs.15/-. A SEWA organiser then assisted the member in obtaining prenatal services from a qualified medical doctor. After delivery the new-born baby was given all the necessary innoculations. Upon satisfying these conditions the mother was given Rs.51/- as cash benefit. Early on the organisers learned that many women were using this to buy ghee, which is traditionally consumed by mothers after delivery, so when more funds became available through the Mahila SEWA Trust, each member was provided with one kilogram tin of ghee in addition to the cash benefit. Initially the scheme was intended to cover only women's first two pregnancies, on the ground that otherwise the scheme would encourage women to have more children. The organisers soon realised that this reflected their own middle class bias towards family planning. The statistics showed that about 18 out of 50 women had had miscarriages, and 40 out of 50 had lost one or more children. When the topic of birth control was broached the reply was invariably »yes, Behn [Sister], we agree, but let my last child grow to be five years old«. As the organisers became sensitive to this concern for the survival of the children, and started viewing the question of family planning from this perspective, their own attitudes changed.

The maternity protection scheme met with considerable success in the urban areas of Ahmedabad, and efforts were made to extend it to the rural areas. In addition to services as in the urban programme the rural scheme, that catered only for landless labourers, included a health education component in pre-natal care. The Bavla Health Centre (a government sponsored health training centre) provided educational facilities. Initiated in 1980, 26 one-day sessions were held at the Bavla Centre on »know your body«. They included lectures and slide shows on basic pre-natal nutrition, health, foetal development, hazards of tetanus and advantages of immunisation. The village »dai«, suitably trained, is the local SEWA functionary for extending the scheme to the members. She is required to register the names of pregnant mothers and take them in groups to the Bavla Centre for a medical check-up, immunisation and health education sessions. Eighty-six village women were recorded as covered under the scheme by February 1981, with no deaths recorded.

The maternity protection scheme demonstrated that government or public institutions can deliver maternity benefits to the self- employed through women's organisations; and that such a scheme can become an entry point into poor women's lives, leading to other development programmes including literacy training, skills upgrading and organisation of grass-roots level associations. »Maternity protection coupled with day care centres for children can help women to resolve the age-old conflict between their role as both workers and mothers and can support women's struggle to take their rightful place in the development of their communities.« (*SEWA Maternal Protection Scheme*, SEWA, 1981)

(b) Creches

The idea of setting up day-care centres originated from an incident in which a hand-cart puller came running into the SEWA office, sobbing that her six month old child had been run over by a truck when she was busy unloading goods from the cart. A network of low cost neighbourhood day-care centres was the beginning of a scheme which SEWA intended to expand, both to help its members and to open new avenues of employment to other women.

(c) Widowhood and Death Assistance Scheme

It is a widely prevalent social practice in most parts of India for the widow to remain housebound for a period of one month on her husband's death. During this time the household is deprived of all income — that of the deceased spouse as well as that of the widow. Under this Scheme, relief of Rs.151/- was given to the widow member to enable her to meet her loss of earnings during the period of mourning; and Rs.100/- is paid to the dependants on the death of the SEWA member.

(d) Housing

In order to improve the living conditions of members in squalid housing quarters, SEWA formulated a Cooperative Housing Scheme as part of the SEWA Bank. »Seven hundred and ninety-four members are already saving for housing and the money accumulated in their bank every month. Meanwhile, SEWA is negotiating with the Gujarat State Housing Board for low-cost housing for 1,000 members.« [Devaki Jain, *Women's Quest for Power*, 1980, p.43]

(e) Functional Literacy

Initial efforts by SEWA organisers to start functional literacy classes for women were not successful, mainly because of the academic nature of the educational programme, which did not relate to the everyday issues and concerns of the women. However, a new urge for education became visible in the group leaders. They found their participation in various organisational activities of SEWA hampered by illiteracy and felt that education would create opportunities for them to improve their skills in the occupations they followed. Special literacy materials based on the needs, interests and problems of women were therefore designed for the functional literacy classes.

Defending the Rightful Place of the Self-Employed

Many of the urban labour force work is the »informal sector« that the modern industrialised sector has failed to absorb. The attitude of urban planners and administrators has been one of neglect and in some cases harassment. Those worst affected are hawkers and vendors. They have no place in city planning. As cities expand they are often treated as criminals, fined, harassed, even beaten. On August 15 1978 the SEWA vendors, exasperated by police harassment, formed a procession of 2,000 women, carrying placards and shouting slogans against police abuse. The procession went to every police station in the city. It ended up in a meeting addressed by the Chief Minister of the State. This was just the beginning of the vendor sisters of SEWA organising to defend themselves against police excesses. In January 1980 the city authorities threw the SEWA vendors out of the Manek Chowk Market, Ahmedabad's main fruit and vegetable market. Hundreds of vendors and hawkers, who had been sitting and selling in the Manek Chowk square for almost three generations, were suddenly rendered jobless. Talks with the Police Commissioner were unsuccessful. The authorities were determined to throw the vendors out without providing alternative arrangements, so SEWA organisers helped the vendor sisters to organise a Satyagraha — a Gandhian peaceful resistance to an injustice. On January 30 the vendors sat in their traditional places while SEWA organisers stood alongside in peaceful defiance of police orders. Despite opposition from the police, municipal authorities, big storekeepers and traders, vendors sat firmly united. This action won them back the places they had traditionally occupied in Manek Chowk square.

The SEWA members had now developed the confidence to bring individual cases of abuse to the notice of the police and public authorities. They showed no fear in approaching higher authorities and demanding inquiries into abuses. When fictitious charges were levelled against the vendors by the police, they took the help of SEWA's lawyer in fighting the cases in the court. Such organised defence against abuse forced the police to treat the vendors with more consideration and respect. The stronger groups, such as vendors of old clothes, reported that the police no longer dared beat them or arrest them on false charges. »Though vendors have not been given official licenses, a SEWA membership card ensures her freedom from harassment by both police and municipal officials.« [Ela Bhatt »Organising the self- employed women workers (an experiment)«]

SEWA's Economic Wing

»Exploitation by merchants and middlemen, unpredictable supply of raw materials, no direct links to consumers, and lack of training in skills and knowledge of markets are problems repeatedly faced by self-employed women in most occupations. The Economic Wing was established in July 1978 as a conscious effort to confront these problems head on. Its aim was to help self-employed women in overcoming these constraints and in reaching towards full employment and full wages.« [*SEWA's Economic Wing*, SEWA, 1981, p.1] The idea of organising such a wing grew out of the union's involvement in the struggles of chindi (cloth scraps) workers, hand-block printers and bamboo workers. After years of exploitation by merchants, chindi workers in 1977 organised to press for payment of minimum wages. After a long series of negotiations a compromise agreement was reached between the two groups. The merchants broke it within 24 hours. Not only did they refuse to pay the agreed rate for doing patch-work; they began to harass them by giving them bad materials, less work and in some cases no work at all. The struggle had begun. With SEWA's support women decided to start a production unit of their own. As SEWA set up the Economic Wing, various problems emerged. Organising the hand-block printers it was realised that these workers could hardly survive because of a declining market for their traditional textile designs. In organising bamboo workers SEWA found that the women were highly skilled but were not making designs and products in demand. Their crude products were sold to merchants at low prices. The women expressed a need for training to upgrade their skills, so as to produce goods in greater demand and that yielded higher returns. They evidently needed alternative institutions through which to undergo training; upgrade old and acquire new skills; manage the purchase of raw materials and the marketing of products; secure storage facilities and workspace; and acquire capital. By February 1981, SEWA was sponsoring several training programmes to develop skills in bamboo-work, block-printing and sewing. Courses in such non-traditional occupations as plumbing, carpentry and radio repair were also offered, with the object of equipping women with skills to break into fields traditionally dominated by men.

Marketing finished products is a major bottleneck for self-employed workers. In some cases a market has to be created through new designs, as in the case of bamboo-workers or block-printers. In almost all other cases there is total dependence on the middleman, who makes vast profits. To eliminate the middleman SEWA sought in various ways to provide marketing services to its members, including organising exhibitions to introduce potential buyers to the goods produced by SEWA members. At the first exhibition, held in December 1980, garments, block-printed materials, bamboo products, toys, khadi cloth, handlook fabrics, carpentry goods, embossed artwork, and incense sticks, were displayed and sold, grossing Rs.11,000/-.

Another strategy was to open shops in the city where self-employed women could sell their products direct, thus avoiding middlemen. Three shops were run on a no-profit no-loss basis, their operating costs covered by sales. A third strategy was to provide a link between self-employed women and large institutions placing bulk orders and making bulk purchases. After seven years of pressure a regulation was issued by the Government in 1980 requiring all government institutions to give first preference in buying goods to women's organisations. Since that time SEWA members have been supplying fruit and vegetables to Ahmedabad hospitals and gaols. The organisers take orders from these institutions and give them to the cooperative of vendors. »This has provided small scale sellers a steady and reliable market for their goods. Each month Rs.40,000 worth of fruits and vegetables are sold this way. Similarly SEWA gets orders for Rs.5,000/- worth of brooms each month from government organisations. SEWA had also helped to link papad makers with government and private organisations.« [*SEWA's Economic Wing*, SEWA, 1981, p.4]

Another constraint on the self-employed was in obtaining raw materials. Lacking capital and knowledge to deal direct with large institutions, the women tended to depend on merchants and middlemen. SEWA sought to help members buy raw materials direct from the source. In 1980 nearly Rs.200,000 worth of chindi (cloth scraps) was purchased direct from the mills by the production unit of chindi workers. Likewise women carpenters and junksmiths have bought leftover scraps of wood and metal direct from local materials.

Yet another acute problem, particularly in the city, is lack of storage and adequate workshop space. SEWA therefore provided workshop space for chindi sorting, bamboo work and block printing. Storage facilities were also provided in different parts of the city.

Rural Wing of SEWA

A small incident one mid-summer afternoon in 1977 led to the creation of SEWA's rural wing. A senior labour leader of the Textile Labour Association found a group of villagers squatted restlessly outside the Union building. They explained that they were poor agricultural labourers from one of the nearby villages. A severe drought had deprived them of their sole source of employment, and they had walked all day from the village in the hope of finding some help. »Can we not be helped in our struggle to survive?«, they asked. Discussion revealed that the plight of rural women labourers during drought was particularly distressing. While the menfolk migrated to urban areas in search of work, the women remained behind in the famine-hit villages to look after the children and other family members.

SEWA thus started a rural programme in villages in Dholke taluk to address two serious problems facing the rural poor: unemployment and poverty. Along with the Agricultural Labour Association (TLA's agricultural wing) SEWA began a local level off-farm income generation programme to help villagers get more regular and secure earnings. The activities included spinning, weaving, sewing, and women's milk cooperatives. Supportive services such as training, banking, legal aid, day-care centres, and a maternity protection scheme were included as crucial components of the income-generation programme. To equip agricultural labourers for employment during the slack seasons and during drought, SEWA provided 150 charkhas (spinning wheels), ten weaving looms and sewing machines to village women. This equipment, along with training in its operation and maintenance, was given to 500 women. Sources of raw materials, and links with marketing outlets, were also provided by SEWA.

Women have traditionally tended the cattle and engaged in dairying, yet they have been excluded from any training programme in dairying, and not registered as members of the dairy cooperatives. After concerted efforts against the local power structure and vested interests SEWA registered the first dairy cooperative of women in 1980, followed by a further nine. The National Dairy Development Board assisted with training in vetinerary care, cattle breeding, and methods to produce higher priced milk.

The Rural Wing also ran creches in three villages. »Women agricultural labourers, relieved of their burden of child-care, are able to increase their productive work on the farms and thus their earning. Elder brothers and sisters can now go to school.« [*SEWA Goes Rural*, SEWA. 1981, p.4] A hundred and fifty mothers and children used these first creches, and the facility was to be extended to each of 30 villages. In order to combat the serious problem of infant and maternal mortality during childbirth, the maternity protection scheme had also covered 500 rural women by 1981.

Some Distinctive Features of SEWA

Influence of Gandhian Ideology

The all-pervading influence of Mahatma Gandhi has been an essential source of inspiration to SEWA organisers. Central to Gandhi's ideas for social action was his belief in the goodness of every man and woman. He believed totally in man's potential to rise above himself — an essentially spiritual approach based on awakening the spirit or the God in oneself. This belief has been central to the functioning of TLA and of SEWA. »Essentially SEWA illustrates the effective use of Gandhian instruments for social change. It emphasises the means by which its members strengthen themselves economically and socially — self-reliance and non-violence being two of the main pillars of this ideology.« [Devaki Jain et.al., op cit., p.67] According to this ideology the poor can be helped to become independent. Economic or social power emanating from their own efforts is the more enduring. Gandhian thinking has even affected SEWA's thinking towards women. »As Gandhi's perception of society was not confined to class categories, it was not confined by sex stereotypes either. SEWA looks upon women as economic agents whose work and income are as vital to society as is their home-bound life. It also attempts to draw them into the mainstream of public life by encouraging them to participate in institutions outside the family such as the union and the bank.« [ibid. p.68]

Mobilisation at All Levels

In its efforts to reach out to the poor, SEWA has had to struggle against the existing public agencies, the banks, government departments, municipal authorities, police officials etc., which cater to the needs of everybody except the poor, particularly the self-employed poor. Each time SEWA had to fall back on its own resources and demonstrate to the agencies that such developmental efforts are viable, that it is possible to extend services to the poor. The keyword is »mobilisation«: of self-employed workers, of public support, of legal support, of all available services. SEWA has shown how vital this is at all levels.

(a) The Use of Surveys

SEWA's first activity in the localities and with workers' groups identified for inclusion in the union was to conduct a survey. Since the organisers were not known to the community, and had no accurate understanding of its problems, surveys were used also as a means of communication. Basically demographic and social in nature, they also included information about the working conditions of women belonging to a particular trade, the nature of exploitation experienced, and how they coped with everyday life situations. During the course of the survey the field workers became acquainted with the women and began to understand their problems. The women meanwhile developed a reciprocal interest in the field workers and the organisation they represented. »Not only is their curiosity aroused but the questions make them aware of their situation. The process of conscientisation begins here. The survey therefore serves simultaneously as an information-gathering tool and a device for establishing contact.« [Devaki Jain et.al. op.cit. p.50]

Data thus gathered through the survey were analysed, providing SEWA organisers with the basic information to start a discussion with the women. SEWA organisers joined the women in »Katha« (a social gathering at which an older person recites religious stories or verses) and »bhajan« (group singing of devotional songs). It was generally after these sessions that discussions were held about the needs and problems. The results of the survey were then shared and solutions worked out together. Experience showed the organisers that use of traditional cultural gatherings was more effective as an entry point than holding formal meetings. The organisers then tell the women about SEWA — of its work with other workers — and make them realise the importance of coming together and consolidating their strength as a prerequisite for overcoming their problems. In other words efforts begin at grassroots level to mobilise women, and to make them aware of the advantages of solidarity and unionisation.

(b) Use of Local Leadership

Leaders of the community, as supported by the local women, are identified by SEWA organisers. These group leaders are natural leaders in their communities — women who have always identified with others' problems in the community, shown willingness to help, protested against unfair practices, and proved capable in dealing with authority, both within and outside the community. They are generally middle-aged, with grown-up children. As such they can devote time to work with the group. Once these group leaders are convinced of the need to form a union, they become a crucial link between the community and the SEWA union organisers. The group leaders, who live and work with the members, articulate the needs and problems of the members and at the same time ensure that the resources and services mobilised by the organisers actually reach the members. Among the various functions they serve are: implementing SEWA programmes, for instance the credit schemes; providing feedback on the success of each scheme; ascertaining and communicating ideas for new programmes; extending SEWA membership in the community. Frequent meetings with these leaders proved a low cost and highly efficient strategy for organising poor urban women who otherwise live out their lives in isolation and poverty.

(c) Use of Public Meetings

Public meetings are often held and processions organised with the participation of leading social and political figures, in order to give greater visibility to the problems of the self-employed women. At these meetings various issues are raised and representations made. Public assurances from the political leaders are then followed up by the SEWA organisers until they are fulfilled.

(d) Use of Publicity Media

At the same time SEWA organisers make a public issue of their members demands, arousing interest in the society at large about the problems of these invisible groups of workers. They regularly use the newspapers, and pamphlets are distributed to sensitise the public and encourage public debate on the stand taken by the workers and those who provide them with employment. Publicising information, as well as the conflict, is a Gandhian way of taking the public into confidence. It has invariably resulted in a better deal being negotiated for the workers.

Some Key Issues

Development of Purpose

SEWA's stated aim was »economic regeneration and social upliftment« of self-employed and other working women of the poorest sections of Ahmedabad and surrounding areas. Thus alleviation of poverty by improving the standard of living of the self-employed poor was one of its principal concerns through the first decade of its work. Alongside economic development, however, the SEWA organisers realised the importance of social development in terms of cultivating women's self-confidence; encouraging more participation; and enabling them to assume responsibilities of leadership. Experience showed that while economic leverage is essential to raise women's status in terms of decision-making power within their families, it is equally vital to develop leadership among them so that they feel confident about their ability to control their environment. Within the broad parameters of economic and social development, SEWA expanded its activities to respond to the needs of the working women: providing credit facilities and health and creche services, upgrading existing skills, and providing market outlets.

Leadership and Rapport

SEWA sought constantly to develop leadership and participation from among the women themselves. Organisers worked largely to this end. Characteristic was their understanding of the women's vulnerability as women. Their work called for rapport with the members, encouraging and helping them, drawing them into SEWA. While SEWA organisers had to take the initiative and sometimes be in the forefront of action, they also ensured that critical decisions were taken by the group leaders. Their struggle together created a mutual learning process. Often the organisers learned that some of their middle class prejudices and myths about poor women, particularly rural women, were unwarranted. Consequently there was increasing openness between the organisers and the women, and a greater sensitivity developed towards the problems of self-employed women.

Flexible Structure

An Executive Committee consisting of the SEWA President, General Secretary, and representatives of various trade groups, was SEWA's major decision-making body. By the nature of its composition, however, this apex body was aware of and responsive to the needs and interests of poor self-employed women. Activities grew in response to needs expressed by members. Despite its varied activities, coordination was not a major problem. Each SEWA member got the services of three organisations — the SEWA Union, the SEWA Bank, and the SEWA Mahila Trust. The Union provided the necessary set-up for organising the trade groups and for engaging in the struggle with various vested interests. The Bank provided banking and credit facilities, and the Mahila Trust extended facilities for legal aid, social security, productivity training and education. By the nature of its organisational structure, SEWA was able to strike a balance between centralised control and decentralised initiative.

Dealing With Vested Interests

SEWA encountered resistance from traders, merchants and middlemen as the members of different trade groups started the struggle for fair and higher wages. But SEWA realised that the struggle for higher wages would fail in those cases where the women were caught between merchants supplying the raw materials and the middlemen selling their products (as in the case of the chindi worker); and in the case of women who were displaced by mechanisation (eg. the hand-block printers); and in the case of those who did not have a regular income (eg. the farm labourers in the rural areas). To help these women SEWA set up its own economic units that would later be organised into producers' cooperatives. These efforts began with a struggle against the existing public agencies — the banks, training institutes, insurance companies, government departments, municipal authorities, and the police. Each time SEWA had to fall back on its own resources and thus prove to these agencies that with suitable modifications their services could be made available to the self-employed poor. What is unique about SEWA is that, guided by the Gandhian principles of Satyagraha, non-violence and negotiation, it often confronted vested interests and challenged their authority, only to persuade them to negotiate and to accede to the demands of the self-employed.

Another kind of vested interest was the husbands of some of the self-employed women. In a male-dominated society women have low status in the family and are subjected to wife-beating and other forms of physical abuse. There were cases of women being deprived of any savings, due either to desertion by husbands or their drinking and gambling habits. Through participation in SEWA activities the women developed more self-confidence, particularly the group leaders, who won better status at home. The incidence of wife-beating fell, and participation in decision-making in the household increased.

Self-Reliance and Motivation

The Gandhian ideal of initiating and sustaining a self-reliant movement went a long way in mobilising human and material resources for SEWA. Initial support came sometimes from TLA, some from philanthropic organisations and from SEWA's well-wishers; but by and large most funds were self-generated. The operating principle was that while the seed capital might be provided by an outside agency or agencies, it is participation of the members which provides the necessary impetus to the activity or programme to make it self-sustaining. Likewise human resources were mobilised both within the community and without to ensure a more lasting impact on the lives of self-employed women.

SEWA's strength has been based in expanding its activities in response to the needs and interests of a well-defined group of women. Consequently there was no problem over motivation. Group leaders experienced a gain in status among their own family members as well as among members of the community. They seemed to strike a balance between SEWA work and private trade, based on their perception of the trade-off between status gain and earnings.

Working With What Is There

SEWA sided with the culture of the poor and tried to use all existing cultural forms and channels. In trying to penetrate various trade groups in order to make the members realise the importance of unionisation, the organisers participated in the traditional religious forms of »kirtans« and »bhajans«. Participation in such traditional activities helped considerably in breaking down barriers to communication between the middle class organisers and women belonging to poorer classes. At the same time the status of women was itself another cultural area undergoing change as a result of SEWA efforts.

SEWA has not favoured working in isolation; rather it sought to activate and utilise existing services and facilities. »Society and the government have created agencies for people's benefit and development. SEWA tries to utilise the services of such agencies — Banks, the University, Institutes of Occupational Health, Design, Management, Housing, Research etc. Individually for women it is difficult to have access to such services or to use them to their fullest advantage. The Association enables each individual member to feel more confident in dealing with an environment which had earlier baffled them, making them feel helpless or overpowered.«
[*Organising Self-Employed Women*, 1981, p.5]

Costs and Cost Effectiveness

By the very nature of the activities of SEWA it is difficult to work out its true cost and cost-effectiveness. It has not operated on the basis of a fixed budget. Rather, the emergent needs and demands of its members have consistently determined priorities and the course of action.

SEWA thus presents a problem that is probably common to most programmes seriously intended to bring about social and economic change. With established credibility and greater recognition of its efforts, financial assistance has been forthcoming; not only from among the members but also from governmental and nongovernmental outside sources. Government assistance is not always from one source; nor has SEWA utilised funds earmarked specifically for its activities. Thus for example in the case of the rural programme, SEWA was able to get assistance from Khadi Gramodyog (a state government undertaking) to provide »amber charkhas« (improved spinning-wheels) and raw materials for training women to augment their income. In the case of dairying the National Dairy Development Board provided some financial assistance. In each case SEWA supplemented this expenditure by providing personnel for the programmes or advancing the deficit amount through its Bank or Trust. In some cases it took subsidised loans from state government or local agencies. Government funds generally came in instalments, or not at all; in such cases SEWA had to fall back on its own resources. It is therefore difficult to calculate the true total budget and expenditure.

Another problem peculiar to such programmes is that, unlike programmes in which cost effectiveness can be worked out on the basis of measurable inputs, it is not possible to determine the economic value of eliminating a middleman, or assign a cash value to the psychological gain achieved through increased self-confidence and sense of self-worth. While it is necessary for programmes such as SEWA to become more cost-conscious and cost- efficient, the yardstick for measuring the cost-effectiveness of such adult education programmes needs to be carefully worked out, considering the important yet somewhat intangible gains of such programmes.

Evaluation and Appraisal

Some quantitative data are available to testify to the impact of SEWA on the lives of poor women. A purely quantitative assessment would however present a very incomplete and unbalanced picture. Certain qualitative changes such as increased self- confidence and better self-perception would be difficult to measure by normal quantitative methods of evaluation. It is essential also to consider qualitative aspects in evaluating: SEWA's major aim has been to reduce poverty by improving the quality of life of its members.

Membership of SEWA Union

One primary concern was to form a union of self-employed women who, unlike those in the organised sector, were deprived of the protection of labour legislation. To bring this whole sector into the fold of labour laws and protective measures, SEWA insisted on being registered as a trade union. Despite some resistance from the Labour Commissioner's Office, SEWA succeeded in becoming a registered trade union in 1972. The task it set itself was to organise the poor self-employed women of various trades who comprise 94% of working women, and help them get a fair deal for their contribution to the economy. By February 1981 SEWA had a membership of 13,000, of which 4,500 were active members. SEWA's relevance to adult education resides in the fact that it has shown how socially and economically deprived illiterate women can be motivated to join a union that will work for their interests.

Banking Services for Women

Among the first development efforts initiated by SEWA was one to create banking and credit facilities for self-employed women. The Mahila Sahakari (Women's) Cooperative Bank, registered in 1974, was still by 1981 the only one of its kind in the country. It was able to explode all the myths nurtured by the organised banking system about extending credit to the poor, illiterate and self- employed women, for it became a viable financial unit with share capital and deposits from its members. It also showed how banking services, suitably modified, can be provided to suit the needs and problems of this particular client group. By the end of 1980 about Rs.500,000/- had been advanced. The experience thus far was that about 50% of the funds advanced were repaid by the members and these had then become available for further advances. The yearly interest rate was 12%; the loan had to be repaid in twenty monthly instalments. Field staff and bank staff provided the necessary technical assistance to ensure that the money was used for economic activities; this facilitated repayment. The fact that loans were advanced to members of SEWA Union and that SEWA assisted its members in becoming economically viable had a significant bearing on the repayment rate. A sample survey of 2,000 comparable borrowers of SEWA Bank and the Bank of India, a Commercial Bank, showed that the rate of repayment in the case of SEWA Bank was very impressive.

During the initial phase in which credit was provided through the nationalised banks, it was the moral responsibility of SEWA and SEWA Bank to assist the commercial banks in recovering loans from members. In these early years private money-lenders made calculated and insidious efforts to prevent SEWA borrowers from repaying loans to the commercial banks, with the intention of defaming and discrediting the small borrowers, and ultimately undermining SEWA Bank's policy of financing the poor. Such attempts did make recovery of loans a difficult task for the field staff. SEWA Bank survived these attacks because recovery of loans was-

Table 3
Repayment Pattern in a Commercial Bank and SEWA Bank

out of 20 required instalments	Commercial Bank	SEWA Bank
paid regularly	16%	87%
missed 1-2 instalments	28%	10%
missed 3-4 instalment	28%	2%
missed 5-6 instalments	15%	2%
missed more than 6	13%	—

Source: *Banking with Poor Women*, SEWA, 1981

not considered an end in itself, but a means to promote self-help and inculcate a sense of responsibility.

As for the impact of SEWA Bank in alleviating problems of poverty: »The Bank has enabled members to come out of the clutches of private money lenders and develop the skills of dealing with formal organisations. In the process, their self-confidence has been enhanced. The vicious circle of indebtedness and dependence on middlemen and traders has been broken, and has changed the bargaining position of women. They can now organise themselves, bargain for higher wages, and if need be also form their own economic units. And most importantly through their savings accounts the Bank provides them a secure and sure way to control their own income. It has also provided the badly needed infrastructure to the commercial banks to serve the self-employed and the small ones. The members become trained in the banking habit, inculcating a sense of thrift and making their money more productive.«
»A large number of them now have their own hand cart, sewing machine, loom, tools of carpentry and smithy to work with. Many of them have upgraded their skills and developed more business such as vegetable vendors, who used to sell with baskets on their heads, have their own little street corner shops with a municipal licence. The SEWA Bank has thus contributed greatly in achieving to some extent the larger SEWA goals of organising and creating visibility for self-employed women, enabling them to get higher wages, and to have control over their own income.« [*Banking with poor Women*, SEWA, 1981, p.7]

Maternal Protection Scheme

The success of the Maternal Protection Scheme has been ascertained partly by comparing the findings of a survey in 1975 with one covering the period 1975-80 under the scheme. The 1975 survey showed 15 maternal mortality deaths out of 500; in the period 1975-80 there were 36 deaths, 15 due to childbirth, out of 2,600

cases. The records maintained on the causes of death among 2,600 women covered by the Scheme, 1975-80, show the following:
causes other than childbirth (poisonous snakebite 1; tuberculosis 3; suicide 2; accident 4; fever 3; weakness 7; insanity 1)
total 21 childbirth: 15.

According to the organisers, even though the scheme brought about an overall improvement in maternal health, there were shortcomings. The major problem was inadequate post-natal follow-up. Consequently, while the mothers have survived the infants have not always been safe. Among 2,600 infants born, the infant mortality rate was very high at 356. A major problem was that mothers generally had to resume work within two weeks of delivery, and the infants suffered greatly from lack of child-care facilities. Of the 356 infant deaths 314 were within the first year of birth and 208 within the first three months. Despite these problems the organisers considered that much had been gained from the Maternal Protection Scheme. Maternity protection together with day-care centres for children »can help women to resolve the age-old conflict between their role as both workers and mothers and can support women's struggle to take their rightful place in the development of their communities«. [*SEWA's Maternity Protection Scheme*, p.4]

The Economic Programme

SEWA's Economic Wing showed how women could gradually become self-reliant. Through participation in various economic activities they gained confidence to enter various non-traditional occupations and activities. Women who had never dealt directly with the public before came to work in SEWA shops; some went direct to the mills to buy chindi, and to hospitals, gaols and other institutions to take orders. These are small but important steps in developing confidence in the ability to take more control of the work environment, and to strive for better conditions and higher income. The greatest change however was in the women's attitudes. To home-based women in particular, self-managed production managing all the steps in the process, from acquiring raw materials to the final sale of the product, was a totally new idea, for they were used only to the idea of producing for one owner. At first they had difficulty defining themselves in relation to SEWA as anything but labourers. After working for a time, they would say »we are neither owners nor labourers, we are somewhere in between. But now, after time and struggle they say »it is our own production unit« [*SEWA's Economic Wing*, p.6]

The next step was for the production unit to become a cooperative, with the women from the commmunity its shareholders, managers, directors and workers. The bamboo workers were making plans to form their own cooperative, as also the block-printers and the vegetable vendors. Women felt that when they developed confidence in themselves and the skills to become owners, managers and workers, then they would truly have their own cooperative unit.

SEWA's Rural Wing

The Rural Wing promoted income-generating activities in rural areas. It encountered several problems, which were aggravated by exploitation by local elites and vested interests, and by the suppression of women in a male-dominated culture. Thus it was difficult to get women to travel outside their villages for training. Organising and managing women's milk cooperatives posed unforeseen challenges. As each hurdle was overcome, a change in the role and status of rural women was perceivable: as they gained economic leverage and took on increasing leadership responsibilities within their communities. »Families who several years ago slept on empty stomachs are now secure with direct supply of raw materials and links to markets; training in cattle care, access to loans to purchase cattle and organisation of milk cooperatives also have led to direct increases in household earnings for many families. But the results of our efforts go beyond purely economic gains. The flow of income through women's hands has raised their status and decision-making power within their families. Developing leadership among the women has built confidence in their ability to control their environment and to take initiative. With the development of women's economic power and leadership in the community, we see a golden line on the horizon.« [*SEWA Goes Rural*, SEWA, 1981, p.5]

Status of Women

One perceptible change brought about by SEWA was an improvement in women's status. The constant discussion of various issues relating to their status made SEWA members more aware of them, including that of the declining sex ratio. There was a new urge among group leaders for education. SEWA members were able to command some respect in their families. SEWA meetings provided an opportunity for women of various communities to forget their caste and class differences and to share one anothers' sufferings. As SEWA was recognised by banks, the press, and government, its members developed more self-esteem and their neighbourhood status was enhanced. No quantitative evaluation can adequately ascertain these inscrutable changes.

SEWA showed that the agencies and services which had been inaccessible to poor women could be meaningfully utilised as soon as they felt more confident in dealing with their environment, less helpless and powerless. SEWA thus aimed at bringing about qualititative changes in the perceptions, attitudes and behaviour of its members. There was a conviction that women must be given opportunities to take part in socially and economically productive life, enhancing their economic and social utility in the eyes of their family and of society. SEWA has achieved considerable success towards this end.

General Impact

SEWA's programmes produced a tangible impact on the local population, and earned a reputation nationally and internationally. Its membership was open to any working woman above the age of 15 resident in the State of Gujerat. SEWA worked not only to alleviate the symptoms of poverty. It tackled some basic political issues as well. Thus it recognised the need to influence government policies and decisions if the poor self-employed sector was to be made successfully part of the mainstream of the economy. One issue related to the definition of »worker«, which had to be changed to include the self-employed. Only then would the labour legislation protect this sector. The Gujerat Government finally set up an Unorganised Labour Board in 1980, after continual lobbying by SEWA for five years.

At the time the Sixth Five Year Plan was formulated, SEWA drew the attention of the Planning Commission to the need for a radical change in government attitudes and policies towards the self-employed and recommended changes in policy that would help the self-employed in their struggle sgainst poverty. Internationally SEWA was able to achieve visibility for the cause of the self-employed right up to the level of the International Labour Organization. The SEWA Bank has become a model for setting up a Women's World Banking system to provide credit and banking facilities to poor women all over the world. »SEWA's struggle is on for a long time to come, to tackle the issues of non-recognition of work, low wages, and no control over their income for the self-employed women.« [*Organising Self-Employed Women*, p.4] It was in recognition of the efforts of SEWA that its general secretary, Mrs Ela Bhatt, won the Magasaysay award for community service for 1977. Ela Bhatt provided dynamic leadership to SEWA from its inception and continued to work unstintingly, along with other women, in her crusade to promote the cause of the self- employed women.

Possibilities for Replication

SEWA was the first concerted effort in India to form a union of women workers in the unorganised sector. This sector is economically important in the production of goods and services, constituting 40-45% of the labour force in the metropolitan cities. Yet this work is not seen as legitimate by government, so government policy and public attitudes are biased against it. The task SEWA set itself was to organise poor self-employed women of various trades to get a fair deal in return for their contribution. To secure their recognition SEWA had to make them and their work visible; organising into a union was the means to ensure this.

Beyond this the relevance of SEWA for adult education lies in the fact that, unlike most programmes for women, its organisers had a long-term vision of effecting women's economic and social development. Programmes for women tend to be short-sighted ad hoc efforts to ameliorate conditions affecting their lives. For SEWA the struggle for fair and higher wages was certainly the economic motivator that helped to bring women of various trade groups together. But it was soon realised that an integrated set of services was needed to help the various trade groups become self-sustaining and in control of their struggle. The ultimate aim, not just alleviating poverty among self-employed women but making them self-reliant by improving their quality of life, provided the long-term perspective necessary for any such programme.

It is true on the one hand that ad hocism has not characterised SEWA's growth and development. It is also true that SEWA has grown in response to the needs, interests and problems of self- employed women. The organisers made no attempt to prepare a blueprint for action on behalf of the self-employed women. Rather did programmes emergé through mutual consultation, mutual learning and exchange. SEWA went a step further. It showed how the existing government machinery and infrastructure could be made to deliver services to the poor. Initially confrontation with various vested interests might be necessary; thereafter the struggle for the poor can gradually be won through persuasion and negotiation. SEWA's operational techniques, backed by Gandhian ideology, provide a suitable model for others working for the cause of the poor generally.

Another feature of SEWA, and one which also owed its inspiration to Mahatma Gandhi, was that of self-help and self-reliance. The concept of self-help permeated all the activities and services developed. Any adult education programme can draw important lessons from the way this was fostered and promoted by SEWA.

Finally, a question can be asked about replicability. Granted the spirit of dedication and commitment to the cause of the poor self-employed women that characterised Ela Bhatt as General Secretary, and other SEWA organisers, if such commitment and dedication can be assumed in other organisers elsewhere then it should be possible to replicate SEWA at any rate in other parts of India. It has provided a viable model for organising self- employed women. Realising its potential replicability SEWA has organised training programmes for women from different parts of the country. These included internship programmes at SEWA and sending spearhead teams to initiate similar work on other towns and cities. It was in recognition of this potential too that at the time of formulation of the Sixth Five Year Plan, the Planning Commission elicited the views of SEWA organisers and members on planning strategies that would help the self-employed in their struggle against poverty.

References

Bhatt Ela »Organising the self-employed women workers (an experiment)«, paper for Regional Consultation on Strategies for Women's Development, Colombo, 1979
Convergence XIII, 1-2, 1980
Jain Devaki et.al. *Women's Quest for Power*, Vikas Pub. House, Ghaziabad, 1980
Organising Self-Employed Women: the SEWA Experiment, SEWA, Ahmedabad, 1981

Banking with Poor Women, SEWA, Ahmedabad, 1981
SEWA's Maternity Protection Scheme, SEWA, Ahmedabad, 1981
SEWA's Economic Wing, SEWA, Ahmedabad, 1981
SEWA Goes Rural, SEWA, Ahmedabad, 1981
»Manpower and Employment«, in *Sixth Five Year Plan 1980-1985*, Planning Commission, Govt. of India, New Delhi

Chapter Six

Learning and Action in Rajasthan — The Work of Seva Mandir

Introduction

In *Combatting Poverty Through Adult Education: National Development Strategies* Ramakrishnan shows how the Indian National Adult Education Programme (NAEP) was allowed to abandon its more ambitious, and politically sensitive, awareness-raising purposes. »Redistributive justice«, »a fair deal to those in greatest need«, gave way to the safer concentration on functional skills and especially pure literacy work. Ramakrishnan concluded that at least in the circumstances of India a mass movement cannot be orchestrated and managed from above. His story also suggests a failure of will and nerve when it came to mobilising the poor.

The study which follows provides a more optimistic view of NAEP from the other end of the telescope: as it appeared to those working in one of the many nongovernmental organisations (NGOs) which took part — Seva Mandir, in Udaipur, Rajasthan. Seva Mandir was perhaps the best known of Indian adult education NGOs, a Mecca for overseas adult educators eager to learn and be inspired by the Gandhian tradition of service. Om and Ginny Shrivastava describe its work during its rapid growth and flowering. Since then its founder, Mohan Sinha Mehta, has died, and the Shrivastavas and other Seva Mandir workers have moved on to found and work in other Indian NGOs. The voluntary sector is especially prone to reliance on charismatic and dedicated individuals, but generally spared the frustration of a cumbersome bureaucracy which Ramakrishnan found so ill-suited to handling NAEP.

This second Indian case study in this volume, like Anita Dighe's, has a sharp local focus, although Seva Mandir reflected national events, drew on outside expertise (notably from a Delhi-based Institute, for training), and belonged to an informal national network of adult educators sharing a commitment to radical social change (there is a passing reference to SEWA at Ahmedabad in the text which follows). The underlying value system resembles that of SEWA: humane, socialist, participative, Gandhian. The study again reveals a sense of quiet purpose and considerable courage, as well as a similar tactical sense: confronting authority yet seeking to work with and modify the established power structure in an effort to effect both short-term amelioration and longer term change. The authors are evidently politically aware and in a very practical way politically literate. At the same time the account suggests a consistency, a congruence, between purposes and processes, making it pragmatic only in a most positive sense.

This congruence shows itself most clearly in respect of the staff training and development which preceded and accompanied the work. The Shrivastavas' account of their approach may be compared with what Stacy, Clark and Dighe have to say on the same subject and also, particularly, with Miller's and Wijetunga's accounts in *National Development Strategies*. Here too congruence between ideology, or value-system, and practice, shines through. Seva Mandir, like Sarvodaya in Sri Lanka and the Sandinistas on their Literacy Crusade, conveys the sense not only of a mission- oriented organisation but also of an organisation effectively committed to its own learning. IAD in Alice Springs, SEWA in Ahmedabad, Seva Mandir in Udaipur: each in its own way displayed an openness to experience, a capacity to adapt to new experiences in terms of objectives as well as means, which is a strength of the voluntary sector at its best. In other ways too the reader will find echoes of earlier themes in this story: the role of women, their exploitation and their capacity for uniting and challenging injustice in the most difficult circumstances; the dedication and learning of middle class workers engaging with a tribal or other exploited community; and the shift of such work, and workers, from an urban to a rural setting — a pattern replicated in the third Indian study, by Felix Sugirtharaj, with which this volume concludes.

Summary

Seva Mandir is a voluntary non-governmental organisation engaged in adult education and rural development programmes in Udaipur district, Rajasthan. »Seva Mandir is for all mankind but, in particular for those who are victims of social, economic and political injustice and oppression. It strives for a new social order based on equality, truthful and open means. Seva Mandir believes that the people, specially the poor, have the capacity and strength to take their destiny in their own hands and that a truly egalitarian and democratic social order can only be established through people's own efforts. In a spirit of humility and compassion, Seva Mandir seeks to exercise a catalyst role in bringing about this sense of liberation and self-confidence in individuals and in communities.«[1]

Seva Mandir promotes literacy for all-round development of the deprived and underprivileged, evolving new techniques for the training of animators and other workers to eliminate illiteracy and awaken in the illiterate a spirit of self-reliance and a consciousness of how much they suffer from the disadvantage of illiteracy. This particular project operated in Girwa and Jhadol, two Development Blocks [a Development Block has a population of 150 — 200,000 people] of Udaipur district. Here literacy was an essential component, though work in two other Blocks concentrated on people's education for development. The approach was to foster community organisation and local leadership among community groups. generating skills in analysing situations, and supporting people to initiate action based on their analysis of the resources available. Most of these groups were formed while the literacy programme was going on.

There were three hundred adult education centres in the two Blocks. Their activities were as follows:

- provision of literacy and numeracy skills;
- provision of information on agriculture, animal husbandry, forestry, cooperatives, health, village industry and other government schemes;
- where learner initiative was high, helping develop projects such as minor irrigation, building community centres, small-scale industry, animal husbandry camps, social forest plantations;
- making learners aware of their civic rights and duties, and providing an understanding of laws and government policies affecting them;
- wherever possible, promoting organised action to bring local people the benefits implied in the laws and policies of the government.

These activities occurred in the project area. Another important activity of Seva Mandir was organising conferences, seminars and training, and workshops for workers, thinkers, and administrators in the field of adult education locally, statewide, nationally and internationally. Seva Mandir sought to combine conceptual clarity in adult education with human values of equality, justice and freedom among participants, and to provide them with skills to enable the people with whom they were working to transform their environment through an understanding of the forces which had enslaved them in the past. Seva Mandir also contributed to developing national and state level plans for adult education, with the bias spelt out in its philosophical stance.

Seva Mandir: Philosophy and Evolution

The Origins of Seva Mandir

Seva Mandir originated in the social and educational concerns of stalwarts of the independence (swarajya) movement of India. The seed germinated in the mind of Dr Mohan Sinha Mehta in 1925, when Udaipur was the capital of Mewar State, a feudal kingdom where education for the poor was considered an act of rebellion. He came into contact with the Servants of India Society and later with the Settlements of England, Europe and the United States. At that time his wish was »to collect a small group of closely knit, disciplined, enthusiastic and educated young persons of character, who would devote their energy and talent to the cause of social progress and the task of national building«.[2] The organisation took physical form in 1966 when Mehta was able to muster the resources to start its activities, although he had bought a parcel of land in 1930, and the foundation stone had been laid by Pandit Hirday Nath Kunjru in 1931.

Objectives of Seva Mandir

The objectives were:
(i) to provide opportunities and to create an atmosphere for the understanding and promotion of human, social and cultural, values by study of trends, events and problems of the country, and of human society in general, and then to help people's groups to make plans and programmes to overcome the problems;
(ii) to make efforts and undertake measures for promoting social, economic, educational and intellectual development and social justice (covering both rural and urban society, specially groups of the rural poor) and to offer support and cooperation in general schemes of people's development, social reconstruction and relief attempted by other individuals, institutions and organisations.«[3]

Credo of the Organisation

Seva Mandir works for the poor and deprived, holding that the essential force for a radical transformation of society is the poor. Only they will gain in moving towards the desired order; they alone embody the values and impulses for this order. They lack competence and organisation to bring about the new society on their own initiative. It is the role of Seva Mandir and kindred organisations to develop these in them.

Development is primarily and essentially people's development: not only for the people but by and of the people. The importance of participative modes derives from this principle. People's development on an individualistic or self-serving basis is neither viable nor just for the poor, who need an indigenous basis for cooperation and mutual aid which can be further rationalised, strengthened and updated. The primary concern and constituency are the people, but Seva Mandir cannot avoid dealing with the state and market forces. It is dependent on these for its existence and functioning, yet has an autonomy of role, helping people to create institutions and modes of economy which will improve their standing vis-a-vis the state and market forces. Meanwhile they have to retain relations with the state and the market forces, to obtain resources as well as to exert pressure.

Experience has shown that development projects tend to become bureaucratised; the onus of responsibility tends to remain at the institutional level, not involving the people. Seva Mandir strives for consciousness, capacity and will for change to be generated amongst the people themselves, beginning modestly in small pockets, but gaining in intensity; bringing forth local leaders and spreading through their efforts in a larger area.[4]

Background: the Area and Activities

The northern part of Udaipur district is a broad plateau, while the eastern portion has fertile plains. The southern part is mostly rocks, hills and fairly dense jungles.

and the west comprises the Aravali ranges. Rainfall is erratic, and this has great impact on agriculture. Generally every third year is a drought year, causing a shortage of food for humans and animals alike. Some areas have heavy rainfall during the rainy season; because of the destruction of the forest the rain takes away the topsoil, also creating a water-logging problem in low-lying areas. The main occupations are agriculture and animal husbandry, for example goats and sheep. People also engage in daily wage labour in agriculture, road construction and building contract work. Many depend on the wooded areas for their income; forest products include beedi leaves, white radishes, gum, bamboo, mahua, charcoal, firewood and honey.

There are three categories of land ownership: absentee landlords, middle peasants, and small and marginal farmers. These last comprise over 60% of the population, but have only about 20% of total holdings of private land. They are very poor and own mainly hilly land. The tribal people are among the poorest in the area. They depend on agriculture, manual labour and collection of forest products. Some have no job for more than five months of the year. Their annual income averages Rs. 2,000/- to 2,500/- per family. Money-lenders and landlords are the richest people of the area, owning the best lands. The majority of the people are in debt to money-lenders, bigger farmers, contractors, cooperative societies and banks.

Specific problems include: lack of water in this hilly, rocky terrain; deforestation of the hillsides; small landholdings and dearth of supplementary income-generating activities, leading to migration for work in the winter; lack of schools, roads, and community meeting places; diseases like guinea-worm, scabies, diarrhoea, malaria and tetanus that could be controlled and cured through public health knowledge and simple preventative medicinal practices; exploitation of labour by contractors working for small irrigation schemes, mineowners, Food for Work Schemes, and village landlords; exorbitant rates of interest charged by money-lenders; lack of leadership among women; illiteracy, particularly among women and girls; widespread superstition; caste customs that adversely affect the state of women; the unequal distribution of resources and opportunities between the rich and the poor. Most crucial is the lack of: a positive self-concept, and of self-confidence, amongst the communities of the poor; appropriate leadership and related organisation among the poor; skills and know-how for appropriate technological advancement; and resources for investment in development.[5]

Since 1966 the organisation extended from voluntary workers in Udaipur city and some nearby villages to four Development Blocks of Udaipur district and the city. The major activities came to be in rural areas but with some activities also organised in the city, particularly with women and Harijans. Initial activities were concentrated in the city. There was always an urge to work in the rural areas, but lack of resources made it impossible at first. The approach was to initiate small-scale activities, identifying people who might later help in the development of Seva Mandir: the Discussion Group, Youth Group, Women's Association, Student Forum,

Publication, Adoption of a village for comprehensive development, and Amateur Dramatic Society. Seva Mandir also acted as a local unit of Amnesty International and Radical Humanism.

In 1969, with the help of Literacy House, Lucknow, the first adult education project was started in one Block of Udaipur district. Objectives at that time were general in nature. The methodology used for training the worker usually provided information which could help people generally. Soon the State Government provided funds to organise the Farmers' Functional Literacy Programme (FFLP) and Seva Mandir started work in earnest. At that time the Green Revolution was the key to solving the food problem, and FFLP was used for educating the farmers. Seva Mandir engaged a progressive farmer along with supervisory staff. It also developed a primer based on high-yielding varieties of crops with the help of the Agriculture University at Udaipur. The programme was successful for those who had land and water, could afford the inputs and so take advantage of them, but small and marginal farmers and the landless did not benefit. Around 1975 a severe drought in the Udaipur region prompted a review of the work. This made clear that the work was mainly with middle or small farmers. Other problems needed immediate attention, such as water, afforestation, animal care, and exploitation. The programme needed enlarging to help solve these. At this time Seva Mandir was also looking for ways and means to work with tribal communities more intensively.

An Experimental Literacy Project was launched in the Kherwala Development Block with a population 90% tribal. [Also a unique project for neoliterate readers of the Udaipur District within twenty miles' radius using motor cycles to take books to the villages. Nearly 3,000 readers were enrolled in this programme.] Several projects complemented the adult education programmes, in land improvement, minor irrigation, forestry, regeneration of rural crafts, rural school building construction, mobilisation of credit from the banks, etc. Another important project was nonformal education for out-of-school children, mostly from tribal or backward communities. This and other projects provided experience of the working of development with poor, tribal and backward communities, and of how an adult education can be instrumental in educating the poor. This brought us face to face with the problems of exploitation, unjust distribution of resources between the haves and the have-nots, the deficit situation of the poor, and socio-political and economic relationships in rural communities. It caused us to develop a new type of follow-up programme, the »Peer Group Rural Development Programme«, launched in Kherwala as an action research project, and based on people's development through people's participation. The process involved a cycle of learning, experiencing, reflecting, analysing and new learning. Evaluation convinced us that one important method of work with the poor is education, organisation and action; this became the key idea in further adult education work. The concept of development was undergoing a transformation nationally and internationally at this time, being seen as more than just material. In this context it seemed important to revise our approach in the adult education programme.

India's National Adult Education Programme (NAEP) was launched in October 1978. Seva Mandir took part in a big way: helping organise 450 adult education centres; organising an International Training Seminar which prepared the training document for the workers; and working on several national committees to help create the operational plan. The policy document of NAEP, though national in approach, spelt out clearly that it was meant for the economically and socially deprived. Our understanding of adult education, and the resultant philosophical position, emerged from continuous review and reflection upon our work. We may have said correct things, but it was fifteen years of experience which brought the action closer to the thought.

Aims and Objectives

»Literacy is not just the process of learning the skills of reading, writing and arithmetic, but a contribution to the liberation of man and to his full development. Thus conceived, literacy creates the conditions for the acquisition of a critical consciousness of the contradictions of society in which man lives and of its aims; it also stimulated initiative and his participation in the creation of projects capable of acting upon the world, of transforming it, and of defining the aims of authentic human development.«[6] Seva Mandir's programme covers the larger purposes of social change, economic betterment, and broad awakening among the people. It seeks to follow the spirit of government policy which states:

(a) that literacy is a serious impediment to progress, both individual and social;

(b) that adult education should go on in all situations in life, and all the time;

(c) that learning, working and living each acquire a meaning when correlated one with another;

(d) that the means by which people are involved in the process are as important as the ends;

(e) finally, that the poor and the illiterate can rise to their own liberation, through literacy, dialogue and action.

In harmony with this participants should be able to understand the social, cultural, economic and political environment in which they live, and to act accordingly. Literacy is considered an essential skill in creating this understanding. The components of the programme are literacy, which includes skill in reading, writing and numeracy at a functional level, functional skill development, and awareness-raising. These programmes are seen as the medium whereby functional education — useful, life-centred and oriented to development — is imparted. Such education, by its very nature, is intended to lead to social, cultural and political change as well as economic growth. Because Seva Mandir has made a special effort to work with the poor and the oppressed most adult education centres opened under this project have the tribal and other poor men and women as learners.

Features of the Project

Planning the Project

Earlier experience had convinced us of the need to organise and plan adult education with the participation of the people and the workers. Seva Mandir therefore started work on a new basis. Several meetings with the old adult education teachers were organised, and experienced workers at all levels involved. The role of the adult education workers included preparation of materials and curriculum development, as well as motivation of the learners. The following description is from the project outline.

»(i) *The Adult Education Worker*
He or she is the frontline person in this operation. On his or her performance depends the outcome. Their concerns have to be: development, organisation and literacy. He/she has to be a literacy worker, as much as a functional leader. Given the uniqueness and specificity of each group, he/she has to be able to adapt, innovate and improvise materials and curricular patterns within the framework of the overall objectives and basic principles of the programme. He/she has to have deep sympathy and a sense of worth and respect for the learners. Ideally he/she has to be one of them, but outsiders with proper orientation can also be found suitable...
(ii) *Material Preparation and Curriculum Development*
In a programme where the emphasis is on adaptation, innovation and improvision by the workers in relation to the specific needs of the particular groups of learners... there has to be a close working participation between the field level workers, supervisors and the support staff of the project... Training, materials preparation and curriculum development have to be carried on in a concurrent and integrated manner with the implementation of the programme, after the minimum basic preparations have been made and broad guidelines developed.
(iii) *Motivation*
This can be enhanced through making the learning functionally useful and incorporating literacy into it as a tool element. This learning of the group can be linked with larger goals such as agricultural improvement, higher incomes, better functioning of the cooperative movement, more effective role in local government, etc. A well-designed programme with consistent and regular contact between the project staff and the field workers usually helps to maintain a common sense of purpose. It is visualised that it will take 10 months to cover the basic literacy-cum- functional education work.«

Participation of the People

To involve those who would be participants in the programme Sasharta Chetna Yatra, or Awareness for Literacy Walk, a consciousness-raising walk by workers of Seva Mandir in eight teams, was evolved. The teams walked through villages holding discussions with people on the farms, at worksites and wells, in tea-shops and village centres, talking with the people about the objectives of NAEP. Wherever they stayed for the night they organised meetings with the villagers, sometimes also cultural programmes and film shows. Cooperation was obtained from local bodies, eg. Panchayata, as well as from the Department of Agriculture, Family Welfare, and other organisations. The Block Development Officers also helped.

This Walk created a new environment in the area; it also helped the workers to understand the problems of the villagers who would be taking part in the NAEP. The workers visited three hundred villages. As the NAEP was a mass programme it was necessary to identify educated men and women who could become adult education teachers and who would also be acceptable to the village community. During the Walk the workers of Seva Mandir asked about such people. The last day of the Walk was 8 September 1978. On that day people from the surrounding villages assembled for a mass meeting, when the importance of the programme was spelt out: it was a programme not merely to make people literate but also to involve them in understanding their own environment and organising projects which might help them in their development.

Preparing Materials in a Local Dialect

Material developed for the project included interesting basic learning materials in the local dialect. We had a primer in Hindi based on the learners' needs and problems, but material in the local dialect was thought more useful, using the »lead sentence discussion method«: the teacher initiates discussion on the basis of a key sentence, which is based in turn on a problem or an agricultural concept. Along with this sentence there is a big charting depicting the idea in the sentence. The picture and the sentence lead to discussion. Primers were prepared in Mewari and Wagadi, the two local dialects, with the help of instructors and other literacy workers.

A meeting was first held with instructors in a Mewari-speaking area, and a proposal put for preparation of the primer. Most supported the idea. A workshop was organised to prepare the first draft. When the instructors and the learners realised that they had actually to be involved in this task there was considerable uncertainty on their part. They had never done such a thing before. Neither, the organiser told them, had he. He pointed out that at least they had the advantage of having Mewari as their mother tongue, which he did not.

Fourteen posters used in the FFLP, conveying certain key concepts in improved agricultural practices in this region and other social problems, provided a basis for primer preparation. The contents of each poster and problems, both economic and social, were discussed and a lead-sentence evolved in the two local dialects for each poster. From this sentence a key word was selected by the group. Each key word was broken into its constituent consonants and vowels. From these letters new words were constructed in each case. The last step involved the construction of new problem- and concept-based sentences from the new words. Before a new word or sentence was accepted the question was asked whether it could be understood by the learners without the instructor's help. There was considerable excitement among the instructors and learners as each word and sentence was examined and analysed for its relevance and meaning. It was often difficult to find a word acceptable to groups representing local variations in the dialect. The primers included a portion facilitating transfer to learning to read and write Hindi at a later stage. The drafts were revised following advice from a panel of experts with a background in linguistics and adult psychology, and again reviewed by the literacy instructors and supervisors of each mother tongue.

Training Programmes for Adult Educators

Proper implementation of the NAEP, with its new thrust towards social awareness and functional improvement for the weaker sections of society, required workers at project level with a deep sense of responsibility to the poor in the community; a faith in adult education as an instrument of social change; and a high degree of self-reliance, initiative and capacity to innovate. Few workers embody these qualities readymade. More often newly appointed workers are dependent, self-serving and lacking in enterprise, as a result of authoritarian upbringing in extended families, reinforced by routinised schooling and oppressive working conditions. Traditional training dominated by prominent personalities, heavy inputs of academic information, and passive learning in comfortable living arrangements, tend to discourage active thinking and analysis, and to perpetuate dependence.

Seva Mandir therefore tried new approaches to training adult education workers in place of the earlier Field Operational Seminar. In the Peer Group programme in Kherwala behavioural techniques were evolved to give skills in situation analysis, group organisation and self-reliant planning and action. Dr Rajesh Tandon, then of the Public Enterprises Centre for Continuing Education in New Delhi, gave valuable help in this. Subsequently further new techniques were tried in preparation for launching new projects. Salient features of the new training approach were as follows.

(a) Opening and Introduction
The formal opening with dignitary speeches was dispensed with. Instead participants were put in the forefront through exercises for self and mutual introduction which highlighted their own and others' attitudes, interests and qualities. The public address system was used with good effect to enable participants to gain confidence in the use of this medium. A questionnaire exercise initiated thinking on one's own responsibility in religious, educational and family contexts.

(b) Familiarisation with the Objectives and Scope of NAEP
This was done through guided self-study assignments on an individual and group basis, followed by discussion and clarification in a common session.

(c) Perception of Own Role in the NAEP
Participants were next asked to define individually their own perception of their role in the new adult education programme, starting them thinking about their own place, functions and responsibilities and articulating their ideas about these. These were shared in small group sessions and a sample presented in a general session. Even at this early stage perceptions began to go beyond the stereotypes and reveal new possibilities.

(d) Exposure to Field Situations
With a tentative idea of their role in mind participants were exposed to the field situation to look afresh at the rural reality. This was done through direct field experience, a simulation game called »Monsoon«, and open-ended case studies depicting real problems in the participants' communities. These exercises sought to give an objective understanding of natural conditions, the social structure, power groups, development efforts and agencies, opportunities and problems for the poor and the decision-making processes in the rural areas. Observations were checked and systematised in groups, and supplemented by data and case studies given for self-study assignments.

(e) Matching Role Perceptions with Field Knowledge
Participants' role perceptions were re-examined and refined in the light of new understanding gained from the field analysis individually, in groups and in the general session. This brought the problem-solving, assistance and organisational role to the fore, and put literacy work in context. For the first time in Seva Mandir's adult education experience, the workers began to see themselves as leaders in development and change in the communities of their concern.

(f) Identifying Capabilities and Skills for New Roles
Following the new role definition, participants were asked to identify the skills and capabilities needed to carry out the new tasks visualised. They also listed the various areas of development work about which information was needed. Apart from skills in literacy instruction, other capabilities identified were: Managing the adult education centre; communication skills; mobilising the learners; mobilising help and resources from the community; establishing links with government functionaries; demonstrating improved techniques in farming. Further training was planned to start developing these capabilities.

(g) Developing Capabilities and Skills
The main responsibility for this was located with the participants; the initial training only began a process which had to be continued by participants on their own, and in subsequent training sessions. Literacy instruction skills were imparted through explanation and demonstration of techniques, using the charts and primers. Record-keeping and reporting were practised, and resource persons from agriculture, health, industries, home science and banking agencies apprised the participants of programmes for weaker sections, and how help could be obtained.

Simulation games and exercises were used to develop communication and cooperative functioning skills.

(h) Institutional Values and Principles of Work
Two sessions elucidated values and principles through illustration, anecdote and dialogue. Seva Mandir's focus on the weakest as the »pole star« for the direction of our work; workers' self- reliance and capacity for self-help; institution as an instrument serving the society; openness and freedom in planning and review, and discipline in execution; attitude of perpetual learning; limiting personal needs and interests for social betterment, and voluntariness of spirit: these were highlighted as guiding principles.

(i) Planning for the Next Phase
Finally participants prepared plans for their work in the field during the month after the training. These were discussed in groups and some were presented in the general session.

(j) Concluding Function
This consisted of reports by the participants and some words of advice and encouragement. The training was experienced as a nursery in which some tender seedlings of ideas, desires and capabilities had sprouted. They had to be careful in the selection of friends and supporters for the new work. They could expect more response and help among the poor who were also the primary concern of their work. They had to be vigilant about the direction and basic principles of their work, and seek help from Seva Mandir workers when in doubt.

This realisation led to this kind of learning being renamed »Ankuran« (germination) instead of »Prashikshan« (Training).[8] The training preceded actual teaching, but orientation training was also organised during the project year. Monthly meetings with the instructors were treated as learning experiences; simulation games, role-plays etc. were used as a form of experiential learning. There were also five-day orientation training sessions every three months, mostly used as an opportunity to foster conceptual learning on the basis of case studies drawn from field situations. The case study became a useful method of training.

Literacy Games and Proshika (Project Journal)

During the project period, with the help of literacy instructors and people from the National Council of Educational Research and Training in New Delhi, some interesting games were developed for the three NAEP components — literacy, functionality, and awareness-raising. They proved useful and easy to handle; Seva Mandir then produced them for the use of other agencies too. The games were used to evaluate literacy and numeracy skills as well as functional knowledge in such areas as agriculture, animal husbandry and health. Another interesting experiment was the news- sheet »Proshika«, a short form of Adult Education Programme, produced with the help of learners, instructors and other workers who wrote about their experiences. Small letters written by new learners were published just as they were, although they contained many mistakes. The idea was to create a feeling of confidence to express themselves among people.

Adult Education and Development Programme

Several development programmes, taken up on the basis of need, succeeded in helping the people as well as the area. They included afforestation, agriculture, and soil conservation. Learners were taken to attend the annual farmers' fair, organised by the Agriculture University of Udaipur. Several camps were organised with the help of the animal husbandry hospital in the field area, where animals were taken when in need of attention.

Cost Effectiveness

There are definite figures for amounts spent on project officers and supervision, on training and lanterns, books and kerosene, on instructor stipends, etc. There is also an accurate figure of the number of persons enrolled, and the number who successfully passed the testing and evaluation procedures to determine literacy skills and functional knowledge.

For 1981-82 the total expenditure on the programme was Rs.463,533.03 (about $ 58,000). 309 centres were opened with 9,051 men and women enrolled; of these 7,787 passed the tests at the end of the ten month course of instruction. This puts the cost per participant at Rs.51.00 ($ 6.30) and the cost per »functional literate« at Rs.59.00 ($ 7.30). For comparison, in 1975 the Farmers' Functional Literacy Programme in Seva Mandir cost Rs.31.50 ($ 4.00) per participant, and Rs.72.00 ($ 9.00) per graduate. The narrowing of the difference between participants and graduates indicates a lower dropout rate; the adults who joined the centre were better motivated than those in 1975. From the institution's point of view, with less experience in running programmes the cost per graduate is higher, and with more experience in training, motivating, supervising, etc., the cost per person falls. Stopping and starting literacy campaigns ultimately costs the government more to reach the same standard of functional education. International comparisons for functional literacy showed the lowest cost per graduate for Tanzania with $ 32, the highest for Iran at $ 442. Seva Mandir, after twelve years' experience, had a per graduate cost of $ 7.30.[9]

Seva Mandir continued to run about 300 centres under the government's functional literacy programme, but was in addition able to support some centres initiated and run by hamlet level groups themselves. There were certain constraints in the government scheme: 30 adults per centre, meeting nightly for 10 months, being visited by a District Education Officer who has his own sets of criteria for »success«, etc. In many tribal hamlets the houses are spread over the hills as people live on their farms, not clustered together in compact villages, so it is difficult to get thirty people together regularly, or even enrolled. Some such communities ran their own adult education centres, contributing money to a group fund and then, as a group, deciding that some of that money would go towards a stipend for the instructor, and/or for kerosene. Seva Mandir loaned such centres, at no cost, old lanterns, cotton mats to sit on, charts and learning materials, also providing training for the instructors. Timing and frequency of meetings were decided by the communities, usually in hamlets in which an adult education centre had been run earlier. The numbers of learners varied upwards from eight per centre. Seva Mandir matched the group fund contributions each month on a 50:50 basis, up to Rs.100/- per month, and provided the training and supportive supervision. It is however not possible to calculate the cost per centre for this area.

One final comparison is perhaps relevant: the cost of adult education compared with primary schooling. Recognising that costs more than doubled since 1968 when the cost per pupil in the primary school system in India was Rs.49/- ($ 6.53), and that per »successful« adult participant in the adult education centres in 1982 was Rs.59/- ($ 7.30), it can be seen how cost-effective is non-formal adult education. The ten-month adult education programme imparted functional and general knowledge, and brought literacy and numeracy skills up to the level of class 4 or 5. Four or five years of schooling, even at 1968 rates, would cost roughly $ 26. If rates doubled, that is $ 50, compared with $ 7.30.

Issues for Consideration

Clarity of Purpose

It is easy to mobilise policy-makers in the realm of objectives once they are convinced. When it comes to bureaucrats, particularly in the lower ranks of the hierarchy, it is more difficult. Sometimes there is a time-lag in their understanding; often the understanding is never there. For example, a national programme launched and offered by a voluntary organisation is treated by other development agencies not as part of a total development effort in nation-building but as a sectoral activity. The important common national objective is not recognised, nor the role of each agency in supporting and achieving it. This happened many a time with Seva Mandir in implementing the NAEP.

A nation-wide people's programme involving voluntary organisations in the implementation requires objectives to be spelt out clearly to all levels through all channels. There should be political will as well as people's will to achieve the objectives. With the NAEP neither the people's nor the political will was developed adequately. This made the NAEP a sectoral programme, like other physical programmes such as irrigation or public works, although the objectives were national and oriented towards people's development.

NAEP was suspended in 1980. Although the objectives were adopted after thorough discussion at the national level, the programme was suspended prematurely, demoralising those involved. In earlier programmes people's development was approached thus: »we know best about their welfare, hence they should do as we say«; involvement was important to the extent that people benefitted from the programme. The new concept was that people should think, initiate, plan and implement the programmes themselves. The former type of programme had a »we-versus-they« relationship; the latter was »we-altogether«. This means major change in the attitudes of organisers at all levels, and raises questions about the behaviour of organisers towards the people. If the organisers at project level understand the objectives and act accordingly, this may challenge other development workers who do not really understand people's development. This has been a problem particularly when the poor and oppressed start questioning and acting to change their own environment. These problems occurred with Seva Mandir's own workers as well as with government agencies with which Seva Mandir worked.

Participation as a Methodology in Adult Education

If adult education programmes are people's development programmes, then participation of learners, workers, administrators and policy-makers should be developed. Telling people to participate, or beckoning them to become part of a programme, may be considered participation, but an understanding of the idea must be created before real participation can occur, fostering an atmosphere in which those participating feel they are partners in the event. Seva Mandir has organised training sessions and tried in many ways to develop skills in creating an atmosphere in which people can become partners, with some success. One interesting result was a change in our own institutional structure: workers became to a greater degree partners in decision-making. Our new strategy meant working **with** the neighbourhood groups of poor and backward communities, analysing their environment and resources, and helping to develop action programmes. We spent a lot of time organising village meetings before launching the programme, not just waiting for a village community to approach Seva Mandir, but not imposing on an unaware community either. Choosing an adequate teacher was the village's responsibility. The training of workers was planned using a participative methodology. Throughout this process we became more aware of the perceptions, attitudes and image of the poor people, despite frequently slipping back into our own former assumptions.

Women's Adult Education Programme

We had encountered great difficulty in organising women's adult education programmes, both from the social and cultural attitude of the people (including women themselves) towards women's education, and organisationally. One needs to persuade community leaders of the importance of women's education, and also to spend time with women in groups where the programme is to be implemented. A major hurdle was attracting women workers. Most of the educated urban women did not want to go to the villages and in most of the villages it was difficult to find a local woman literate enough to be an adult education instructor. Outside women could not be placed there because of the cost involved, so men were used who were acceptable both to the community and to the women learners. This was found by a research study to be suitable and satisfactory.[10]

Leadership was not the only problem. The status of women was so low that it was hard to convince people to send the women to the centres. If they came they had to bring their children with them. This reduced learning as half the time the attention was shared by the child. The site of the centre was also a problem. It needed to be near the houses so that the women could come and go easily at night. In some cases the instructor had to escort the women to their homes, and in tribal areas the houses are not clustered together.

The women's programme had to be organised somewhat differently from the men's, particularly in poor communities; the women work inside the house, and need to supplement household earnings. The programmes needed extra attention and more money. For example intermediate technology can help; a bio-gas plant can save women hours of fetching firewood. The instructor's qualifications, the number of learners in each centre, and other administrative requirements had to be varied; only thus could the women's adult education programme operate effectively.

Problems of Implementation

Preparation of the environment proved very important. It had to be such as to stimulate people's will. The programme needed to be seen as an instrument of social change. This meant increasing people's understanding, as well as involvement with their problems. In many case this hits at vested interests in the area as well as at the power structure at village level. This can be difficult for village-based workers, both from the point of view of community support and from the point of view of other agencies and government departments. These see adult education only as making people literate; in fact it extends far beyond literacy skills. This then poses a problem about the organisation of adult education centres for the poor and oppressed where exploitative systems prevail. India is a socialist country, so the laws and political rhetoric support work with the poor. Resources and programme however too often fail to reach their intended destination. Seva Mandir tried to keep working relations with the power structures, without compromising the essential task with the poor.

It proved hard to find good instructors. Most instructors used by the adult education centres were young, belonged to that community, and had no formal education beyond grade 8. They needed continuous support in teaching not only literacy skills but also other functional education and consciousness-raising skills as well. This reduced the time available to the field supervisor and project officer for tasks other than training. Due to NAEP project constraints the supervisor had to visit thirty centres, and could not give effective support to all of them. Wherever such support was given by a supervisor, some of the young instructors became real community animators and helped to get people thinking about their own development. Many went on in later years to work with groups in their areas, planning and implementing development programmes.

Another issue was the language used. Generally it is thought that the local dialect should be used for initial learning, with a shift to the popular regional or national language later on. According to a recent research study[11] this method does not significantly affect achievement scores when compared with continuous instruction in the regional or national language, but it does help to generate and sustain learners' interest in the programme. In many cases participants showed interest in learning the regional language because it is the language of power — all transactions in business, banks and government are in this language and not in the local dialect.

The relationship with government development agencies proved very important. Sometimes it was possible to create a good personal working relationship with a worker in a development agency, but once he was transferred it became a problem again. The programme explained to the people might be changed for some not always rational reason, creating a problem of trust and confidence. There was also the issue of coordination with other agencies. Finally, economic pressures on the learners affected their attendance. This problem could not be resolved. It caused high attrition, which reduced the cost-effectiveness of the programme.

Evaluation and Appraisal

Instead of evaluating the training, the materials used, the supervision, etc., we chose to evaluate the effect of the adult education work on those involved in both teaching and learning. Although in some villages nothing remarkable happened, on the whole the efforts made a difference to individuals, to village life, and to the workers of Seva Mandir. We all became stronger, more aware of our strength individually and collectively. Both leaders and learners who benefitted from the programme efforts moved solidly into a life-style of continuous learning, action and reflection.

We did not evaluate the programme by the number of people made literate, although such figures were available: 15,000 men and 3,500 women attended Seva Mandir adult education centres, and passed the functional literacy tests at the end of the ten month sessions. Nor did we evaluate on the basis of functional knowledge learned and put into practice, although more than 500 families in the small and marginal category adopted improved agricultural practices through the efforts of Seva Mandir.

We have seen individuals take hold of their lives, growing in self-confidence and feelings of self-worth. The feelings and ideas communicated by Rajkumari [see Appendix 2], a young woman in a learning group, reveal elements of growth common to many touched by the work. The self-concepts of women attending the adult education centres increased considerably. Before the centres were really under way women interviewed indicated that they thought men were better at all things than women, that men and women did not have equal rights in India, that they did not love girl children and boy children equally, that the village panchayat did not need to take the opinion of women before making a decision, and so forth. After the operation of the centres for about eight months, the same women had shifted by about 25% in the direction of perceiving women to be equally as important as men.

Surveying the hamlets where groups were running, we found many groups continuing to meet and expand their membership, and working on other development issues. The Pai village group began with a functional literacy centre, moved to soil conservation work and, when last contacted, were collectively pooling their time, labour and resources to deepen a community well which would irrigate the land of about 30 farmers. The women of village Channi continued to meet. They formed a self-help loan society and fought successful struggles againt daily wage labour exploitation.

The adult education programme helped leaders to come forward at all levels. At hamlet level, most of the leaders of groups moving on to work on agricultural exploitation, the development of cottage industry skills, and credit started as adult education instructors and initiated these programmes. Tulsi Bahingi, an instructor for two years, was leading the tribal people of her village in a fight for hand pumps in the hamlets, and against exploitation at the government ration shop in the village. Another instructor, Amar Chand, continued to build up a group of village people, men and women, who met regularly to work on soil conservation and wage exploitation of labourers in the soapstone mines. Similarly Sattoo Linga was organising several villages around a reafforestation programme. Shanta Devi had built a federation of the poor in her area, organising around self- employment skill training, community centre construction, small- scale credit, and abolition of bad social customs. All began their leadership work as adult education instructors.

As for leadership at the institutional level, we all continued to grow in understanding of the task of organising people for rural development and fostering continuing education, both from outside contacts and from our own work. The »functionality« of the adult education programme meant that we contacted forestry, agriculture, irrigation, medical, legal, nutrition, engineering and other resources. We continued to build on these many areas. We learned from our own experiences and used case studies from our own work in training programmes, cutting them up and putting them together again in analysis sessions.

Evaluating the programme as a whole, we judged that adult education was still the best way to open up an area for further development work, whatever its size. No one development or educational effort will solve all the problems of an area, so the programme must be judged as a medium for beginning work that will continue in other ways. Adult education seems to work thus: a local leader is identified and attends pre-service and in-service training programmes in instructional techniques, functional knowledge, and awareness-building. Those constituting the learning group were by definition illiterate or neo-literate and, therefore, not likely to be the upper class people of the area. Improving the lot of the poor must ultimately involve them in the struggle for liberation.

Does such work reduce poverty? First one must ask why people are poor. Discussions with the poor in this area of southern Rajasthan revealed several reasons: exploitation; feelings of helplessness and fatalism; an unjust social system that perpetuates exploitation by the rich and powerful; internal fights that prevent unity; lack of income-generating skills and opportunities; not maximising income-generating possibilities; caste and social customs; and lack of education generally. If these are the causes of poverty, clearly starting with adult education work does contribute to the process of integrated rural development and ultimately reducing poverty. A meeting of self-employed women in Ahmedabad in 1981 [see chapter 5] agreed that production units were not very effective in providing a base for continuing and integrated work for development. The group cited health and adult education as the best media for development, and health meant, mainly, health education rather than curative programmes.

In all the group activities mentioned above, including the work by old functional literacy instructors, the adult learning component is still very high. People learn how to work together to resist exploitation; taking control of their lives through group action and group strength; trying to solve problems in the village and work together on commonly identified tasks; learning about government schemes of employment, about government laws related to daily wage labour rights, which will help them to create and maximise income-generating possibilities; learning how to reduce and abandon harmful social customs like drinking at marriage time, reverse dowry, death feasts, etc.; and remedying their own lack of education by gaining literacy skills, learning about agriculture, government schemes, development work in other areas, etc. Our experience has been that adult education is a good way to begin work in an area, and an integral part of the further work of groups of the poor to remove poverty from their own and other lives.

Conclusions and Implications

Seva Mandir opened adult education centres, ran agricultural extension programmes, trained village health workers, began a mobile library scheme, and helped communities with digging wells, constructing community centres, establishing small credit unions, etc. This experience showed that adult education is the best medium for opening up an area, and laying a foundation for further continuing education and action for development.

Why did we find the adult education centre to be the best approach? Implementing a programme of 150, 300 or 450 centres means that young people are identified, trained and supported in leadership roles in running a programme of which literacy, functional knowledge and awareness-building are the content. Many of these young people become involved with the problems of the poor locally; if even half show some interest and aptitude in providing continuing leadership among the poor in their area, there is a not insignificant network of contact people for further action with and for the poor.

When the educational level of the population is generally low, it is necessary to start with a programme that is specific enough in task for a local village person to understand, From there we can help people to grow, to lead, and to be part of groups with less definite but equally urgent objectives. The learner group that comes together to work on one or two problems of poverty (illiteracy, lack of agricultural knowledge) and experiences the value of working at these things in groups, gains confidence and a desire to continue to work together. The first year of the adult education centre will not in itself make a significant change to the poor and in exploitative conditions in the area, but it proves to be a good beginning. People gain confidence. They get into the habit of meeting together, come into contact with a voluntary organisation prepared to help them, and lay a foundation for future action.

Through leadership training and group training programmes people come in contact with government officers in charge of programmes that are supposed to be for the poor. They get some glimpse of schemes and resources that could be brought to their area. This exposure itself starts people thinking about further action. Not only do people see resources in government departments outside the village; they also begin to see resources in their own midst. Adult education centre groups have gone on, together, to build community centres, to start small credit unions, to clean up their villages and homes, without intervention from any government department.

It has been our experience, too, that after a year or two, when the literacy component has been dealt with, groups continue to meet at least twice a month, often more frequently. Membership expands as others are attracted. These groups go on study tours, take advantage of short courses in agriculture or cottage industry instruction, work together to change caste and social customs, and fight outside forces of exploitation over daily wages, police or settlement officer bribes, etc. Learning to solve problems together; gaining specific knowledge of laws and programmes; skill development; collective agitational action for justice: all are part of »continuing education« and »lifelong learning« as we see it.

We see the causes of poverty as: lack of economic skills for maximising production; lack of knowledge of sources and resources: exploitation by the rich and powerful; lack of organisation of the poor; social customs and personal habits that impoverish the poor; and lack of self-confidence of the poor to stand up for their rights, and work together on plans to end poor conditions. Thus adult education centres are an important part of the process of overcoming poverty. The centres, by definition, are groups (the beginnings of organisations of the poor); have some leadership development (from the village or hamlet itself); expose the group members to knowledge and resources beyond their experience; and lay a foundation for further education and action. From such experience we firmly believe that adult education is the medium for launching and supporting the movement of the poor to end poverty and exploitation.

References

1. Seva Mandir, New Constitution, 1981, p.1.
2. Seva Mandir, Udaipur Pamphlet, 1966, p.1.
3. Seva Mandir, New Constitution, 1981, p.1.
4. Seva Mandir, *Newsletter*, June 1980, p.3.
5. Seva Mandir, Project Proposal, »Integrated Rural Education and Development Project«, 1980-82, p.5.
6. Persepolis Declaration, Tehran, 1975, p.1.
7. National Adult Education Programme, Policy Statement, 1978, p.1. 8. Seva Mandir, *Newsletter*, October 1978, p.8.
9. *The World of Literacy — Policy, Research and Action*, ICAE, Toronto, 1979, p.75.
10. Shrivastava, Virginia, »Nonformal educational programmes for women in Indian villages. A study of social change and leadership patterns«, 1980, p.237.
11. Shrivastava, Om, »The use of spoken languages in an adult literacy programme in India«, 1980, p.170.

Appendix 1

Seva Mandir — Basic Data

I. *1966-68*
Total staff 1

Urban Activities

(a) Discussion Group	membership	30-40
(b) Youth Group		18
(c) Student Forum		60
(d) Women's Club		20-30

Rural Activities

(a) Adopted Village   one nursery school; road construction

2. *1969-72*

Total staff 10

Urban Activities

(a) Discussion Group	membership	35
(b) Youth Group		18
(c) Student Forum		60
(d) Women's Club		30
(e) Amateur Dramatic Society		30
(f) Harijan Work	literacy centres	3

Rural Activities

(a) Badgaon Literacy Project	centres	100
(b) Farmers' Functional Literacy Project		60

3. *1977-80*

Total staff 92

Urban Activities

(a) Discussion Group	members	18-25
(b) Women's Club		35
(c) Publication & Communication	books	35
Media Department	film shows	60
(d) Harijan Work	creches	1
	nursery	1

Rural Activities

(a) NAEP Badgaon-Girwa Blocks	centres	300
(b) NAEP Kherwara	..	150
(c) Non-formal Education Project	..	30
(d) Rural Mobile Library (to April 1977)	..	100
(e) Rural Devt. Project Badgaon Block	agric. work	150 families
	cooperative & banking	156 ..
	minor irrig. schemes	7
	rural eng. works road	40 km.
	schools	3
	anicuts	3
	rural industry	190 families
(f) Peer Group Development Project	villages	50
(g) Community Education for Devt.	village clusters	3
(h) Rural Women's Devt. Unit	block areas	3

4. *1981*

Total staff 112

Urban Activities

(a) 1000 Household Industry	families	60
(b) Harijan Work	communities	3
(c) Urban Women Devt. Project	work with families	1,000
	to develop programmes	30
(d) Women's Club		30

Rural Activities

(a) Integrated Rural Ed. & Devt. Badgaon	village groups	47
(b) Integrated Rural Ed. & Devt. Kherwala	..	57
(c) Rural Ad.Ed. Project Jhadol-Girwa	centres	300
(d) Resource Support Units: Women's Devt. Unit		
Rural Industry Unit		
Rural Engineering Unit		
Agriculture Unit		
Non-formal Education Unit		
(e) Rural Marketing Centre Girwa	communities	3

Appendix 2

Women's Development in Chhani Village: by Rajkumari

[The following remarks were recorded by the supervisor of the women's adult education centre in village Chhani, Kherwala Block. The young women interviewed had made remarkable progress in many aspects, but was not atypical of changes that take place in women who had never been touched by development efforts earlier. The English translation of Rajkumari's own report of her growth and development is presented as an example of what can happen through adult education and women's development efforts.]

The name of my village is Chhani. It is 10 km west of Kherwala. The population of this village is approx. 2,500 which includes different castes of people. Only a few in my village are rich people and all the rest earn their livelihood through farming or manual labour. I too belong to a poor farming Rajput family and my father owns only one Bigha (half an acre) of land. My father works as messenger (Chaprasi) in the village panchayat. My younger brother works as a domestic help in Ahmedabad in a rich businessman's house. During most of the year, my mother and myself work as labourers. looking at our situation, we can say that without labour it would be difficult for us to make both ends meet.

It has been a tradition in our area of not sending girls to school and also not allowing women to talk and mix with people. In the old days, the women had to remain veiled, and any kind of outside influence on them was unthinkable. Gradually, with passage of time, the traditions are slowly changing. Because of the traditions, even I was deprived of studies. Seeing my other friends going to school I often wondered at my fate that I was letting such a beautiful opportunity go past. I used to blame my parents for this but after all they were also helpless in front of social circumstances.

In this moment of regret, Seva Mandir opened an adult education centre in my village. I still feared an opposition from my parents and they did object. A teacher of the centre, Chandrkanta Devi, would everyday come to my house to persuade my father to let my study, telling him that there was no harm in doing so, but he would always say »what will the community think that I was sending a girl to study?«. In the meanwhile without the knowledge of my parents, I would go to the centre along with my friends. Whenever my father would come to know of my going to the centre he would scold me; despite this, my interest in studies kept growing. Slowly and slowly my parents understood the importance of literacy. I learnt not only to write my name but other things too. I would meet the teacher of the centre in the afternoon at her shop and gradually learnt to sew there. My friends also faced the same problem as mine in the beginning, but being together we gained a degree of confidence and courage in ourselves, and slowly even the parents agreed to send them to the literacy centre. At the centre we got the opportunity of meeting and talking to other people and gained some knowledge of the outside world. Whenever an outsider came to the centre and asked us questions, we were very scared and apprehensive about answering. Even some people of the village did not stop at making fun of us and would say »so you are this«, and I would answer back. Whoever got an answer from me would not have the courage to tease me the next time.

Seva Mandir often organised cultural programmes and with my colleagues I would enthusiastically participate in them. Whenever I got the time I told my neighbourhood women to study too. But they being older than me would not give serious thought to it; still I was not discouraged. With the close cooperation of my friends I continued to study, sew and embroider. With the help of Seva Mandir I went to Udaipur for training and learnt about the nutritional value of food. Going outside the village also gave me a chance to see the city, meet people and learn new things, and I reached a conclusion that without studies everything is meaningless. One advantage of being literate is that I gained a lot of confidence. Before this, I was scared and answered only questions I was asked, but now I could answer my parents on something that I thought to be right.

There was a tradition in our society of all the family members sitting together and consuming liquor. I raised my voice against the custom and told my father that by his consuming liquor he was ruining our lives. Gradually my father understood my point of view and stopped consuming in front of us; and even if he did consume some, it was less, and he would go to sleep.

There were about 15 other girls from my village who came to study at the centre with me. Being with them and talking to them every day, we exchanged our ideas, we listened to each other and respected each ones's ideas and points of view. The village people did not like the formation of our group and often criticised us. We would sometimes give reply but often had to tolerate their criticism. I had full faith that we would have to be ready with an answer for the right cause.

Last year in the neighbourhood village of Chitter, the work of road construction started, in which about 100 workers from Chhani also worked. Nowadays in every department and place corruption is growing. While listing the wages of the labourers, the supervisor and foreman keep an amount of Rs.2-4 from each labourer's salary in their own pockets. I felt like fighting against this corruption but I did not receive the cooperation of my co-workers and neither did I have adequate knowledge of the law etc. I kept quiet and remained a silent spectator to all this. God knows how much money these corrupt people stole from the illiterate poor labourers, and how they indulged themselves in luxuries. Although this work was a government department project their workers also had a hand in this malpractice and they too enjoyed themselves at the cost of the labourers. When the due money had to be paid to the labourers the foreman forged their thumb print and exploited them once again; and with that money they indulged themselves in the »luxury« of wine and chicken. During the discussions at the literacy centre in my village, we had learnt not to put our thumb print on false papers and to maintain a private copy of our attendance. So, when the turn came for me to put my thumb print on the false papers I refused to do so and told my colleagues to abstain from doing so, but they were scared that the foreman would strike out their names off the master roll, therefore, they continued to put their thumb print wherever the foreman wanted them to.

A similar kind of roll call was made one day at 10.00 pm, because the department people knew that at night whatever wages would be given to the labourers they will accept without protest. This is what really happened. That night the 500 labourers accepted whatever was given to them as wages during the roll call. We discovered one or two days' salary less after reaching home and looking at our personal attendance register. We wondered: is this what we get after carrying 20 kgs. of stones throughout the day? At the Adult Education Centre I told this incident to all my friends and the teacher in charge of the centre. When I discussed this with the incharge and the workers of Seva Mandir, they wrote a request letter. When we were busy signing this request letter, the foreman came to know about it and Shri Ram Singh came to threaten me and said it was not the right thing that I was doing. He also said that he would not take me for work next time. To that I replied back that we are the people who work, while you are busy exploiting us. At this point my parents were very angry and asked whether I went to the centre to study or fight with other people. The teacher in charge and myself tried to explain that this was reality. All my other friends got scared after listening to these things. But I was adamant that when we work, then why should anyone else receive the money! The request letter reached the department. However, because the departmental people were also responsible for all these things, the request letter had virtually no effect on them, and when the work of threatening started all over again, we 12 people who had put forward the request letter were not taken on the job. We all decided that if they would not keep us on the job for a year, and would not give us the money that they owed us, we would still continue to keep contact with the department and press them. We saw the muster-roll three to four times in connection with the proceedings, and also met the Sessions Judge thrice, and sent back the request letter to Kherwara. Seeing that we were adamant about this and would not leave them, they gave back our money which they owed us, and took us back on the muster-roll.

When these foreman were working in the forest department they refused to take us as labourers. This was a needed drought relief project in our area. We continued our efforts and gheraoed [surrounded] the sarpanch [the elected village leader], and the forest official. Due to these incidents, the villagers grew quite angry, but I feel we took the right step, which is why they had to bow down. I believe in continued joint effort, hence I am for ever working for it, and keep explaining these courageous ideas to them. Gradually these ideas are having an influence on the rest of the women force of the village. While before only girls of the age group 15-20 came to study at the centre, now this year women of an approximate age group of 30 years, who have children, are also coming to the centre. Besides, this year they have opened a sewing centre in our village, where I am working as an assistant sewing teacher.

In all this work I have got continued cooperation and advice from the Seva Mandir workers, because of which my ideas and arguing power have been on the increase. I am sure, in the future, I will work for these developmental works and help in the upliftment of my village people.

From the above incidents I have learnt the following:

- to read and write;
- realise the real position of women in society;
- continued effort can undo the impossible;
- indulging in developmental programmes assures continued increase in courage.

Chapter Seven

From Health Care to Community Development: Broadening the Base of Gonoshasthaya Kendra

Introduction

The first case study in this volume is by a trained nurse. This one is by a qualified doctor. He was among the dedicated group who founded the People's Health Centre in Bangladesh in the special circumstances following a War of Liberation, and stayed with it through and beyond the period reported upon here. Valerie Miller's account of the post-liberation Literacy Campaign in Nicaragua, in the earlier companion volume to this, shows how popular will and energy can be mobilised, there on a national level, to serve educational and political purposes. Rezaul Haque's study, spanning a longer period, also explores problems of relating to a less-than-ideal government, while sustaining the original sense of vision and purpose. The theme is replayed, fascinatingly, at the microcosmic level within Gonoshasthaya Kendra (GK). Here those who created the Centre in the heroic days of 1972 had to come to terms with its growth, and with the »generation gap« encountered as younger and more recent recruits joined the organisation. On the one hand, then, this is a study of the evolving relationship between a small, energetic and high profile NGO and the State and society which it sought to serve and to change. On the other it constitutes a natural history of a new NGO as it learns and evolves.

The sense of mission, or destiny, is reflected in GK's primary aim: nothing less than »to provide a plan to upgrade the national Public Standards and eventually to release our country from its dependence upon foreign aid by becoming self-sufficient through community support«. One detects in the account a congruence between lofty ideals and day by day living. Haque's account of the principles and practices for managing the GK community is almost painful in its sense of integrity — self-analysis combining discipline with democracy. Here is a self-consciously »learning organisation«, changing in the light of experience and mistakes while seeking to sustain an egalitarian and value-driven community. It had, perhaps painfully, to compromise on some issues of staff selection, lifestyle and reward systems in order to attract and hold a membership still dedicated but perhaps rather less single-minded than the founding cadre.

At the heart of the study is an account of how a medical volunteer group created a community institution which sustained medical education and services at the core; but which found it necessary, as it engaged with the particular locality and communities of Savar, to widen its remit until it encompassed just about every aspect of work with the poor and the disadvantaged for amelioration and ultimately for structural social change. At the core remained the remarkable achievements in training paramedical workers, traditional midwives, and then also medical students whose regular courses gave them too little contact with the facts of life in rural Bangladesh. To this was added work in agriculture and vocational training — including »para-agros« on the analogy of the paramedicals modelled on China's barefoot doctors. The Centre also provided special training for women and a women's centre; an experimental school for young illiterates which spilled over into wider community education; support for cooperatives and a loans scheme to make possible independence from moneylenders during the annual hungry season; publications to inform both specialists and lay persons about drugs and related matters; and even a pharmaceuticals production unit to make good drugs available.

Although GK received significant funds from overseas aid agencies — such that lack of human resources rather than funds was the problem — it also required its village clients to pay what they could afford: part of the long-term aim of removing dependency on any outside aid and thereby fostering self-reliance. Budgetary information shows how cost-effective the operation was. It suggests that in principle GK could provide a model for health delivery and community development for the whole society, providing Government perceived it thus, and behaved accordingly. At the least however this would call for a clarity about priorities and target groups similar to that developed by GK, and perhaps barely conceivable at the State level.

Other features of this study include the quite extraordinary achievements in terms of quality health care, including simple operations, on the part of semi-literate boys and girls; and the very tangible measures of success which were quantified. One asks how far the particular circumstances of Bangladeshi society made possible the impressive take-up of good health practices — contrast the failure to put health teaching into practice as documented in Chapter Two above.

One is impressed also by the courageous and open recognition of the need for radical and indeed revolutionary change, alongside a capacity to survive and win support from Government. This support was expressed in such simple and homely, yet courageous, acts as the women's bicycle ride into Dhaka — to win the right to cycle to the villages and so work more efficiently. Not only was GK formally recognised; it won a Presidential Award, and was used by Government as a training facility. On the other hand the murder of the health worker Nizam symbolised the realities of brute power and the danger in seeking to effect change. The People's Health Centre study provokes further reflection upon abiding themes concerning adult education for development: the role of the educated urban elite; the delicate relationship with Government and lesser powerbrokers; the modes of networking and exerting pressure to bring about substantial change without major destruction.

Summary

Savar, 22 miles from Dhaka, capital of Bangladesh, is the site of the non-governmental organisation Gonoshasthaya Kendra (GK), or People's Health Centre. Savar Thana (an administrative unit comprising 150-300,000 people), area 133 square miles, had a 1974 population of 204,988 (106,534 male, 98,454 female) according to the census that year, in 309 villages, 14 unions, and 34,000 families.

GK originated out of the Bangladeshi liberation war in 1971. Operating in a participative mode, it quickly moved into first one and then another area of training and development, as further needs were identified. Besides its training programmes for health personnel, the project came to offer: classes in literacy and consciousness-raising for villagers and staff members; an experimental primary school for children of landless farmers; and a vocational training programme for villagers in which both men and women were instructed and employed. These multifaceted educational opportunities were designed to increase the quality of life of the poor majority.

The main activities included the following.

A *Health Programme* encompassing

- the training of paramedical workers, basic health workers, medical students, and doctors, in rural health care delivery
- curative care through a system of sub-centres staffed by doctors, technicians, and paramedics, and offering operating theatre, sickroom, pathology, X-ray and dental care facilities
- preventive care including immunization programmes, mother-child clinic, pre- and post-natal care, nutrition, hygiene, and basic health education, carried out through a regular programme of village visiting
- family planning, providing contraceptives (pill, IUD), sterilisation, and abortions, while carrying out a programme of motivation and follow-up
- an insurance scheme for users of the health care services
- publication and distribution of literature to assist medical practitioners in effective health care delivery in rural areas
- a pharmaceutical plant manufacturing drugs under their generic names.

Education in the form of:

- classes in literacy and consciousness-raising for adult villagers and staff members
- an experimental school for children of the landless, combining practical training with formal study.

A *Vocational Training Programme* for villagers instructing and employing both men and women in: agriculture; jute handicraft manufacture for export; shoe manufacture for export and local markets; metalwork including welding, bending etc; woodworking and finishing; management of a canteen which caters to a sizable public clientele.

A *Credit Union* providing loans for marginal and landless farmers.

By August 1980 GK had 136 staff including 16 at Bhatsala. Among these were 14 village-based paramedics. The four sub-centres had 22 health workers. Twelve tube wells had been installed and eight experimental latrines. A quarter of all married couples were using modern family planning methods, and a further 10-12% traditional methods. In the previous year 67,000 patients had been treated in outpatient departments, and a further 21,000 at Bhatsala. Those trained included 120 female IRDP cooperative health workers, 168 medical students, 12 post-graduate doctors, and 40 UNICEF health workers.

The expanding programmes of Gonoshasthaya Kendra reflected its widening awareness of the needs of poor communities, the causes of poverty, and the prerequisites of development. At the same time political and other interests represented real constraints on what could be attempted.

Rezaul Haque

The Origins of Gonoshasthaya Kendra (GK)

It might seem unlikely that volunteers who set up a field hospital during a liberation struggle would take up rural development programmes at the end of the war. Yet such were the origins of GK. Soon after the start of the liberation war in Bangladesh on 25 March 1971, some young Bangladeshi doctors in Great Britain established the Bangladesh Medical Association, mobilising the resources of nearly one thousand Bangladeshi doctors who were working in different parts of the world, and sending assistance to the freedom fighters in Bangladesh. This led to the formation of a field hospital in Bishramgonj, Agartala, India, named Bangladesh Hospital. From among the refugees, Bangadesh Hospital recruited medical college and university students, and other volunteers, and trained them in staff clinics in the camps to treat the usual diseases resulting from close confinement and insanitary conditions, as well as to care for wounded freedom fighters.

The hospital was geographically isolated and lacked sophisticated medical facilities, so it had to be self-sufficient in all its pathological, surgical and other requirements. These conditions favoured a policy of emphasising outpatient departments, preventive medicine programmes and general health education. Small outdoor clinics set up near the war front provided both preventive and curative services.

This experience awoke the hospital workers to the socio- structural problems of the country, and convinced them that any concrete effort to correct them had to be initiated at the local rural level. After the war the Bangladesh Hospital started functioning at a local level in Dhaka. The workers committed themselves together to post-liberation development work. Since the initiators were a group of doctors, medicine seemed to be the priority and a viable entry point, given the inadequacy of the existing medical system for the majority in rural areas. How could their medical facility be taken to the villagers effectively? The achievements of the Chinese »bare-foot doctors« were a source of inspiration, and also provided a basic framework for the project programme. A project proposal was submitted to the Prime Minister and the Health Ministry early in 1972, and finally approved on June 8 1972. By November that year the People's Health Centre at Savar was staffed by: four doctors; six trainee nurses; two trainee pathology technicians; a trainee pharmacist; and 150 trainee volunteers including four »quacks« and some primary school teachers.

Structure and Functioning

GK operated as five projects. Each had several departments, some with more than one division, and each department, division or section had a number of ordinary workers. The first project consisted of health, agriculture, library and general administration. The general administration department included an accountant, cashier and other workers such as guards. The second project comprised the department of women's vocational training and instruction, the third the departments of education and publication. The Bhatsala project at Jamalpur District was the fourth project, and the pharmaceutical company the fifth. In the early eighties a management board of four members, heads of the different projects, was set up to run all the Savar projects except the pharmaceuticals. One member was selected as Chairman, and the position rotated every six months.

The autonomous Board of Trustees of GK consisted of two representatives of the Bangladesh Medical Association and three eminent social workers. The project coordinator was a member of this Board, which overviewed annually the programmes run under the project director and managers. The Board of Governors, with executive responsibilities, comprised representatives of each of the major categories of project staff together with a representative of the Bangladesh Medical Association, the Red Cross, and the faculty members and students of the local Jahangirnagar University.

A method of self-analysis combining discipline with democracy was introduced through the general monthly meeting, meetings among the departmental heads, and other intradepartmental meetings. In the general monthly meetings it was also possible to secure the participation of the lower level of workers, who for the first time in their lives became acquainted with the idea of expressing themselves in a gathering including higher ranking workers. The process was gradual and the level of articulation initially low, but the effort was definitely there. On the other hand the general meeting largely took over the constructive functions of a trade union. The chairman of a general meeting was elected by the meeting. Attendance was compulsory. Absence without proper explanation could attract disciplinary action. The project director could initiate such action in consultation with the chairman. Democratic practices at GK were not confined to participation in decision-making by means of discussions at the general and other meetings. Many organisational rules and arrangements — eg. in matters of pay, food, accommodation, provident fund — strengthened the practice of democracy.

Excluding pharmaceuticals, the project had three categories of workers, apart from the trainees. Those totally illiterate up to those with as much as ten years of education had a monthly salary of 300 — 1,500 taka (15-20 taka approximately equalled one US dollar through the period described, falling to 24:1 in the early eighties) The second category was professionals with a salary scale of 1,200 — 2,500 taka. The third included the project coordinator, director, etc., in a 2,000 — 3,000 taka salary range. In 1978 provision was made for an annual increment of 50 taka per person, irrespective of category, so long as the person's work remained satisfactory.

Everyone contributed 10% of salary to the Staff Welfare Fund. For workers with a salary up to 600 taka a month, the contribution was matched with 10% by the project. For those upward from this to 1,200 salary a month the project contributed 5%, and for those above 1,200 taka. 2 per cent. This welfare was refundable to any worker who remained three years in the project service. Mess contributions were also scaled to salary, but everyone got the same food. Housing was according to need (single, married, with family) irrespective of salary. Health insurance benefits were the same for all. Literacy classes were available to illiterate workers. Training in various skills was available according to the abilities and interests of the workers, at the project's expense. Thus one boy was studying under the electrician, one man learning mechanics, and another driving. Similarly cashiers and storekeepers were trained for their present jobs.

At GK centres the workers lived together to form a community. At the main Savar centre there were about 200 people. Initially most of the working members were young and unmarried. The number of people living within the GK compound was much smaller and the community much more compact. With the passage of time members got married. new people joined GK. and as GK expanded compact communal living was no longer possible. A canteen was established in 1973, owned by the GK workers and run on a cooperative basis available to everybody. A messing system was also established. All the workers ate together in the dining hall. but married couples and families could eat on their own.

General Staffing Policy

The idea behind recruiting unpaid volunteers was that if volunteers were paid their sincerity in labour would diminish, and there would be created another class of servants. However, experience taught the leadership that too much was being expected. Unpaid volunteers can only devote so much time to training and paramedical work; and there were too few doctors to give the amount of supervision needed. These circumstances drove GK to recruit full-time paid workers with more intensive training than the volunteers, and capable of working independently. The usual practice was to select as a trainee someone whom another GK worker knew, but newspaper advertisement was also used for recruitment. The trainees received free board, a modest living allowance, and subsidised food in the official mess. After the training was over they were recruited as full-time employees. Part-time workers, like vocational trainees and midwives, received pocket money during the training period. Midwives continued to work part-time, while the vocational trainees after completion of training worked on a piece-rate basis. There were no fees for the educational programmes, and all books, slates, pens and chalks were free. As an added incentive small lunches were provided in the primary school.

Training Programmes and Other Activities

Gonoshasthaya Kendra offered education and training to a wide range of participants, with subject-matter varying from adult literacy to vocational training, from non-formal education for children to training programmes for health workers.

Paramedical Workers

The training of paramedical workers naturally assumed early and high priority. Ninety-two per cent of the population lived in rural areas; 50% were effectively landless, and trapped in poverty, disease and malnutrition. Ninety per cent of the total health budget of Bangladesh was going to medical colleges and urban hospitals; rural Bangladesh had one doctor per 30,000 people. This maldistribution of medical manpower affecting rural Bangladesh, it was assumed, could only be altered through developing a cadre of basic health workers, or paramedics. Conventionally, paramedics assist doctors. GK's concept was quite different. Paramedics were not merely assistants to the physician, but professional women and men in their own right, possessing special skills, methods and fields of activitiy in which the doctor was not trained to perform. Perhaps the most important difference between the village health worker and the doctor was the health worker's background and training, as well as membership in and selection by the community, which helped reinforce the will to serve the people.

After instruction the paramedics performed a wide range of activities. Each paramedic, in charge of the health service for approximately five square miles,

generally with a population of 3,000 in three to five villages, was called on to provide the following services:
- family planning to approximately 600 couples;
- immunisation against tetanus (post partum and neonatal) for 600 women;
- assistance at approximately 14 pregnancies per month with 3-4 requiring special attention and possibly referral;
- BCG and immunisation against diphtheria, whooping cough, tetanus, and poliomylitis to 15-20% of the population, those under five years;
- smallpox immunisation for the entire population (in total, 15-20 immunisations daily);
- treatment for 40-50% of children under five years of age for diarrhoeal diseases, and teaching mothers to make rehydration fluid (a few serious cases may have to be treated at the sub-centre and given saline drips);
- treatment of 97% of all children for helminth infestation, which if not cared for can undermine general health;
- 30 adult cases of frank tuberculosis, periodically supervised;
- one or two cases of leprosy, syphilis and gonorrhoea to be treated.

Health workers had also to keep accurate records of births and deaths, which must be registered, and of their own activities. They had to be prepared to assist in the maintenance of tube wells, look after sewage disposal, offer health and nutrition education to the villagers, and work closely with rural development workers in the area.

At the sub-centres the paramedic was prepared for the following:
- 5-10 sterilisations (with or without abortion) per month;
- boil and abscess draining;
- dressings;
- suturing of small cuts;
- burn treatments;
- fractures, mainly of feet, clavicle, wrist, and forearm;
- foreign body removal from ears and eyes;
- difficult labour.

The instruction was for a period of no longer than one year, three to six months if the candidate proved capable. The programme offered gross anatomy, physiology and pharmacology, sterilisation technique and simple surgical procedure including tubal ligation and vasectomy. Immunisation techniques (BDG, smallpox, tetanus etc.) were considered essential, as well as record-keeping of these. The course of study, started in 1972, was set out to include:
- Health Survey (statistical data collection etc.)
- Basic Human Body and Gross Anatomy
- Basic Physiology
- Health Education (personal health and hygiene, community health, communicable (local) diseases, immunisation. nutrition)
- Environmental Hygiene and Sanitation (water-source and treatment. disposal of

refuse and excreta, air pollution, industrial and agricultural health problems, etc.)
- Problems of Overpopulation and the Need for Family Planning Rural Community Development (including Cooperatives)
- Practical Work (use of microscope, sterilisation, first aid, visits to paramedical centres etc.).

Training of »Dais«

Dais are women known to be skilled in assisting with deliveries, who are called when a birth is imminent. The role is usually inherited, and the skills passed on by a mother-in-law or other female relative. Such a village midwife may deliver one or two babies a year, or up to one or two a month, and her remuneration varies similarly, often according to how welcome the new baby is to its parents. Since the 1950s dais have played a role in a number of family planning programmes in different countries, helping for instance with the distribution of condoms, spermicidal agents and oral contraceptive pills. Dais linked to existing health centres are extremely helping in spreading information about medical and family planning services offered to the villages, since they pay frequent visits to the centre to obtain supplies. They are also on close and friendly terms with many of their fellow villagers, some of whom may be relatives.

Their role makes dais suitable motivators for female sterilisation. Their presence can be invaluable to the village client, as the dai provides comfort and reassurance during the inevitably frightening experience in an unusual environment. The dai can also play an important role in post-operative follow-up: removing stitches, providing treatment in cases of infection or other complications, and helping with tetanus immunisation. She can offer pre- and post-natal care and promote breastfeeding.

The training of dais capitalises on their traditional role and skills. Areas covered in classes include the following:
side effects, advantages and disadvantages of various methods of contraception;

- the value of immunisation, especially against tetanus;
- prenatal care, especially signs of pre-eclampsia;
- features of common ailments such as diarrhoea, skin diseases and simple treatment (eg. giving fluids to a child with diarrhoea rather than withholding it, which is traditionally believed to be the corrent treatment);
- simple knowledge of nutrition;
- Sterilisation of syringes and needles, and the dangers of unsterile procedures for intra-muscular injections;
- correct antiseptic behaviour in the operating theatre when accompanying a sterilisation client.

Training of Integrated Rural Development Programme (IRDP) Cooperative Health Workers

There were 303 thanas under the government's IRDP, 28 with women's cooperatives. One course at GK was designed to train 120 women of these cooperatives from 12 thanas. On completion of the course they were to act as health workers in their respective villages. The first programme began in August 1978: ten women came to Savar GK and ten to Bhatsala GK (see below) for an initial one-month training period. Most were married women aged from 17 to 50 with a mean age of 31 years, and an average of three living children up to ten years old. Instruction included general health, with emphasis on maternal and child health and the treatment of four diseases commonly found in Bangladesh's villages — worms, scabies, diarrhoea and simple fever. After the month the women returned to their villages for five months to put into practice what they had learned. During this time they were evaluated by a team of GK staff, usually two paramedics, or one doctor and one paramedic, to see how much they retained, to identify the particular problems they had to contend with, and to arrange subsequent training accordingly.

When they returned to the centres for a further month's instruction there was a review of what had been taught previously, and an introduction to two more common diseases. This was again followed by five months in the villages. The third and final month of training was then given in the various sub-centres. It included familiarisation with the vaccine programme, and dealing with another two common diseases.

Medical Students' and Postgraduate Doctors' Field Programme

Early on GK began to consider the possibility of using its staff, buildings and health programme as a field practice training centre, to bring greater relevance to medical training in Bangladesh. On 6 May 1978 the Syndicate of the University of Dhaka finally approved the programme. Training was offered to the undergraduates of three Medical Colleges in groups of 12 — 15. The programme was designed to give realistic exposure to the health situations of the students' own country: who receives treatment? Who cannot receive it, and why? Does the background of medical students make their effective involvement in change impossible? In the morning students made visits to the villages and interviewed people regarding their health problems. Afternoons were spent discussing the visits and possible methods of treatment for common diseases.

The field practice and dissertation section of a National Institute of Preventive and Social Medicine (NIPSOM) course leading to a Diploma in Community Medicine was also conducted by GK. Graduate physicians, health administrators and other clinical medical officers in hospitals attended the course. In the introductory week students were taken to the villages to become acquainted with the situations there, subsequently discussing their possible choice of thesis topic with people responsible for the GK section of their course. Mornings were spent collecting data from the survey areas and evenings discussing health needs of Bangladesh. Students pursuing other NIPSOM courses came for variable periods to get experience in specific areas.

Literacy Programme and the Experimental School

The urban elite feel they know the correct path for development. and consider restructuring the »ignorant masses« for development as their civic duty. The masses are not seen as individuals with dignity and intelligence. Consequently the real problems of rural Bangladesh remain untouched. Nevertheless, basic intelligence and numeracy are necessary to reinforce and use natural intelligence. The man who signs by thumbprint is cheated easily, and there is no hope for him to improve his life simply by developing farming methods. He will not become adequately aware of the economic and political context of his oppression.

A sample survey by GK in 1972 showed that 78% of males and 92% of females in the area could not read or write. Ten per cent of the population attended or had attended classes I-IV. Spot tests showed that 80% of these could not read functionally, and 50% could only just write their own names. Less than 5% of the population were truly literate. According to government statistics, 46% of school-age children in Bangladesh did not attend school. Only 41% of boys and 33% of girls completed five years of schooling, the minimum necessary for a person to maintain the ability to read, as was found in a GK survey of dropouts in 1976.

Poor villagers did not send their children to school because they learned little, and what they learned was irrelevant to, or indeed a disadvantage for, village life. Subscribing to the traditional view, the educated boy does not participate in manual labour in the fields. Having a secondary school certificate the boy cannot find a job which pays enough to feed the extended family. On the other hand the enormous cost associated with studies in the city-based university prevents the peasant boy from participating in higher education. To marry a girl who attended school up to class V, her father will not find anyone with less than ten years of schooling willing to take her. Such bridegrooms are expensive. Education therefore becomes a part of the conspicuous consumption of the better off, not a tool for ordinary living.

GK decided to establish a school for the children of poor peasants which would take into account, as far as possible, and be able to address, the factors which keep poor children from coming to school. In 1976 it started an experimental school for children from villages near the project who were selected, with the help of the Centre's survey, from landless families. None of them was attending school.

Teaching of reading and writing was combined with discussion about village life. Health and nutrition education were emphasised, along with learning to grow nutritious foods. Older children, including girls, learned vocational skills. In the evening the older children organised classes for their brothers and sisters, as well as for the elderly people around their homes, including their parents. The top class spent one day a week in the villages and fields, teaching their siblings and friends who did not come even to this school. Apart from the adult literacy classes conducted by the children in the evening, literacy and consciousness-raising classes were offered in the village cooperatives and vocational training sections, and for the staff members. The curriculum incorporated literacy and numeracy, discussions on health, nutrition and family planning, the general socio-economic context and political structures, reasons for poverty, disease and malnutrition.

Vocational Training

»We have admitted to our sickroom, in the last 18 months, 11 cases of attempted suicide by married women. Sociologically, these cases are highly significant. They represent an unaccounted number of village wives whose position drives them to despair.« (5th Progress Report 1975) Far from being unique, this is a common phenomenon throughout Bangladesh. If she has a considerate husband and a fair mother-in-law, a wife in a Bangladesh village may be no worse off that a housewife anywhere. A housewife in rural Bangladesh is treated as a free servant by her husband and in-laws, and may find nobody to turn to. Any woman trying to resist the tyranny of her husband is likely to become an outcast. She is not received with pleasure at her father's home. A woman separated from her husband is abhorred, irrespective of her reasons for leaving him, and brings disgrace on her parents. Trapped between the cruelty of her husband and the lashing tongue of society, many a wife finds no way out but death. Such a society does not allow women to give of their best. Women, as mothers, are the prime educators in any community. Cultural and moral impoverishment, in addition to personal tragedy, result when society condemns women to a mute, subordinate role.

At the root of the weak position of women in village society is their dependence on father or husband for their daily food. A degree of economic independence would greatly improve their lot. This thought lay behind GK's vocational training programme. By providing village women with a money-earning skill, GK aimed to strengthen their position at home, give them some respite from exploitation, and enable them to enlarge their spiritual as well as economic contribution to the community. Emancipation of women, and engagement in pursuits other than childbearing and housework, may also result in a lowering of the birth-rate.

Training was initially confined to sewing and jute handicrafts. Expectations for long-term employment which were raised in the women trainees could not be fulfilled in this way: jute was seized upon by most of the charitable organisations and women's cooperatives during the post-liberation period as a suitable occupation for women, quickly saturating the tiny internal market of resident foreigners and city people with westernised tastes; while export was difficult to organise and unreliable, depending as it does on rapidly changing fashion. GK therefore rethought its approach to women's employment.

The unrestricted migration of skilled manpower to Middle Eastern countries caused a shortage of carpenters, plumbers, blacksmiths and the like. Training women in some of these trades might open new employment possibilities for them, as well as meeting a need. GK therefore initiated a number of training programmes with primary emphasis on young women who were taught metalwork, carpentry, sewing, shoe-making and baking. Literacy classes were held alongside the vocational lessons, and matters of home economics, hygiene and family planning covered incidentally.

Training in Agriculture and Nutrition

Poverty and underdevelopment, added to disease and illiteracy, create a vicious circle. Malnutrition is one sign of this syndrome of poverty. Not only do deficiency of certain elements and lack of knowledge of concomitant infestion cause malnutrition; non-availability of food itself is the major cause of under- and malnutrition in rural Bangladesh. In a country where more than 20% of the population cannot afford two meals a day throughout the year, malnutrition resulting from starvation should be a major concern.

GK's concern with the health of the community led inevitably, therefore, to concern with its food and hence, since rural Bangladesh is predominantly an agricultural society, to the way food is grown and distributed. Recruitment was sought for a category of agricultural workers on a par with paramedics. These «para- agros» were local people, locally trained at an entirely practical level. They were available to advise and assist right in the villages. They provided a much-needed link between the thana agricultural officer and the peasant: helping farmers to form cooperatives and avail themselves of the services offered by the government, keeping tubewells in running order; and carrying out other small but necessary tasks. They used land at the project site, and gave demonstrations of what could be grown at the sub-centre. Certain introduced crops were exhibited in this way, also increased yield of existing crops by improved farming techniques. Participation in GK's own agricultural programmes was mandatory for all GK staff, to promote better understanding of the exploitation involved with agriculture

Loans and Cooperatives

The number of landless and marginal farmers was increasing in rural areas of Bangladesh, to more than 50% of the population. Chronic insolvency placed poor peasants at the mercy of unscrupulous money-lenders. In the lean period between winter and spring harvests, small farmers are forced to borrow money for food and agricultural inputs. To cut through the downward spiral of debt, GK in 1976 started giving loans to poor sharecroppers, on the following easy terms. For each 100 taka loan, the creditor had to pay back the capital within four months, together with 10 kg of paddy, but he was free to cultivate whichever crop he wanted. Five kg of the »interest« was deposited as a saving on behalf of the creditor, who could borrow two kg of paddy for each one kg deposited in time of need. GK hoped that within a few years of this compulsory saving, the farmers would be able to tide themselves over the hunger periods of the year and become independent of GK's loans. The other five kg of paddy was used to set up a fund for giving further loans without such capital input from outside. The operation of the programme was organised through cooperatives; only a cooperative body could nominate new members, and repayment of the loan was also a responsibility of the cooperative. Literacy, numeracy and consciousness-raising classes were also organised for these village cooperatives.

Publications

Publishing a monthly health bulletin, producing mass communication materials' and books of related interest, developing curriculum and teaching-learning aids for the education programme, were the responsibilities of the publications department, which came into being in 1978. The persuasive marketing of drug companies sways the minds even of highly qualified medical personnel, and leads ultimately to unscientific and unethical medical practice. Their lead is followed by numerous unqualified village doctors, who are consulted for treatment by the vast majority of the rural population. To stop such exploitation the health profession needs continued education, and consumers need access to the »restructured« information about drugs they are prescribed to take.

The department's research programme included 66,000 Bangladeshi villages. Information was collected on how many qualified and unqualified persons were practising medicine in the country, what their practice habits were, and what information they would find of value in carrying out their work. Using this information GK started publishing the monthly health bulletin *Gonoshasthaya*, or People's Health, completely in Bangali. This described the major issues of ill-health in relation to the socio-economic condition of the people, and helped protect consumer interests. It also promoted the use of quality generic drugs. The bulletin, with a circulation of 20,000 copies per issue, attracted an estimated 100,000 readership. Qualified and non-qualified doctors, medical students, paramedical personnel and students in paramedical schools, as well as lay people, read the bulletin. The publications department also published books of related interest, and developed teaching aids and curricula for the Centre's education and medical training programmes.

Bhatsala project

»Bhatsala«, the »daughter project« of GK, came into operation in 1977. Originating as a health care programme, it too branched out into other areas of development to help people raise their social, economic and educational status. The project, 120 miles north of Savar Thana, was located in the village of Shapmari, in Jamalpur District. It offered an intensive coverage to 18,000 people, with services also available to an additional 10,000. With a staff of twelve female and four male workers, the main thrust was similar to that of Savar GK: preventive health care, nutrition education, and family planning. There was a theatre for minor operations, and a few beds for emergency patients; an out-patient clinic was conducted twice weekly at the Centre. The paramedics as Bhatsala offered health and nutrition education to the village mothers. The maternal death rate for Bangladesh was 8 per 1,000, but at Bhatsala it was down to 2.7 per thousand. Bhatsala also began an agricultural extension programme following Savar GK, to assist landless farmers. Within three years sixteen cooperatives had been formed, with 122 members.

Priority Groups

Experience in the field helped GK in shifting the emphasis within its objectives, as well as in defining the target population. In view of the increasing number of landless and marginal farmer families, officially fifty per cent of the population, GK's leaders aimed at social transformation. They therefore sought to pay attention mainly to the most exploited sector of rural society, the landless poor marginal farmers, and women at large.

This shift of emphasis is evident in GK's different programmes. For instance, during the first few years the health insurance scheme levied a subscription of two taka per month and was open to all in the area. Later it was found that the rural rich and the middle class could easily pay this subscription, but not the poor and landless. In 1977 the health insurance scheme was thoroughly altered. The new method divided the service population into three groups by economic condition. The first priority was those families which could not afford, from any source, two meals a day throughout the year for their members. The second was those who had up to five acres of land (not necessarily arable), and the third group included those with more than five acres.

Members of the first group received registration cards free and paid 50 paisa (about US 3 cents) per patient visit. Other services such as pathology, operations, X-ray and admission were included in the 50 paisa. For members of the second group the registration card was 12 taka, and 10 taka per year for renewal. They paid two taka per patient visit and also bore the subsidised cost of other services. For members of the third group registration charge and renewal was as for the second, but they paid 5 taka per patient visit as well as bearing the cost of the other services at a higher rate than did the second group. This system ensured that the poor would get health care at a minimal cost, which was GK's main concern.

The agricultural programme and credit offered loans and assistance to the cooperatives of marginal farmers, sharecroppers, fishermen and women's groups.

The primary school also exemplified identifying the priority target population. It was specifically for the children of landless and marginal farmers who otherwise had no opportunity for education. One count showed the following primary school families, including children, by land-holding:

amount of land	number of persons
landless (not even a homestead)	80
homestead only	50
6-17 decimals* of land	98
18-33 decimals of land	72
34-66 decimals of land	104
67-100 decimals of land	90
101-166 decimals of land	35
total	529

* 100 decimals = l acre

The Position of Women

Family planning is an effective means to free village women who are poor, illiterate, sick and persecuted, from exploitation. GK's health and family planning programme promoted self- confidence among women, thus making an effective contribution in the long run to their emancipation. Women paramedics proved much more suitable than men for work among village women, especially when the paramedic has to engage in intimate and frank discussion of female diseases. Moreover a woman paramedic is a shining symbol of social transformation. In a situation where most village women suffer constantly from crippling panic born of general social backwardness, and physical and mental torture at home, female paramedics can signal emancipation and raise confidence among the downtrodden women.

It may be impossible to make an effective contribution to social transformation without raising women's self-confidence. This requires some measure of economic independence, which will make men somewhat respectful towards women. By providing village women with a money-earning skill through vocational training, GK aimed to strengthen their position in the home, give them some respite from exploitation, and enable them to enlarge their spiritual, as well as economic, contribution to the community.

Some Distinctive Features of Gonoshasthaya Kendra

Evolving Aims and Objectives

»Our primary aim is to provide a plan to upgrade the National Public Standards and eventually to release our country from its dependence upon foreign aid by becoming self-sufficient through community support.« Thus proclaimed GK in 1972. The intention was to implement this through: preventive medicine; health education; paramedical training; family planning; curative medicine, with emphasis on education and community involvement.

It became increasingly apparent with experience that health was not a problem to be dealt with in isolation, and GK began to expand, not to any pre-planned pattern but branching out at different points where it encountered opposition, in order to bring about necessary changes in response to this opposition. Thus the 7th *Progress Report*, 1980, declared:

- Gonoshasthaya Kendra came into being with the birth of Bangladesh and its development cannot be separated from the life struggle of the country itself.

- Since independence, Bangladesh has been the recipient of an increasing amount of foreign aid, while at the same time the number of landless peasants has considerably increased. The price of food has risen sharply. In a country where 70-80% live below subsistence, this does not mean denying oneself some delicacy, it means that there are millions of families who go one or two days a week without anything to eat. In an agricultural country, a farmer without land is a discontented man, but a man whose wages no longer buy enough to feed himself and his family, is a dangerous man.

- GK's ideas and ventures have often been a response to different problems in the country as they came to be perceived in the course of its work.

- The structures of the country still oppress women and GK's programmes are weighted towards them.

The objectives of GK might therefore be summarised as: to provide adequate health service in the rural area of Savar Thana; to increase the independence and bargaining power of women; to bring about a change in the infrastructure and thereby allow for the economic and social development of poor villagers, ie. 90% of the population of Bangladesh.

Paramedical training

The basic approach to paramedical training is supervised practical experience of trainees paired up with experienced paramedics as they perform their normal duties in the clinics or on village rounds. The trainee paramedic, with an educational background varying from uncompleted primary education to one or two years of college education, accompanied the experienced paramedic and, despite having no theoretical input, started receiving practical training through observing the procedures and actions of the senior colleague. After thorough exposure to the health problems of the people in the area and seeing how the general socio-economic situation affects the health and welfare of the rural population, the trainee attended a series of formal instructional sessions guided by either a physician or an experienced paramedic.

Evaluation took place throughout the training by means of several oral, practical and written tests, coupled with careful observation of performance. After general paramedical training participants were selected according to their special interests and aptitudes for further specialised training. This included training in simple surgical procedures such as tubectomies, menstrual regulation, abortion, vasectomy, pathology, X-ray, out-patient, sick-room and administration. The training, mostly through demonstration, was of variable length, upward from six weeks. *The Lancet* on September 27 1975 provided this account:

- The tubectomy training itself begins with learning to sterilise linen and instruments, followed by circulating assistance in the theatre. During this initial period the trainee learns the function of the different instruments and memorises their names. It is an advantage that the method requires only a few types of unfamiliar instruments: blades, scissors, and non- tooth forceps are already known to most trainees from their daily lives. Later on she is instructed in scrubbing up and the correct handling of sterile garments and gloves. She assists in several tubectomies before being allowed to handle the knife itself. As far as possible, explanations are given with objects and actions already familiar to the trainees. For example, the necessity for catheterisation of the bladder is explained by describing the bladder as a balloon-like organ which collapses when empty and can thus be removed from the field of operation. The ovary has to be identified on both sides without fail (this is easy, owing to the distinct appearance of the organ) and both the trainee and her assistant have to ascertain that the same tube runs between ovary and uterus; this ensures that the fallopian tubes rather than the round ligaments are excised. The first 10 to 15 tubectomies of each trainee are performed under close supervision, which is relaxed only when she has gained sufficient self-confidence and skill. A qualified physician is always on call.

Education was considered ongoing for both trainer and trainee. Recruitment of the paramedics also played an important role. GK required that candidates for paramedical training be proposed and selected by their own communities since, to be fully effective, they needed to possess the confidence and esteem of the people they were to serve. Unfortunately, in a situation where a few wealthy families control resources and public opinion, this probably leads to one of two extremes. If the job carried prestige and adequate remuneration the sons, daughters or other relatives of the better-off families would be chosen, if the job was considered beneath their dignity, it would carry little authority for the duties to be performed. In practice therefore selection was left with the staff of the health centre, who were careful to apply criteria of intimate communication with the common people of the village, and dedication to the projected task, rather than insisting on scholastic achievement, although basic literacy was a definite necessity.

Other Training

The training of dais capitalised on their traditional role and skills, and was uncomplicated. Since many were illiterate, illustrations and practical demonstrations played a large part. The dais usually came once a week to the main health centre or sub-centres for classes of about one hour, given by a paramedic or a physician. Instruction attempted to convey a basic understanding of how the various contraceptives work.

The Field Study Programme of medical students and postgraduate doctors began with exposure to the health situations of rural Bangladesh. It was organised through interviewing people regarding their health and related problems. This was followed by discussion of the findings from the field, and of relevant experience.

GK's main emphasis with the experimental school and adult literacy work was on extirpating the factors which prevent the poor from attending school. Children were selected for the school with the help of GK's survey, from the families of landless and marginal farmers, so that they could form a homogeneous group. The school did not insist on uniforms or decent clothes. Slate, pencil and books were provided by the school. In a free government primary school children have to buy their own notebook, pencil and reader. Children over six or seven years of age are useful to their parents: they can collect cowdung and firewood, go fishing, take their father's lunch out to the fields, look after the cow or goat. To accommodate these needs children were allowed to bring their animals to let them graze with the project herd. During busy farming seasons they were allowed time off to carry food to the men in the fields. Children of this age often find paid employment outside their homes, as servants, cow-boys, or restaurant helpers. Since GK could not provide them with a paid job, as compensation they were given one meal a day.

In the morning, after arriving from their villages, the children first looked after their vegetable plots and chickens. This was to avoid the traditional break between work on the soil and school education. Simple health measures were taught, like the importance of washing, with a daily bath, as scabis was endemic. Students learned how to deal with diarrhoea, restoring lost fluids with a simple mix of water, salt and local sugar. Reading and writing were taught by the look-and-say method, starting with the recognition of short whole words taken from daily village life. Wherever a local dialect diverged from standard Bengali, the dialect word was used.

How things are taught is also important. The monitor system — children teaching other children — was used extensively. The most advanced older pupils helped other children to practise what the teacher had taught them. The children worked in self-chosen groups of about ten. Promotion to the next class up was not automatic, but had to be earned by the group as a whole. If there were one or two laggards everyone concentrated on helping them to reach the required standard. Discipline too was through social pressure from peers. There was no corporal punishment. Misbehaviour was discussed by the child's own group, and appropriate measures taken

Issues and Implications

What Political Stance?

Those building GK knew the limitations of vertical top-heavy development programmes. An integrated approach to development was therefore assumed. Nevertheless
> within the existing overall structural set-up, the work continues in an encapsulated manner. Gradually, the realization that it is not possible for GK to proceed further in this set-up has gained ground among the workers. According to the majority of the workers, the answer lies in a revolution. Now the question arises as to GK's role in the process to this revolution. In this context a consideration of the GK's relationship with the existing political parties, especially the left-oriented ones, is necessary. There does not seem to exist any empathy between the two. The political parties are very suspicious of the work done by these foreign-funded projects, whereas these microexperiments have a contemptuous regard for the rhetoric-based political parties. Under these conditions two trends of thought seem to be emerging at GK. One advocates waiting out the period, whereas the other suggests going in for greater concerted effort along with the other existing macro-experiments in the country. But the dilemma persists. (Jahangir, 1979)

Internal Dynamics

Through its democratic processes the project sought to develop leadership and greater participation among the workers. In part this appears to have succeeded. Common girls and boys were running the programme, taking part in decision-making, managing complex situations and conflicts. They demonstrated, moreover, that organisations like GK are indeed replicable. Nevertheless, for GK also, despite all the pitfalls of the urbanite education system, the initial and sustained leadership of self-sacrificing educated middle class people cannot be ruled out.

GK started its programme with a limited number of dedicated workers who really had to bear the pain of birth. Emotional attachment, therefore, dominated the scene and won their selfless motivation, sacrifice of time and money. This created a »generation gap«. The first staff members were bound to one another by the shared experience of pioneering days of struggle, individual courage and insecurity. They felt that this gave them the right to set the tone for conduct and work performance. New members saw the older ones as arrogant, and feared for their own chances of promotion and recognition. The growth of the project naturally limited personal contact between the project leaders and the large number of new staff, who felt powerless in a seemingly powerful organisation, in spite of the various departmental meetings.

Rapid expansion of the project's activities required division of responsibilities. Thus the project was divided in 1976 into three:
- health, family planning and nutrition in Savar;
- education, women's vocational training and workshop;
- Jamalpur family planning and mother and child health project.

In 1977 Projects I and II were combined and the whole project divided into five sections, each with a section chief:
- Health and Family Planning;
- Education;
- Agriculture and Nutrition;
- Vocational Training;
- and Research and Evaluation.

In 1978 the whole project was again reorganised into a new five-project form. These changes in the structure of the administration suggest dynamism as well as weaknesses. Lack of coordination was supposed to be the primary cause behind repeated reorganisation of the projects. However GK was evidently aware of the situation and trying to resolve it by trial and error.

GK also tried to strike a balance between over-centralisation and too little central direction and control. Flexibility and adaptability to new circumstances were considered guiding principles of the project.

External Resistance

GK faced initial social resistance from the villagers who could not accept the communal living and free movement of the women workers of GK, especially female paramedics riding around on bicycles — a shocking sight. GK workers however succeeded in reorienting villagers' views, bringing them gradually to a point of acceptance.

Resistance came also from vested interests, when GK started organising the poor peasants and landless of the villages. An extreme example of this was the murder in 1976 of Nizam, a paramedic in charge of Shimulia Sub-Centre. His dedication, selfless service, inspired leadership and growing popularity were too much for certain vested interests to tolerate.

Sometimes opposition presented itself disguised in the form of participation, as was well illustrated with the establishment of another sub-centre. The land for the sub-centre was donated by one of the local landlords who, along with his brothers and other relatives, owned almost the whole village. As such he virtually controlled the whole community, since the landless depended on him for their livelihood. When GK started constructing mud houses for sub-centre staff quarters and a clinic area, the landowner attempted to force GK to purchase earth from his highland, though earth was being offered free of cost by another party. He then requested a tubewell free for the exclusive use of his family from GK's village cooperative tubewell programme. This was meant to be exclusively for the poor, with 20-25 families sharing one tubewell. He also wanted his children's tutor appointed as a paramedic. When this failed he embarked on a course of harrassment, trying to obstruct the paramedic's work, being especially rude and aggressive towards the girls. He used the poor village men, telling them that unless they did as he told them they would have no land to work. One paramedic who was in charge of the sub-centre had to be transferred from the post, as he resisted this attempt to interfere with the sub-centre's work.

Similar opposition was encountered with the Women's Centre, School and Bhatsala programmes. This reflected the existing social system. It may not be possible to resolve it without social transformation, which is only possible after winning the confidence and creating awareness among the poor majority, through sustained activities.

GK did not believe in working in isolation. It maintained a good relationship with government, non-governmental and other relevant organisations. For obvious reasons GK tried to understand the role of a particular organisation first and then take the decision whether to cooperate or not. One observer of GK commented that it was »yet another example where confrontation tactics have been skilfully deployed and yet selective cooperation from different agencies has not been dogmatically rejected. Bangladesh Government too, although initially not involved in this experimental venture, has started utilizing the services of GK.«

Resources

GK faced problems over human resources rather than over funds or materials. It is not easy to get trained doctors to work in a project like GK. They either concentrate in the cities or fly to industrial Western or Middle Eastern countries. As Ivan Illich points out, doctors concentrate »where the climate is healthy, water is clear and people can pay for their services«. It is difficult to recruit trainers for other disciplines as well. Either the traditional education system does not equip them with the knowledge and skill to train people in rural situations, or they find it difficult to cope with the lifestyle of GK. GK also faced problems in retaining its own trained people such as paramedics, handicraft workers and teachers who can easily find better paid jobs in the city, which GK cannot afford or does not consider.

GK's problem in recruiting outside trained personnel, doctors, engineers, agronomists, accountants and the like, and retaining people trained in its own facility, may have been due to different causes. For instance a person who joined the Centre with the intention of doing a nine to five job would find the lifestyle of GK quite frustrating, for workers' involvement with the project activity was assumed to be continuous. Nor did GK want to pay a salary which was much higher than the prevalent government scale. There was also an attempt to reduce the gap between workers in the higher and those in the lower echelons in terms of facilities and benefits offered by the institution. This acted as a disincentive to someone able to move to another organisation.

Motives and Attitudes

GK channelled its programmes towards well-defined groups; these grassroots programmes enjoyed good motivation. Where GK could not employ its own criteria there was lack of motivation. For instance the Women's Centre vocational trainees dropped out of the adult education programme when GK could not provide them with work. Not infrequently dropout occurred in paramedical, school-teacher and other related training programmes basically from lack of motivation. The name and fame of the organisation initially attracted workers but the long working hours and lifestyle at GK, and their own preconceived values, disappointed those in particular from a middle or upper class background.

GK sided with the culture of the poor, trying to utilise all existing cultural forms and channels. For instance it used years, months and dates in accordance with the Bengali calendar, having initially used the European calendar. GK workers faced tremendous difficulties in communicating with the villagers, especially on such subjects as family planning and agriculture. In 1974 it corrected its mistake and switched to the Bengali calendar in all its dealings. In addition local arts and crafts were patronised. Folk songs and other cultural media were explored, to incorporate into GK's own activities.

GK designed its programmes to suit and solve the problems of real life, and it had the courage to admit its mistakes and accept challenges for rectification. Despite its firm belief in science and innovation, it did not ignore traditional ideas which had passed the test of time. Ironically it had at times to take decisions against expert opinion as when, following expert advice from Dhaka, it dug a tank which was too deep for fishing. Realising this one expert proposed bringing the fish to the service by stunning them with sub-lethal electric shocks. GK workers preferred to turn for advice and help to the local people.

The Achievements of Gonoshasthaya Kendra

Researchers usually seek quantitative data when assessing rural development and adult education organisations. Reliance on quantitative data is perhaps unavoidable in the evaluation of more conventional organisations. Qualititative data may be inaccessible, or inapplicable. In the case of GK, in addition to quantitative data it is essential to make a qualitative evaluation, since the major aim was to reduce poverty through social transformation. In order to attempt this GK adopted a variety of programmes concerning health, nutrition, family planning, education and agriculture. If hunger could give birth to social transformation, the famine in British-ruled Bengal in 1943 and in independent Bangladesh in 1974 would surely have produced it. GK stressed that it might be impossible to bring about change until reformist measures significantly improved the health and nutrition of the masses, making them receptive to political education which was conducive to change.

Value for Money?

The income to GK came from donations from external philanthropic organisations; from local donations, both cash and kind; from service charges, a health insurance premium, and other receipts; from project activities such as earnings from the women's centre, agricultural produce and publications. The major external donors were Oxfam (UK), Oxfam (Canada), NOVIB in The Netherlands, the Canadian International Development Agency, and Terre des Hommes, a Catholic relief agency. Smaller grants were made by the Ford Foundation, UNICEF, Concern, and Unitarian Services of Canada.

Much of the project resources during the initial years was spent on capital items. Recurrent expenditure recovered through services, such as insurance payments and charges made directly for treatment and services, amounted to 65% of total expenditure in 1974-75, and 44% and 47% respectively in the two following years. Expenditure included drug bills, salaries, transport etc. Returns from vocational training centres, agricultural produce and publications are not included.

The cost of Basic Service Delivery in Health and Family Planning for the fiscal year April 1979-April 1980 was as follows (taka):

salaries (43%)	398,637.80
stationery and printing (2.5%)	22,773.00
transport (including fuel, maintenance etc.) (6%)	56,497.89
post and telegrams (0.2%)	1,276.46
electricity, light and fuel (1.9%)	16,914.90
drugs and reagents (29%)	268,145.86
maintenance of equipment & miscellaneous (2.4%)	21,596.00
expenditure on trainees (14%)	129,589.00
	914,430.91

Income included 150,000 taka from health insurance, clinic and dental fees; 171,000 taka from outside training programmes; 53,000 taka in subscriptions for in-patient services; 22,000 taka for pathological services and 20,000 for operations; 9,000 taka for family planning services; and 31,000 taka in local donations. The total (local) income for that year was 456,442.11 taka.

The costs exclude cost of vaccines and family planning material. The per capita medical expenditure in the GK area amounted to 11.02 taka (approximately US 50 cents). This covered the health and family planning services for 82,958 people under intensive care, and the health insurance scheme. This was well below the national expenditure of 26.89 taka per capita for health and planning, including capital and non-capital expenditure, as proposed in Bangladesh's Second Five Year Plan for 1980-85, not including the 5.50 taka per capita income as earned by GK. This demonstrates the feasibility and cost effectiveness of a national programme based on GK's model.

The Health Programme

The following extracts from *Progress Reports* in 1975, 1977 and 1980 indicate the achievements of this programme.

- Some successes of the primary services have been ascertained by surveys of the sample villagers and also by more random observation of disease incidence. Thus, there has been a dramatic fall in the incidence of serious diarrhoea and dehydration. This is probably due to our intensive teaching of oral fluid therapy to mothers of small children, who now give the »shorbot« to their infants as soon as they notice the first symptoms of diarrhoea. Since diarrhoea in children is still the commonest cause of death in Bnagladesh as a whole, our success with preventing serious cases may well account for the lower overall death rate in our area which has been established by a sample survey (12 per thousand as compared with the national average of 17 per thousand). There has also been a marked decrease in scabis and other forms of skin diseases. Care of pre-eclampsia has resulted in no maternity death for the last year in the area fully covered by our services.

- Of 600 tubectomies carried out in three centres, 366 were performed by female paraprofessional workers with an average of only two months' part-time training in tubectomy surgery. The rest were performed by qualified physicians. The infection rate in tubectomies done by paraprofessionals was 5.5%; in those performed by physicians it was 6.4%. Comparison of other factors indicates that the results of paraprofessionals were in no way inferior.

- Most villages in the project area have less than 60% coverage of BCG, DPT and Tetanus immunization, but a small number of paramedics have reached 70% in their work area.

- From April 79-80 a total of 66,948 patients were seen in our outpatients' clinic (this is excluding treatment given by paramedics in their village work). 1,090 were admitted to our sick room, giving a bed occupancy rate of 97.4%

- In our insurance area, 25.4% of married couples (population 100,000) are active users of modern family planning such as Depo-Provera injection, pill, menstrual regulation and sterilization. Equally important are the traditional methods of withdrawal, abstinence and breast-feeding which account for another 10-12%. Consequently our population growth is one of the lowest in the country.

Women

Many of GK's programmes are weighted towards women, as was stated in the 1977 *Progress Report*: »apart from nightguard duty, there is no single task which women have not been engaged in on equal terms and on equal pay with their male colleagues, be it the daily agricultural labour, health work, welding in the technical workshop, teaching or office work«. A woman riding on a bicycle was not a common sight in villages, or indeed in cities in Bangladesh. GK wanted to make a breakthrough, not for cosmetic reasons but from practical necessity, since riding to a village reduced unnecessary travelling time. To boost courage and create greater awareness, on 1 May 1977 23 women from the project cycled all the way to Dhaka to demonstrate solidarity with the women's movement all over the world.

Another indication of change resulting from GK's efforts was the disappearance of »burkas« (veils) among the female patients as well as among those women attending the vocational training centre. It was stated that »...recruitment of female workers for those types of work and training which do not require much school education, no longer poses a problem; indeed, we have to send many home for lack of places and during our recent procession to Shimulia sub-centre to commemorate the death anniversary of Nizam, many village women, as well as men, joined the ranks of the project staff«. *(Progress Report*, 1977) Furthermore, GK's work with women contributed to government decisions to recruit women for village work in family planning, and female primary school teachers.

Education

In addition to the children in the experimental primary school, village cooperative members (529), vocational trainees, basic health workers and some staff members benefitted from the education programme. Siblings, parents and friends of the children coming to the GK school also benefitted, since the students organised evening classes and once a week, guided by the teachers from the centres, conducted outreach classes in the field.

By 1980 the experimental primary school had had 218 admissions with 46 dropouts: 14 boys (13 of them aged 9-12, one younger) and 32 girls (26 aged 9-12, and six younger) dropped out. Of the boys dropping out two took up farm duties, eight became servants, three day labourers or assistants, and one worked as a cow-boy at GK. Of the girls. 17 cared for domestic animals, collected firewood and cowdung or looked after the home and small children, one became a servant, three took up paddy watering in the rice husking mill, three got married, one died, four worked in the Women's Centre, and three took up other activities. In fact seventeen of the dropouts (5 boys and 12 girls) continued occasional classes in the village and were in touch with the school. Another four girls working in Narikendra (Women's Centre) attended functional literacy classes conducted for the GK staff.

Agriculture

The agriculture programme included demonstration and training in improved techniques for crops, cattle, and fish and poultry, as well as helping to seek assistance in terms of cash, chemicals etc. The basic instruments for operation were the cooperatives. By 1980 there were 529 cooperative members in 47 cooperative groups, 34 male and 13 female. Of these 21 had 5-9 members; 13 10-14; 10 15-19; and three had 20-24 members. Loan utilisation in relation to land-holding was as follows:

number of loans taken:

Land holdings	1-3	4-5	6	7	total	and %
up to 1 bigha *	200	62	11	9	282	61%
up to 2 bigha	58	17	2	4	81	18%
3 bigha	48	22	5	2	77	17%
4 bigha	3	8	2	3	16	3%
5 bigha	4	2	—	—	6	1%

* one bigha = 33 decimal, or one third of an acres

Overall Impact

Gonoshasthaya Kendra's programmes produced a tangible impact on the local population and earned a reputation nationally and beyond. The population of the entire region of Savar, and the adjoining thana to some extent, benefitted from the health care and family planning services offered by the project. Women, landless and marginal farmers and their children were also direct beneficiaries of the project. GK's institutional facilities were being utilised for training IRDP workers, government officials, UNICEF health workers, medical students, postgraduate doctors and others. There was an increasing demand from government, voluntary and other organisations to send their workers to be trained at GK. Untrained and partially trained doctors and health workers were receiving educative information through the health bulletin.

GK offered advisory and extension services to various organisations, an indication of their appreciation of its experience gathered in the field. GK also received a Swedish Youth Peace Prize and Bangladesh Presidential Award for its success in development activities.

More specifically, GK started out as an experimental project intending to work for the basic health needs of rural communities in Bangladesh. Gradually, through experience, it investigated underlying factors which prevent proper application of health programmes and this took it to the areas of education, agriculture, vocational training etc. Poverty was identified as the root of the causes pertinent to underdevelopment, and its eradication received attention. Villagers came to accept the programme and to participate in health, family planning, vocational training, education and cooperative activities. One attempt at robbery at one of the sub-centres was averted through cooperation from the neighbouring villagers.

Despite all these encouraging events, the achievements cannot be described as a complete success. Vested interests persisted:
- the Nizam murder case could not be resolved;
- the land donor episode continued to haunt the workers.

Unless subtle changes created in the mind of the poor peasants can be translated into articulateness, confidence and action, tangible transformation will not take place.

The reduction of poverty was considered as an implicit objective of the project. Devices for its evaluation were not instituted and the validity of the results in this sense are therefore difficult to substantiate. GK however demonstrated commendable success in training paramedics, semi-literate boys and girls performing extraordinary works normally done only by the professionals. The school programme was designated by *The Guardian* in 1979 as »one of the boldest experiments in the world«. Though not all the programmes were economically self-sufficient, the stated goals seemed to be attainable.

General Conclusions

It has been said that adult education and development programmes as a whole are »merely ameliorative«, that they »take the heat out of the system« while failing to address the basic problems. A health programme may turn into failure if it does not consider the diarrhoea-malnutrition-poverty cycle. An education programme may prove ineffective if it puts more poor children out of school. The »success« of the Green Revolution is condemned since it widened the gap between the rich and the poor. Without considering socio-economic and political factors no such programmes can be judged to have produced the desired effect. GK was conscious of its role and ready to learn from its failures; this should lead it to be a real organisation for the people. Lack of motivated and properly trained manpower delays and hampers programmes. The organisational set-up, despite ceaseless effort, could not ensure people's full participation at every level of activity. Willingness to admit faults and to learn from mistakes is however a key to future success.

GK approached the task of developing villages on a basis of self-reliance, with programmes projected towards poor peasants who are the majority. Its staff thought they were not in a position to succeed unless they began by learning important lessons from the villagers themselves, poor and illiterate though they were. They thought it impossible to attain success in the intricate task of rural development without the flexibility to change predeterimined ideas and methods in the light of evolving experience. Realising the inextricable links between ill- health, illiteracy, malnutrition, superstition, unemployment, agricultural backwardness and poverty helped them to design a comprehensive needs-oriented scheme.

The Savar project demonstrated an eminently sensible approach to bringing basic health care and family planning services to rural people in a poor country. It used paraprofessionals for certain essential tasks conventionally performed only by highly trained and highly paid professionals. Contributions from individuals for health care removed the stigma of charity and created an awareness of the value of health in the mind of the beneficiaries. GK proved how a technical service such as health care could be conceived as part of a total package , in a country which is among the poorest in the world and with a conservative outlook among its people.

Training and education, as well as general perception of the existing situation, were incorporated in all GK programmes. One important lesson concerns demystifying technical and professional knowledge, putting it in the hands of ordinary people. An egalitarian culture was sustained by attacking the distinction between labour and mental labour. Professional knowledge and skills- differentiation did not create a hierarchical system in GK: the politico-administrative structure as institutionalised in the development system can therefore be challenged by the approach adopted by the Centre

Poverty is not a natural phenomenon. The causes lie in the structure of society. The poor are deprived of facilities vital for survival, including food, clothing, shelter, education and health. To have impact, an education programme must serve the poor majority. Adult education programmes designed for the reduction of poverty should not only consider social and economic rehabilitation of =peripheral man=, but take care also of his psychological and cultural revitalisation. If the existing system cannot accommodate this, the poor themselves will have to win power and make their own decisions. This can be gained through increasing awareness, in which education can play a vital role.

Adult education programmes like that of GK which honestly intend to do good for the majority can disseminate experience and lessons through a concerned circle, exchange ideas and develop empathy with organisations having similar objectives. This may finally convince and guide the government in implementing programmes. Though GK's programme expanded and was replicated in another area of the country, its broader impact depends upon political will and national policy. The existing political system did not seem to be helpful in promoting the concepts generated by GK. Finding the solution politically was beyond its capacity.

In terms of social transformation it is difficult to judge the impact of the programmes. Quantitative data are inadequate to measure social change. It may take a long time to initiate certain changes, but the time comes when a situation conducive to change is created, and transformation takes place rapidly. The work was directed towards creating that critical situation which is conducive to change. Its partial failure demonstrated the need for the change, and so reinforced the process. Adult education programmes at GK earned the confidence of the local people, won the attention of national and international bodies, and produced tangible change in the knowledge, attitudes and practices of the population they served.

Notes

Gonoshasthayakendra Progress Reports: April 15-June 20 1972; June-November 1972; December 1972-July 1973; July 1973-April 1974; April 1975; December 1977; August 1980.
Jayanta Kumar Ray, *Organizing Villagers for Self-Reliance: a Study of the Gonoshasthayakendra in Bangladesh*, December 1979.
B.K. Jahangir, *Local Action for Self-Reliance Development in Bangladesh*, December 1979.
Zafrullah Chowdhury, -Health Auxiliary Workers: Their Training, Supervision and Evaluation-, 20th International Hospital Congress, Tokyo, May 1978.
Susanne Chowdhury and Zafrallah Chowdhury, -Medical Highlights — The Role of Midwives and Paramedics in Voluntary Sterilization Programs-, Third International Conference on Voluntary Sterilization, Tunis, February 1976, published in the conference proceedings: Marilyn Schima and Ira Lubell (eds.), *New Advances in Sterilization*. Assoc. for Voluntary Sterilization Inc., New York, 1976.
Manzoor Ahmed, *The Savar Project: Meeting the Rural Health Crisis in Bangladesh*, Essex, Connecticut, Int. Council for Educational Development, 1977.
Susanne Chowdury and Zafrullah Chowdhury, -Tubectomy by Paraprofessional Surgeons in Rural Bangladesh-, *The Lancet*, September 27 1975.
Paul Harrison, -Windfalls under the Mango Tree-, *The Guardian*, January 30 1979.
Zafrullah Chowdhury, -Under the Law: In Bangladesh, GK occasional paper.
Nitish R. De, -Organising and Mobilising Some Building Blocks of Rural Work Organisations-, *Human Futures*, Winter 1979.
Rezaul Haque, -Incorporating the Concept of Adult Education in Paramedical Training Programme: Savar Experience-.
Malcolm S. Adiseshiah, -Functionalities of Literacy-, in Leon Bataille (ed.), *A Turning Point for Literacy, Adult Education for Development: the Spirit and Declaration of Persepolis* Pergamon, 1976.
Kamal Islam, -In Search of Relevant Health Care. with a View from Gonshasthaya Kendra-. Anthropology and Primary Health Care Symposium, Amsterdam, 1981, published by Holiday, Dhaka, 1982.

Chapter Eight

Organising Agricultural Labourers in Southern India: Association for the Rural Poor

Introduction

At the other end of the Indian subcontinent from Dhaka, Felix Sugirtharaj's account of the rationale for and approach to »development from below« of the Association for the Rural Poor (ARP) reads quite uncompromisingly, yet quite congruently with Haque's account of GK. There is no softness or sensitivity here about what might be the proper limits for education, no equivocation over the need for social change and the application of adult education to this end. Sugirtharaj is explicit about the ideology underpinning his and his co-workers efforts, and the strategy which derives from this. Despite concern about what he calls over-ideology »ideologies can and do play a crucial role in promoting social change as well as in perpetuating the status quo. In other words they are key instruments in promoting and retarding social change.« The inclusion of Alinsky along with Freire, Gandhi and Marxism as sources for ARP's »ideology for the transformation of unjust structures« suggests how naturally strategy and tactics flow out of the basic value mix drawn from Christianity and Marxism which also characterises Freire. Disarmingly, the author also reports that »truth to tell, we succeeded in making out only a few lines of Freire's writings, finding the abstract terminology unintelligible«. The method as described, however, with 444 basic or key words, does appear closely to follow the Freirean approach to conscientisation, leading on to direct action.

Sugirtharaj is quite clear that the problem of development is the problem of people's liberation: »groups have, therefore, to try to create revolutionary consciousness and a continuity of action that together change the oppressive structure«. As a »pragmatist with vision« he is convinced that there is a humanising and conscientising way to bring about radical change which does not cause destructive social disruption through violence, but does not on the other hand result in quietism and acceptance of the status quo. Real structural change is required, going beyond what is seen as the norm of voluntary development aid agencies, namely seeking »to improve living conditions by taking away a small amount only from the superfluous excess of goods of rich people«.

For Sugirtharaj the change agent, or animator, seeks to awake the masses from their »culture of silence« to see the world anew. »Animators do not believe in relief work, in compromises that betray the poor.« Like Haque, he is sceptical about politicians and political parties, which he finds suspicious of genuine grass-roots mobilisation, although the question of political affiliation is not ultimately dismissed. The articulation of »micro-group« projects into an effective force for change remains an unresolved problem in this paper. Sugirtharaj is scathing about the empty rhetoric of national intellectual leaders: »phrases borrowed from Marx, Ghandiji, Gramsci; Freire and others bring occasional applause but grass-root workers realise the emptiness of the show, and the first meeting to bring together different grass-roots workers becomes also the last«. The success of Sarvodaya Shramadana across the water in Sri Lanka is all the more impressive when cast in this light. There is concern too about reliance on overseas aid, described as »only a dream«, partly because of the compromises that this tends to involve, but also because »we have the right to use the resources of our own country«.

Among other themes from earlier case studies which find an echo here, one of particular interest, and almost global significance, is the identity and role of the middle class animator, which Sugirtharaj and his colleagues clearly were. They set out quite deliberately, from working with slum-dwellers, to mobilise and organise the still more deprived rural poor. Reference to the »House Church« recalls somewhat the spirit of Sarvodaya, as well as the determination in Gonoshasthaya Kendra to practise living congruently with the Centre's public purpose. The ARP workers pledged themselves to accept all hardships and difficulties in living with and working alongside poor oppressed villagers. No »hit and run« methods here: the animators stayed with the poor and shared their difficulties and dangers, it is claimed, in contrast to irresponsible activists or agitators who come in and stir up the people, then leaving them to bear the brunt of reaction and live with the consequences. Interestingly, however, Sugirtharaj concludes that the change agents, in not wishing to foster dependency, moved on too soon and left some of the new groups too weak and unsure of themselves. At the point where this particular narrative ends, it was decided to send one animator back to each old area to provide a continuing stiffening of resolve. The contrast with those educationists who determine to disengage before the point that learners draw particular conclusions and commit themselves to one or another action could not be more stark. Not only is the extrinsic end, and the ideology behind this, made explicit; the educator cum animator role is seen as carrying ongoing responsibility with the groups thereby mobilised into, in this case, local political action.

Summary

The problems are discussed of organising for development from below, via a diverse multitude of small groups, in the context of great deprivation and exploitation of the rural poor, and of scepticism about political parties and intellectual leaders alike.

Three phases of the work of the Association for the Rural Poor to organise agricultural labourers in Tamilnadu and Andra Pradesh, in Southern India, are described. They run from 1974 to 1977, from 1977 to 1979, and from 1980. There was a religious commitment to equality, and to working with people for their liberation , in circumstances of great economic disadvantage and exploitation, which had social and cultural as well as political and economic causes. The Christian basis for the work is explained, along with the influence of Paulo Freire, Gandhi, Alinsky and of Marxism. The process of politicisation and the objectives beyond the educational programmes are set out. The central purpose of conscientising for action was tackled through a system of key-words which is explained and illustrated. The philosophy and methodology of Freire were thus applied to altering the oppression and sufferings of the poorest, especially landless labourers and Harijans. Mobilisation and liberation from the local community level upwards were seen as the key to individual advancement through community organisation.

A summary of achievements lists very specifically the different kinds of gains made during the period studied. Direct costs are set out, together with the estimated economic value of the change brought about in each case. More broadly, the case study concludes with reflections on the state of organisation of rural groups, the role of change agents, and the relationship to political parties, the Farmers' Association, and overseas aid. The study closes with some reflections upon the need for conscientisation, and the limitations of functional literacy as a means of seeking to effect change.

Felix N. Sugirtharaj

The Diversity of Micro-Group Projects

There is no history. Life seems to stand still. The burden of misery, hunger and ancestral submission to Destiny crushes man by reducing him to the immediate tasks of animal survival, and shuts him off from any confrontation which exceeds the time limits of his vegetative concerns. Unhappily, this is how we must think of the fate of the majority of those people in India who are living below the 'poverty line'. They are still overpowered by magic, superstition, fear and sorcery.

In India the culture of silence is age-old and has taken the form of a caste hierarchy. This cultural oppression, product of the structural relation between dominated and dominators, must end. There are certain revolts against the dominating castes and classes, but these are sporadic. They indicate the emergence of popular consciousness but this is not enough. Symbolic action and temporary anger do not change society. Groups have, therefore, to try to create revolutionary consciousness and a continuity of action that together change the oppressive structure. The political parties are not doing it. They are content with symbolic actions and temporary anger, having neither the will nor the capacity to create revolutionary critical consciousness among the poor. Political leaders and revolutionary intellectuals try to create such consciousness through learned and not-so-learned articles. In a country like India where the majority of the poor are also illiterate these articles have little impact.

A number of institutions have been trying to impart knowledge of new agricultural methods to the small and the poor farmers. Their efforts also appear to have achieved little success, excepting cases where local people were involved in organising such programmes. They also suffer from the defects of government efforts: paternalism, control, and non-reciprocity between experts and laymen. A number of crisis theoreticians have come to the fore, creating social assistance institutions and employing armies of social workers. These will never solve the problem of development, which is really the problem of people's liberation. What is needed is not just finance or physical inputs to the poor, but going to the people to create critical consciousness and help them enter the struggle to change the socio-economic reality.

There are however various micro-level groups working with the people and organising them against oppression and exploitation. Some cover large areas of about 150 villages, while many limit their activities to about 10 villages. Some have been working for more than a decade, while a number of groups are very recent. Several such groups are formed every year. These groups have different ideologies. A few believe in the immediate annihilation of class enemies. Their attempts win immediate sympathy of the poor, but sympathisers soon become targets of police aggression. Some have a clear perception of the structural changes to be made, with a clear but broad leftist egalitarian perspective. Some are started by persons with rather romantic ideas of work, while others began their work only on a broad humanitarian basis.

Some groups organise people for implementation of progressive laws, like an employment guarantee scheme in Maharashtra, minimum wages acts for agricultural labour, laws giving land rights to the poor. Some have also taken up the harassment of the lower caste by the higher caste, while others avoid such social issues. Some groups engage in medical aid and education, others help people to obtain bank loans and government aid for different schemes. Many groups are taking up the issues of exploitation by traders, money-lenders, landlords, police, and other village officials.

Most of these groups have no direct links with any political party, although some individual workers have leanings towards one party or another. Political parties in turn look at the groups with suspicion. Local leaders of all political parties see them as rivals; political parties try to woo them at election times. Some groups take a strong stand and denounce all political parties; the more reasonable know their limitations and admit the necessity of political parties in present circumstances.

Problems of Organisation for Development from Below

The groups tend to be separate and scattered. Even those working in close proximity lack contacts and common strategy. Several efforts are made to bring together groups to form a common front, but most of these have failed. Intellectuals try to convene meetings of group leaders to bring them together. Any attempt on an All-India scale invariably fails. First the convenors know only of the large groups whose activities have received publicity. Secondly the absence of common approach between the groups makes it impossible to create an all-India platform. All-India meetings end with revolutionary speeches, resolutions but no action. Even at state level attempts to bring different groups together have achieved little success. Here again differences in approach and the methods of work get in the way, but the real hurdle is that the inviting agency has nothing to offer. Organisers of different groups may initially attend such meetings, but the really active among them gradually drop out, and annual meetings become a ritual attended mostly by the not-very-active. Some funding agencies also try to bring different groups together, also with no real result. Grassroot workers refuse guidance on perspective and method of work from the donor agencies, which are mostly foreign-based and unable to guide in respect of structural changes. Their meetings are mainly attended by their clients. They are comfortable, and nothing more.

Some universities and institutes of social work have also tried to build up a sort of co-ordinating organisation of micro-level groups, also with little success. Their meetings may start with an an elaborate and learned lecture by the chief of the Institute, or a professor who has never been at grass-roots for a single day in his life. Phrases borrowed from Marx, Gandhiji, Gramsco, Freire and others bring occasional applause but grass-root workers realise the emptiness of the show, and the first meeting to bring together different grass-roots workers becomes also the last. Several groups are led by Christian youths belonging to the different orders. Attempts are made by the senior persons of these orders to bring together organisers belonging to their order, and such attempts do have limited results. However, these gatherings are attended not only by non-Christian organisers but also by organisers belonging to different Christian orders.

All groups feel the necessity of having some contact with others, particularly in the present political context. The agency or the group which really desires to make an attempt to bring these groups together must have something to offer in return beyond finance. The agency must be ready to visit micro-level groups in the field, to organise tehsil or district-level meetings. A group which is not itself a grass-root organisation can do this work more effectively than any grass-root organisation. Small groups hesitate to attend meetings called by big grass-root organisations, as they are afraid that the latter will swallow them up rather than help them.

Revolution from below appears to be the only solution to the problem of socio-economic stagnation. Different grass-roots groups can definitely help to accelerate this process. They need bringing together on an information basis, and also to help the creation of groups in areas where there is no such work, not an easy task. Micro-groups have their vanities and prejudices. However, the fear of repression prompts them to seek wider co-operation.

It is possible in the beginning to create informal fronts of different groups doing similar types of work. This requires tact and humility. A genuine sense of friendship and lack of paternalism is necessary. Groups may develop new activities and perspectives in the process of coming together. This may take up a few years but will really help to build up people's power, without which there can be no development or liberation. This is not an easy task but knowing a number of grass-roots groups reveals rays of hope.

Situation in the Project Area

We found the following different land-holding circumstances in Chinglepet and North Arcot District, when we began our work in 1977.

(i) Feudal landlords, who do not physically participate in the major agricultural operations. Income from tenancy and feudal extractions is generally more than what one gets out of cultivating land. A feudal landlord might possess 200 to 300 acres of wet and dry land, sometimes more.
(ii) Capitalist landlords, who do not physically participate in the major agricultural operations but exploit wage labour in agriculture to a great amount of surplus. 50% of income may be derived through labour, the rest through rent. Typically 100 to 200 acres of good cultivable land is owned.
(iii) The rich peasant can be defined as one who physically participates in the major agricultural operations and is not content with supervision alone. Sometimes the rich peasant working on his own farm saves a considerable amount of money by his work.
(iv) Progressive farmers are those called capitalistic. This new class of farmers have become powerful through the green revolution and the benefits offered by banks and credit societies. Most are either Panchayat Presidents or local party leaders; many are staunch supporters of the Farmers' Association.
(v) The small farmer possesses five to ten acres of cultivable land, does most of his work by himself and hires wage labourers whenever necessary. He might possess additional acres of dry land and might earn more income through cash crops.
(vi) Marginal farmers might hold one or two acres of wet or dry land and live in perpetual debt.

How does political power and social status relate to the caste structures of these areas? With this information to hand, and studying the different kinds of agricultural labourers and their wage patterns, it is not too difficult to find out about the oppressive situation and the level of exploitation. The facts of injustice, atrocities to Harijans, raping of women, burning huts, beating up of labourers, etc. are collected to decide whether this area should be chosen for conscientisation or not.

In both the Panchayat Unions, the poorest of the poor consist of the agricultural class. They are regularly beaten up. Harijan villages have been burnt whenever there has been resistance by the landless labourers. Landlords control five to six Harijan villages and nothing occurs without the approval of the so-called goondas landlords. Poor wages are given to the agricultural labourers irrespective of Government wage fixation. The labourers neither demand nor protest for higher wages. Many cases of caste discrimination go unnoticed. Each rich peasant has at least four to five families as bonded labourers. Harijan women have often been assaulted and raped. Most of the landless poor simply accept this situation. Harijan youth who speak against injustices are often beaten and threatened. Lands allotted to the poor by the Government have been forcibly and illegally taken by the landed class. The backward villages are kept in inhuman conditions. House pattas are denied to many Harijan villages, schools maintained only to very poor standards. Intelligent children from the landless class are often discouraged from studying further. Though the Panchayats have provision for making available lights, drinking water facilities, burial-ground, etc. for the untouchable villages, these are deliberately denied. In most of the villages the elders or headmen are dancing to the tunes of the Panchayat Presidents from the rich caste Hindu groups. Many landless join hands with the rich and squeeze the poor with high interest. Often tenants are not allowed to continue to cultivate for more than two years. Tenancy rates are exorbitant. The agricultural labourers are so afraid of the police that they ran away at the very sight of them. After initiating an Agricultural Labourers' Movement in Tamilnadu the author moved on to the border area of Andhra Pradesh in March 1980, having found the worst problems existing there among the rural workers. When we offered to liberate them they welcomed us openly, offered food and shelter and began a dialogue, a sign of new commitment.

This border area of Tamilnadu close to Satyavedu was very well developed, with intensive agricultural activities. More than a hundred progressive farmers in this area possessed all modern machinery and skills for cultivating paddy, and were able to get very cheap acricultural labour from the borders of Andhra Pradesh. In Tamilnadu the agricultural labourers demanded an average daily wage of Rs 5/- whereas in Andhra Pradesh it was only Rs.2/-. Therefore the coolies from Andhra Pradesh preferred crossing the borders, and were satisfied even if they were paid Rs.3/- per day.

Out of the total population of 66,873, eight per cent of the people are small or marginal farmers, and agricultural labourers belonging to different backward caste groups. Most are employed for only 150 to 200 days a year. At other times half of them cut firewood from the nearby ests and sell it for a very cheap price. The others migrate to various parts of Tamilnadu, especially to the fertile parts of Chiglepet District, and earn much more than they are usually paid in Andhra Pradesh. Some engage in protecting mango orchards and collecting mangoes during March to June every year. But it is estimated that over sixty-five per cent of the poor in the Block live below the poverty line, earning less than Rs.21/- per person per month. They are clustered in one hundred and fifty villages in the Block of Satyavedu.

The extreme poverty of these people has been caused by the survival of feudalistic socio-economic structures, keeping them poor and ignorant of their rights.

Economic and political interest have manipulated the poor Harijans and other backward labourers according to their vested interests, never allowing them to participate meaningfully in the political process.

Most of the land in Satyavedu Block is either forest or barren and uncultivable waste, but over five hundred hectares of mango or cashew nut orchards are mostly owned by absentee landlords, who live in big cities such as Madras, Hyderabad, Tirupati and Chittoor. Sometimes profits from other business and industry are used to buy cheap land for mango orchards. A few rich feudal land-owners live mostly near the river bed where there is an ample supply of ground water. The other rich peasants are scattered all over the Block and are politically very powerful. Most of the small farmers possess dry land and a bit of wet land. They do cultivate bits and pieces, but always become the losers, and are fully controlled by the rich landed gentry. Land ceiling legislation during the emergency did affect Satyavedu as much as was possible. In many places landless Harijans received one to five acres of dry land, but not of a cultivable nature. Many big peasants also divided and sold some of their waste land. But those who own ten acres of land have not substantially contributed to agricultural development in terms of raising any bumper crop. Though the ground water is not very deep down it has not been properly used in dry areas. Therefore the non-progressive middle class farmers who received free government land still lived in poverty and debt. The landless of course suffered worst. Thus the rural rich controlled the socio-economic machinery in the whole Taluk by keeping the poor masses submissive and squeezing all they could from the labour force for their own benefit.

The Project of the Association for the Rural Poor

This case study explains the people's movement in terms of social and political transformation. More should be done to organise the unorganised rural masses before it is too late. Myself and a group of young people decided to leave the slums of Madras where we had been organising the urban poor, and work in the most backward rural areas of Tamilnadu because we felt that the slum-dwellers, though poor and powerless, were still more privileged than the rural poor. Secondly, most of the slum-dwellers were more interested in solving day-to-day problems such as getting water pipes, street lights and latrines for their slums, than in transforming their powerlessness into fruitful action to build up people's power.

Work among the agricultural labourers can be divided into three phases. In 1974, when five of us left the city, we were sure that the little experience we had had in Madras in the techniques of Community Organisation would help us to analyse the rural situation better and start an effective programme among landless agricultural labourers. From August 1974 to 1977, along with four other graduate animators, I organised landless Harijan agricultural labourers in one of the oppressive Blocks of Chinglepet District of Tamilnadu. By means of a regular conscientisation process which included adult education based on issues and key words having historical significance, study-circles to youth for politicisation, mass cultural action or drama programmes for demythologising the myths, taboos and caste values, leadership training for village leaders, etc., we were able to strengthen two thousand Harijan agricultural labourers into solidarity. There resulted a mass organisation in the name of the Rural Harijan Agricultural Development Association (RHADA) completely governed and controlled by leaders who had no status or power previously.

From 1977 to 1979 about ten animators went to another Panchayat Union of North Arcot District at the request of the agricultural labourers. During these three years we again conscientised three categories of powerless people in a class basis: landless agricultural labourers; marginal farmers; and the small farmers. The majority of the labourers in this new place also happened to be Harijans. From our earlier experience, we learnt many lessons and avoided making the same mistakes. In the second place we were clear about our objectives. As a result the long cherished movement of agricultural labourers came into being at the end of 1980 in the form of an Agricultural Labourers' Movement or Union on Tamilnadu level, with three thousand subscribing members, and a Head Office in Vellore, North Arcot District.

At the beginning of 1980, some of us left the old areas and scattered into interior parts of Tamilnadu and Andhra with the purpose of intensifying the rural workers' movement. This includes agricultural labourers, artisans, small farmers and other workers such as salt workers and quarry workers. I worked along with eight new animators in the border areas of Tamilnadu and Andhra, convinced that we would be able to make the same impact in Andhra and create a fervour among the rural workers to form a union of their own to fight for their basic rights.

What are the convictions under which we have been motivating the agricultural labourers' movement?

Faith & Ideology: Values and Objectives

Anyone conscious of the growing and alarming disparity between the poor and rich locally and internationally, and of the inhuman way the masses are marginalised and condemned to sub-human living conditions, cannot but look for alternative organisation of societies favouring greater justice and equality. This should not be the pre-occupation only of a few top politicians and international organisations; rather it should be the concern of every man and women who in everyday life sees and experiences exploitation and dehumanisation.

There is a growing concern regarding over-ideology among people concerned with existing social conditions. Ideology has become a very sensitive word. Both those who are afraid of ideologies and so react negatively to the concept of ideology, and those who speak positively, are well aware of the power of ideology in social change. Ideologies can and do play a crucial role in promoting social change as well as in perpetuating the status quo. In other words they are key instruments in promoting and retarding social change.

Ideologies promote social change by offering a system of social and economic analysis of the existing situation in a society, and by proposing objectives to be achieved, and programmes and methods of social action to be followed in achieving the objectives. On the other hand an ideology can defend and justify an existing social order. Everything in culture, in social and economic relations, in the state, in religion, in education, in mass and even in everyday life, has ideological dimensions. There simply is not anything that is non-ideological. It is a fallacy to speak of a non-ideological stand or a non-ideological approach to social, economic and political questions.

It is our own conviction that, as Christians, we can transform faith and suffering into a deeper knowledge of God's love as was the case with Jesus. Our struggle among the poor is to express the full meaning of the Gospel and to identify ourselves with those for whom Christ dies daily on the cross. Theology according to our understanding cannot be used to justify political situations, but to criticise such justifications. We see politics and economics as decisive spheres for Christian praxis.

As Christians with a concern for the establishment of a new world order, we accept that existence determines consciousness; if we do not create feelings of disharmony between existence and consciousness, social transformation within an ideological framework of love, justice, equality and freedom will be only superficial.

We do not accept that people's faith must pass through an ecclesiastical structure where only the ordained have the authority to decide for the people. We sustain the ideas of the 'House Church', which meets in insignificant places whenever necessary, accepting anyone who suffers, by the sins of society, to understand the cross of Christ in worldly spirituality and be liberated from submission to fate, apathy and exploitation. The concept of 'House Church' is to practise love and forgiveness in the context of inequality, dehumanisation, prejudice, envy and strife, and to create a new humanity as the foundation of the kingdom of God at hand. We pledge ourselves to work together with oppressed, both Harijans and Non-Harijans, and accept all hardships and difficulties to work with them for total change in their own environment. We seek no comfort, accepting simple village life according to the poor standard of the villagers, in the role of servants among the people. We would lead in the way of Christian discipline based on prayer, devotion and corporate worship and understand each other with love, trust and confidence.

To create an awareness in the minds of a landless peasant that receiving Rs.3/- per day for ten hours work is due not to fate or the existence of poverty in India, but to the poor understanding of his own existence (which he believes has nothing to do with the present oppressive organisational structures) we need a theory of social transformation beyond the dogmatic beliefs of religion, culture and tradition. Non-Marxist chance agents may try to change the consciousness of the masses to be in harmony with their existence. The revolutionary Marxist who believes in a classless society, based on State sovereignty, wants to create socialist consciousness by imposing a socialistic historical approach to struggle, without conscientising the oppressed through problematisation. These two approaches have been widely used on an international level to provoke the poorest of the poor for radical change. Most development agencies have become depressed because the first approach has not succeeded. The second approach has led to social disruption through violence.

It is in this context that I talk about creating and strengthening an awareness of social change among the voiceless through a pedagogical approach of conscientisation. As a pragmatist with a vision I am convinced of a humanising process enabling people to think rationally of existence without romanticism floating between consciousness and existence. Man, dehumanised by the rotten structures and system, is able to feel free and engage himself mentally and physically in a forward-moving determination of consciousness which is the solid foundation of a humanistic faith.

Four Sources of Ideology

We are convinced that with a methodology based on the philosophy of education for liberation, the poorest of the poor can think and act independently to change the consciousness of their existence, which has so far been based on distorted views of such capitalistic matters as: competition, divide-and-rule, cut-throat job opportunities, exploitation, myths, false views of caste degradation, discrimination according to skills, outmoded views of production, unequal distributive forces, nepotism, slavery, malpractices, repression, domination of private property, feudal values, animism, fate.

Our ideology for the social transformation of unjust structures has been developed from four sources.

1. Paulo Freire's approach to the liberation of the oppressed through a pedagogy that can make them feel they are not docile listening social animals but conscious beings with enormous self-expression. This has recreating effects on their oppressed existence within an oppressive historical situation. This methodology makes them critically analyse the society, generating a new culture of change through participation. Freire was the most important source of inspiration for the group although, truth to tell, we succeeded in making out only a few lines of Freire's writings, finding the abstract terminology unintelligible. We have met other groups which faced the same initial difficulty.

2. Gandhiji's philosophy of education based on the liberation of the rural masses. Purification of the self and totally committing oneself to the cause of the public.

refusing to comply to a system that perpetuates injustices, learning to suffer and struggle together for the creation of a new community of freedom and equality, and establishing 'commune' types of people's organisations; these are the essence of Gandhiji's precepts of liberation theory.

3. Saul Alinsky's technique of disorganising an organised community to build power has been used as a tactic to help the powerless to build mass organisations. The techniques of role plays, analysing case studies, group dynamics, creating new leadership, pressuring power structures through non-violent means, have all been used day-to-day for problem-solving and for the construction of people's power.

4. The Marxist tool of analysis is often used critically to assess the given situation of oppression and exploitation. With the help and co-operation of the local people a new ideological framework is formulated. If a proper societal analysis is made the vision of a new society will be very much socialistic, and these socialistic principles will not be a replica of any existing model. It is in this context of ideological socialistic principles that a revolution suitable to the given situation will emerge.

Politicisation: Strategies and Objectives

The situation of the Harijans, Adivasis and other backward caste labourers is no longer a local phenomenon. there are upheavals and uprisings all over the country, and signs that people are protesting against oppressive structures. By tackling deep-rooted caste and tribal problems, and organising the rural labourers on economic grounds, we are trying to create a mass class consciousness among the 80% of rural labourers to increase their struggles and intensify their commitment to total change.

If our goal is socialism, we must also transform the socio-cultural structures with all their values and norms. This means redefining people's culture and people's history, understanding the revolutionary potential already existing, and trying to establish a new society, demeriting the values and goals of capitalistic society among the voiceless in the rural areas.

Objectives in politicising people are as follows:

(i) To make agricultural labourers an integral part of society accepted as people with dignity and respect;
(ii) To build labour power through mass organisations for effective political, social and economic participation at the local, Block and District level;
(iii) To consolidate farm labour (the only labour force in our area) around economic issues based on day-to-day problems, and increase and solidify the bargaining power of those currently powerless;

(iv) To politicise and organise landless agricultural labourers other than Harijans to consolidate and participate in struggles of a class nature;
(v) To study, analyse and help to liberate all five categories of landless labourers: agricultural landless labourers on daily wages; agricultural landed labourers with small pieces of land but lack of material resources; permanent bonded labourers in the clutches of the big peasants and small farmers; semi-bonded and contract labourers and share croppers; marginal farmers and small farmers in perpetual debt.

Specific objectives laid down for the phase of work starting in 1980 were as follows:

(i) To continue with the programme of conscientisation to cover at least forty villages during the next two years and to make at least a thousand people conscious of their situation.
(ii) To establish action committees in each village and initiate dialogue on development, conduct regular training programmes for promising youth, and build new leadership for effective local participation.
(iii) To study thoroughly the economic conditions of the rural poor and work out a viable scheme for providing land, employment, technical education and other skill training for the landless on a collective and co-operative basis.
(iv) To acquire forest land wherever possible for the sake of the landless and reclaim the land on a collective basis for a 'Biological Farming System', with appropriate technological skills already available among the villages.
(v) To seek the co-operation of the government and other agencies wherever necessary to help the poorest of the poor out of inhuman conditions.
(vi) To concentrate on health education and women's liberation by appointing a few health workers, health education itself being a conscientisation process Village women to be specially trained to take care of village health needs, with emphasis on prevention rather than cure, and top priority to child care.
(vii) To help rural women to learn their rights and responsibilities by forming small women's groups in villages for various developmental activities; small sewing centres to be started.
(viii) To eradicate mass illiteracy, superstitions, myths, taboos, witchcrafts and such dreadful diseases as leprosy and tuberculosis, and to foster new communities of active citizens.
(ix) Ultimately to form a Landless Agricultural Labourer's Union and enable a few leaders to contest political elections at Block and Taluk level.
(x) To start commune-type collective and community farming and enable the poor to live self-sufficiently by raising at least one meal through poultry, piggery or sheep breeding. To provide credit facilities to small farmers to enable them to cultivate their land and raise a sizable income
(xi) To equip the leaders of the agricultural union to participate in politics and local village Panchayat elections, replacing corrupt and oppressive caste-dominated leadership

(xii) To organise short training courses and All-India Training Courses for activists in various action groups and voluntary agencies throughout the country.
(xiii) To organise seminars for intelligent social workers and agricultural experts on bio-dynamic agriculture, conservation of forests and soil, rural appropriate technology, etc.
(xiv) To create a link between different action groups in Andhra and offer help and co-ordination whenever necessary.

The Conscientisation Process

These procedures differ greatly from those followed by voluntary agencies for development aid. Generally speaking, such agencies seek to improve living conditions by taking away a small amount only from the superfluous excess of goods of rich people. They avoid trying to bring about real structural changes. Such charitable enterprises fall short of what needs to be done. To go about doing good in such a manner, without knowing what one is really un-doing, and to analyse the deeper causes and take stock of the consequences of one's action, can no longer be pardoned.

There is also the practice of some welfare programmes and religious institutions — albeit well-intentioned — to organise, for instance, batches of students who are sent to bring solace and relief to villages and slums, yet behave like visitors in a zoo. Realistic analysis must precede lucid action, if it is intended to effect transformation. This analysis should be radical and without compromise. It should be protracted and cover all different steps, including the motivations and implications of the whole undertaking.

**Conscientisation
as a Communication Process**

The work of the main animators has much to do with the processes of communication. It is of capital importance that, from the very beginning, they get sensitised to theories of communication and be made aware of some elementary concepts and basic problems. Subsequently, they will have to go on deepening this insight. They can never forget that it is through dialogue that one becomes more conscious of reality. The animators should develop their skill and competence at two principal levels. The first is their own relational behaviour within the group of animators, the first companions at hand. Direct and progressive experimentation is called for which has to be somewhat regular and methodical, using the techniques of group dynamics. They have to train and form themselves in a concrete manner, analysing the interactions at work in their own circle. The quality and efficacy of the whole conscientisation project depends partly upon a high standard of healthy internal exchange within this group itself.

The second level is know-how about the elementary problems and techniques of communication; from this knowledge will ensue the capacity to detect the real aspirations of the people, with appropriate methods of observation and investigation. Correct methods are always of a non-directive kind, based on dialogue and unbiased interrogation. One has to rely on the words used by the partner in conversation and to follow closely the internal development of his thought-flow. One has not to pronounce any judgement but on the contrary to respect the other person's own way of expressing himself, of construing his own logic. Afterwards there will be ample scope to make the communication more explicit and render it conscious at a deeper level. Each society is finally but a particular system of communications; the way in which the animator enters into contact with the population pre-determines a certain type of social relationship.

The practice of conscientisation differs from the economic, ritual, financial or political practices, in that it is a full practice of communication. The very milieu in which conscientisation is exercised and the place where it has its desired effects is in the broad field of communication. It intends to promote a reflexive and critical consciousness about the nature of relational systems that unite social partners at the different levels of their collective life. Conscientisation seeks to question and then modify established models which tend to freeze the existing systems of social relation and communication. This effect is produced by an action which of itself introduces a whole mass of new information in the field of communication. This should not be done in a rush. Therefore animators should acquire the ability to analyse and to deal at all levels with the network of forces that permeate the different symbolic layers of social relations.

The Key-Word Approach

A collection of 444 basic words revealed that the population was currently using a vocabulary concerned essentially with the social and economic order. This helped the main animators to gain an awareness of the current vocabulary and, thereafter, together with the village animators, to draw up a more thematic analysis of key-words and types of phrases.

Analysis of the selected linguistic theme made explicit:
— the obstacles opposing the solution of the problem
— the effective means for solving it
— the programme of corresponding actions; and
— the likely cost in money and time.

Here are some key-words and key-phrases which the group catalogued, and an example of the scheme of treatment.

Key Words

WATER	'In this bloody village, there is no drinking water.'
LOAN	'There's land, but no money to cultivate the land. Nobody will give a loan for digging of a well'
ROAD	'There's no road in this bloody village in the event of an emergency'
PRICE RISE	'When the prices go up, it is impossible to buy anything. How are we going to live?'
LIGHT	'There are some electricity poles but no bulbs.'
FAMINE	'Because of the drought last year people emigrated to town
EMPLOYMENT	in search of work'.
RADIO	'People talk of everything and nothing. If we had the radio it would be better.'
RATION CARD	'It's impossible to buy outside the ration shops. We'd like to purchase in these shops but there aren't any here'.
ELECTION	'It doesn't matter who wins the elections. We only eat according to the work of our hands. Each one lives for himself.'
SICKNESS	'What happens? For two days, I've had a head-ache. In the evening, I had a fever. Nobody bothers about me. The hospital's a long way off.'
POPULATION	'We made kids like pigs and there's not even room to sit down'.
UNTOUCHABILITY	'Look, Sir — If we give then a rupee they take it. But if we touch them they say »We are Untouchables«.'
SCHOOL	'Even though our grandparents had no education, we want our children to go to school. But we can't send them.'
AGRICULTURAL WORKER LAND	

Key Sentences

'Even though we work like bullocks from morning to night our salary hardly pays for one meal.'

'They say »He who cultivates the land is owner of it«. Now since my grand-father, we've worked this land and it doesn't belong to us.....They say they're going to give the land to the landless peasants. There's no meeting about this. I've paid taxes for 10 years and I've no right of ownership.'

Obstacles

Lack of collaboration amongst workers.
Workers from neighbouring villages are willing to work for less.
Ignorance of the legislation relative to minimum salary.
No other work possible.
Ignorance of recent agrarian reforms laws.
Loop-holes in the legislation and ways of getting round it.
Corruption.
Ignorance of administrative procedures relative to the claims to title and property.
Objections on the part of village people.
Ignorance of taxes paid but not registered.

Means

Meetings in the village create understanding and co-operation.
Meetings with neighbouring villages for agreement about salaries to be accepted.
Visits to Associations of agricultural labourers in other districts to become informed about their aims and types of action.
To meet the authorities concerned.
To know laws and procedures.
To know the Twenty Point Programme.
To know the law on agrarian reform and the land ceiling.

The Central Issue

Real development is liberation of the oppressed from the cultural burden upon their minds. The oppressed must first be prepared to denounce oppression in all forms. There is no real annunciation without denunciation. While getting prepared to end oppression the oppressed must be ready to build an oppression-free society, not just change places with the oppressor. Critical self-insertion into real action by the oppressed will then ultimately transform the reality of oppression.

The oppressed is made by the oppressor to believe that everything is in harmony with existence and in effect predestined. Unless a man believes that he can change his existence, he will never liberate himself. Since consciousness determines the existence of each individual, we emphasise the disharmony between consciousness and existence. A free person is able to develop all the faculties and find satisfaction in whatever is creatively done.

An animator is one who instigates the masses to wake up from their 'culture of silence' and see the world with new realities. He or she is a catalyser, designer of their destiny. Animators do not believe in relief work, in compromises that betray the poor. They identify and side with the oppressed. They are radical and committed to social transformation through political struggles. They stay with the poorest of the poor instead of using 'hit and run' methods. They are people-oriented, not target oriented They believe in a steady, slow and painful process of social change which is effective and revolutionary. They treat people as subjects of humanisation, not objects of welfare and relief. They work with the people, accepting their decisions and conditions rather than imposing their own intellectual ideas and goals.

They do not wish to stick to one place of work. Believing in the idea of a movement, they prefer to move from place to place, mobilising the unorganised and powerless. Thus they will never become emotionally attached to an area, committing themselves only to establishing justice and truth wherever it is needed most. We therefore commit ourselves to work in any area only for a period of four to five years, and during this limited time, to prepare local leaders to take up the work.

Results

Some Examples of Achievements

On entering the oppressed villages we faced severe problems. It was not easy to win the confidence of the poor villagers and begin a programme. In many instances we were suspected and forcefully rejected by the villagers. Landlords instigated landless Harijans to drive us away, branding us extremists. Despite this we began regular problem-oriented education after picking up key words frequently spoken by the poor. We lived in the Harijan villages and organised the people day and night. Popular theatres were held to highlight injustices. Men, women and youth were brought to understand the oppressive conditions, and as a result many changes took place.

So far we have trained three groups of people at different levels. First we gave training to nearly one hundred activists, community organisers and rural development workers from different parts of India, about half of them from church-related groups, using a well-defined syllabus relevant to transforming local situations. Participants came from Cross-Comprehensive Rural Operations Service Society, Andhra Pradesh; Rural Development

Advisory Service, Hyderabad; Rural Development Association, Midnapur, West Bengal; Society for Rural Education and Development, Tamilnadu: Houng India Project, Karnataka.

Secondly we trained village level animators or cadres and absorbed them into our groups for organising dramas, study circles and leadership training, for people at the grass roots.

Thirdly we trained about three hundred village leaders representing various action committees in three different areas, and helped them to safeguard their mass-based labour organisation. Discussions of case studies, role-plays, sensitivity training, leadership skills: these and other approaches were used to make leaders more articulate and less oppressive. These leaders have now taken charge of the agricultural labourers' movement in Tamilnadu, and to some extent have a broader perspective on planning and legislating for the labour force at local and national level. We also trained eight theological students during their internship training

We organised some twenty strikes for raising wages, redeeming illegal land holdings, and demanding justice against the beating up of Harijans and raping of women. In each strike at least ten to fifteen villages participated with firm discipline and a well planned strategy. Land reforms enjoyed top priority. Any available excess lands were either grabbed or asked for through legal means. Conciliation and negotiation during strikes occurred under the presidency of the police and the thashildar, so that the agreement was enforced.

Instead of protesting against small caste atrocities we gave top priority to economic issues to benefit the majority of the people. A Bhoodan land of 100 acres was released for the benefit of the landless, after a prolonged struggle with the rich landed peasantry, who first gave the land but took it back again, although the Government had registered it as Bhoodan land donated for the poor. In six villages people, mostly Harijans, received house pattas after hunger strikes and picketing in front of the Collector's or Welfare Thasildar's Office.

A Centre to train backward girls not only in embroidery but also in liberation and work skills was opened in 1976. Some twenty-five young women were trained in leadership skills, animation work, rural comprehensive health, etc. Most of them then worked in different organisations in Tamilnadu, promoting women's movements among the agricultural labourers. Nine non-formal schools were opened for children between the ages of six and fourteen where there were no schools. Two were declared to be exclusively for cow-boys. The syllabus was carefully prepared mainly to provide a vocational training which would enable them to remain in their village and work for the development of the rural areas.

There resulted fourteen groups working in various parts of Tamilnadu with the same ideology, methodology and programmes, with the aim of organising rural labourers. Ten bonded labourers were released during the emergency, through rallies and the support of the State Bank of India, Polur, Tamilnadu, and the Indian Overseas Bank, Vellore, Tamilnadu. Four rallies were organised to stress and demand a charter of ten demands of the agricultural labourers' movement at the District Headquarters in North Arcot and Chinglepet Districts. In each rally about 4,000 rural workers participated, showing their solidarity.

Other Specific Achievements

Wages were increased after prolonged strikes in different villages. The wage used to be Rs.3/- for men and Rs.2.50/- for women for all kinds of agricultural work. After three strikes wages went up to Rs.5/- for men and Rs.4/- for women. Through strikes the labourers learnt the techniques of bargaining, negotiating and demanding. People's organisation began to emerge as they learnt to suffer and also fight for their rights. A few bonded labourers were permanently released. In each Harijan village the new action committee began to make decisions affecting total village development. Youth became more courageous and encouraged others to protest. Children began to go to school regularly. Child labour was to some extent discouraged. People learnt procedures for solving their problems, meeting the Taluk Head and the District Head when emergencies arose.

Through the mass consientisation programme in two separate Panchayat Unions of Tamilnadu, we touched nearly 150 backward villages over six years. In each village roughly 50 — 70 adults, both men and women, benefited from problem-oriented adult education classes. They learnt at least to write their names and read a little and also how to solve problems themselves; their civic and political consciousness increased. They learnt to become more participative; to make decisions and stick to them; to protest and struggle to achieve social justice; and understood the process of forming Action Committees in order to go to the government offices and other places to demand what had been denied.

Estimated Gains and Costs

The total cost of the project was very small, with few visible costs beyond the time of the workers involved. The following is an estimate of expenditure on various forms of activity, and the economic value of the final gain.

Problem	Time Needed To Solve It	Estimated Expenditure Rs.	Estimated Economic Value of the Final Gain Rs.
1. Drinking Water The majority of villages have no drinking water (wells lacking or dried up, dilapidated, polluted). 45 cases registered 37 solved 8 pending.	6 months	98000	2500000

Problem	Time Needed To Solve It	Estimated Expenditure Rs.	Estimated Economic Value of the Final Gain Rs.

2. Cultivated Land

The Harijans had received some land with title of ownership through government regulation or under influence of the Bhoodan movement for redistribution of land; but the original owners had taken them back by falsifying the titles. Those plots had to be returned to the true owners.
186 acres reclaimed in 9 villages.
451 acres still to be recovered.   2 1/2 years   2 22 000   37 2 00 000

3. Land for Hut-Settlements

The Department of Harijan welfare had distributed rights of land-ownership to hundreds of homeless Harijans.
109 acres thus given.
 26 acres appropriated.
 83 acres still pending.   2 1/2 years   3 50 000   26 00 000

4. Electricity

220 attempts made at getting electrification of villages.
150 installations.
 70 pending.   2 1/2 years   37 000   4 55 000

5. Collective Radios

Radios supplied to Harijan communities which are utilised by caste people.
17 cases mentioned.
 5 settled.
 12 pending.   2 1/2 years   30 000   2 00 000

Problem	Time Needed To Solve It	Estimated Expenditure Rs.	Estimated Economic Value of the Final Gain Rs.
6. School Buildings			
A school meant for the Harijans, which was left half-finished and badly constructed, has been improved and completed. 7 cases. 4 realised. 3 pending.	2 years	20000	285000
7. School Children			
Programmes of cultural action have convinced parents to send 250 more children to school. Savings for education board.			500000
8. Loans			
Help provided for requests of loans e.g. to dig a well. 80 requests were made. 5 were granted.	2 years	25000	500000
9. Means of Communication			
The president of the Panchayat had sanctioned 3 new roads of about 3 kms to link the colony to the main road in 3 villages. 2 villages waiting.	2 years	18000	800000
10. Landworkers			
In various villages, strikes were organised to increase the pay-scale for both men and women. 60 villages made claims. 50 obtained increase.	2 1/2 years	180.00	55000000

Problem	Time Needed To Solve It	Estimated Expenditure Rs.	Estimated Economic Value of the Final Gain Rs.
11. Untouchability In 4 villages, Harijans were not allowed to cultivate land next to a village of high caste people nor could they cross that village. In 2 villages the situation could not be remedied.	2 1/2 years		
12. Creation of the Harijan Association 65 villages have joined to lay the foundation (700 members contribute). Their number is increasing constantly.			
13. Road to the Cremation Ground The Departments of Public Works and Social Assistance have sanctioned roads leading to the cremation ground for Harijans in five villages.			1500000
TOTAL:		818000	10410 5000

A Broader Appraisal

(i) We left both areas immediately after the formation of the Harijan Labourer's Association and the Agricultural Worker's Movement. Despite our conviction not to dominate the people's organisations we feel that we should have remained somewhat longer. The leaders of the movements requested us to stay longer and guide them but we refused and shifted to new areas. We felt subsequently that these new organisations lacked courage, discipline and perseverance. Some of the leaders became too parochial. Some were influenced by right-wing political forces. The Panchayat Union staff and the landlords in connivance with the Police used repressive measures. But the struggle goes on. We have now decided to send one animator each to the old areas to encourage people to stand firm and continue to struggle for their lost rights.

(ii) We used donations from friends in India and abroad to promote the movements. Now the labourers are asked to manage with their subscriptions only. This is the best way of making them self-sustained, but I wonder whether etc., without financial support. It is however only a dream to think that people's movements would grow only with foreign funds. We have the right to use resources in our own country; why should we not encourage these movements to do so?

(iii) In one area the Harijan Landless Labourers' Association is strong, in another the class organisation of the agricultural workers is stronger. But the Harijans do not want to join hands with the Agricultural Workers' Movement, though it is on the State level, thinking that their identity would be lost; they prefer to remain a caste organisation. In the Agricultural Labourers' Movement, it is too difficult to prevent the other caste Hindus from taking the leadership. The majority of the members are Harijan coolies, but they are often overpowered by the caste Hindu labourers; it is not possible to achieve an equal share in the governing body between non-Harijan and Harijan workers.

(iv) The Agricultural Labourers' Movement has to spread its wings all over Tamilnadu. This needs committed full-time workers to go all over the State and convince other agricultural movements to join. In many parts the small and marginal farmers are not mobilised, remaining outside the movement of the working class.

(v) The question of party affiliation often confronts the leaders. Both the left parties — the CPI and the CPM — want to enlist the support of the workers, and dialogue has started. The Organising Secretary of the Agricultural Labourers' Movement was himself a CPM worker. Whether or not it is too early to have this support is a serious question. The CPI and the CPM have no strong basis in the rural areas, and are afraid of these mass movements among the working class. At the same time they would like to draw the organisations under their party banners. To engage in a serious discussion with the party, a group of labour leaders has first to be prepared.

(vi) How to confront the Farmers' Association is another important question that has to be discussed on a wider level. The farmers are now trying to incorporate the agricultural labourers in their associations, telling them to join the farmers' agitations and fight along with them. But the history of the past three years shows that the agricultural workers have been almost forced to participate in the agitations of the farmers since most of them work on their lands. Sometimes they have been hired on daily wages to participate in the agitations. The majority who died in the police firing during the agitations happened to be the poor landless labourers who were made to stand in the front line and fight against the police and the bureaucracy. In this process of politicking, we, the leaders of the agricultural labourers' movement are becoming very nervous, finding it difficult to counter the Farmers' Associations with a clear-cut ideology. They cannot convince the small and marginal farmers in their movement to show loyalty to the movement rather than to the Farmers' Association. As animators we wonder whether we should infiltrate the movement of the workers and remain with them for a longer time, to motivate them towards right decisions and towards confronting reactionary forces in the disguise of radicalism.

(vii) So far we have not built up any kind of linkage among all the action groups and voluntary agencies working in different parts of Tamilnadu with Harijan and non-Harijan agricultural labourers. Some work on caste issues. Some work on class issues. Some use educational processes to organise tribals. Some are using a lot of economic input. But the problem is whether they are all really working for organising at the grass-roots, or for some other purpose. How to bring them together on a common platform and make them confront the reality of a People's Movement is still a question.

(viii) We have not built any financial base to enable the workers to continue their struggle. Since trade unions are prohibited from receiving foreign donations it becomes difficult for the movement to continue important programmes on a State level. Let us not forget that the members are mostly non-permanent workers with meagre wages. To subscribe heavily is therefore a problem.

(ix) Linkage with other workers' movements all over India has not yet been achieved.

Conclusion

Experience has proved that to confront India's conditions of extreme poverty, it is necessary to abandon the kind of misguided prudence with which welfare institutions carry out economic development projects, when at the very start they refuse to make a critical analysis of society. Development work must start by analysing deeply the clashes of interest, the social disparities, as well as the attitudes of people. One should not make do with humanitarian motivations or ready-made technical solutions, or stick to a party catechism. There is need for a real apprenticeship, which, in the first place, can be assured only by personal involvement in the struggle for social liberation. Secondly, this apprenticeship requires continuous reassessment on the part of the aminators, guided by a set of elementary categories. The concrete contents of these categories can hardly be taught beforehand or formally; they are operative and heuristic concepts whose function is pedagogical. To use them as topics for teaching in isolation from their dialectical moorings (viz., the permanent process of social action/critical reflection) amounts to falsifying the whole idea of conscientisation, which is a praxis, not a subject to be taught.

A Note on Literacy

Education through conscientisation cannot be ranged in the same order as a functional literacy campaign. The latter is not always a real criterion for development. Programmes of cultural action may include a minimum effort of literacy. The villagers' motivation for learning how to write the alphabet may not go further than acquiring the ability to spell and sign their names. A functional literacy campaign may indirectly facilitate the economic progress of the village — though with serious reservation about the usefulness of many programmes of functional literacy in the

Third World, especially if one considers the input of capital. They may perhaps improve workers' productivity or permit the implementation of particular projects with a net increase in profits, but it is certain today that wide- scale literacy campaigns are not of great practical use; they are too costly and provoke a good deal of frustration, if the programmes do not also entail new chances of employment. All this has already been said long ago.

What is the repercussion of literacy campaigns at village level?

The landowners who utilise the labour force will naturally profit most from an improvement of the labour force itself. If we made the simplest presupposition that literacy in general is but an acquisition of knowledge, and that development is but the logical application of that newly acquired knowledge, then progress should automatically accompany all programmes of literacy and one could imagine that the imparting of mere knowledge was a great power for progress. Reality is quite different. Objective knowledge does not alter the collective mentality, nor change a person's attitude. It does not help reorganise the pattern of social relationships. It also does not make sense to speak about literacy as a promoter of development unless the person acquiring literacy also gains an awareness of his increased responsibility and the ability to contribute to the building of his community. In view of the extreme poverty of the masses, literacy in India (where more than 400 million people are illiterate) should mean, first of all, an intense programme of liberation. Conscientising projects should therefore orientate programmes of literacy towards political education and use them as instruments to make the oppressed even more conscious about all sorts of alienation.

Appendix

Agricultural Labourers Union -Tamilnadu demands

1. To fix a minumum wage rate and to regulate the working hours as per wholesale price index. To facilitate the landless labourers and partisans to meet their basic expenses for their survival. The Government should take steps to implement the minimum wage rate and to see that men and women get the same wages without disparity.
2. Though there is an existing law to protect the tenant from not being thrown from the land it is not being practised. This law should be implemented and the tenants should have the legal right to harvest. The courts should refrain from pronouncing an intermediate stay on the tenant before the dispute is being settled.
3. If the workers die due to accidents during the work they should receive a compensation amount of R.10,000/- and in the case of losing any part of their body, an amount of Rs.5000/-. They should also receive money to meet the medical care charges in case of injury and a salary for the days when not at work should be in force.
4. After proper implementation of the Land Ceiling Act the surplus land which has been acquired and the forest and the government land should be made available to the landless labourers and the artisans. The Government should also give financial assistance to develop these acquired lands.

5. For the unemployed landless labourers and artisans the co-operatives should make provision to employ them in village development work. And also start a food for work scheme on days where there is no work.
6. House pattas should be given to the homeless and also houses should be built for them.
7. Education, hygenic conditions, hospitals, protected drinking water, electricity, road and transportation should be made available to the people. Children should be given healthy food.
8. The crop should be insured and when their crops die compensation should be paid out of which one third should be made available to the landless labourers.
9. The landless labourers, artisans and the tenants who cannot work due to old age should be given pension.
10. The nationalised banks should give financial support to the people to start small scale industries and cottage industries which will in turn develop the rural economy. Alternative arrangements should be made to discourage people from borrowing money from private parties.
11. The landless labourers, the artisans and the tenants should be brought under one banner and their problems should be solved. A high level delegation should find a permanent solution to their problem and should be implemented.
12. There should be an implementing machinery to implement the minimum wage rate fixed by the government.
13. For every 2,000 people a doctor should be appointed in the villages and the medical relief should be available to the people. Every district headquarters should have a fully equipped hospital to give medical aid.
14. The surplus land acquired under the Land Ceiling Act which is being distributed should be developed and loan facilities to buy pumpsets and to dig wells should be available on a low rate of interest.
15. The essential commodities should reach the people direct through the Government and not through middlemen. This should be put into practice and properly supervised.
16. The agricultural inputs like fertilizers, pesticides, agricultural implements and seeds should be made available to the tenants, marginal and small farmers at low cost.
17. The produce should be given supporting price which will match the cost of cultivation.
18. In areas where people depend on ground water, dams should be built without any profit motive to promote cultivation.
19. Lakes and ponds should be well maintained and it should also be seen that cultivation is not hindered.
20. In order to develop the rural areas the village Panchayats should be given more powers.
21. Untouchability, caste harassment, bonded labour, and oppressive structures prevailing in the villages should be eradicated from the very root. To this effect a binding law should be enforced.

Chapter Nine

Grassroots Changes — And Some Implications
What Was Achieved?

And How To Measure It?
Performance measurement has become a preoccupation of contemporary educational administration in Britain. Some see the quest for quantitative output and efficiency measures as a threat to quality and effectiveness. Others find it remiss of those in the education business apparently to have left questions of efficiency to its critics. Educational objectives by their nature tend to be complex: hard to define, hard to convert to specific, especially short-term, outcome measures, even when the will is there. There is a danger that in order to protect systems and budgets from immediate Treasury pressure, educational ends may get quite displaced by attention to more tangible, and measurable, means.

It is instructive to review these grassroots, development- oriented, case studies of adult nonformal education with these trends in mind. Participants in the research project were asked to look at visible costs and where possible hidden contributions, and to identify what was achieved by whatever criteria seemed relevant to the particular project. In the earlier set of large-scale, mainly government-led, projects, costs and benefits were superficially easier to identify, insofar as large administrative systems were available to collect and analyse such data. The measures may however be illusory: both because many of the costs were hidden in the form of unfunded, voluntary effort, and because the objectives and outcomes even in a literacy campaign may include long-term, transformational aspirations irreducible to specific literacy measures.

The objectives of the main actors in the different micro-level projects described in this book were generally more radical and ambitious, and sometimes also perhaps less tangible. Several also share the characteristic (claimed as a strength) of setting broad and general objectives which lend themselves to focussing and refocussing over time — see for instance Dighe's and the Shrivastavas' accounts. Of GK, Haque writes: »it became increasingly apparent with experience that health was not a problem to be dealt with in isolation, and GK began to expand, not to any pre-planned pattern but branching out at different points where it encountered opposition, in order to bring about necessary changes in response to this opposition.« Stacy observes that »in November 1973 the objectives changed«. Health »was no longer seen as the absence of disease« but, »involving the well- being of individuals in relation to their whole environment, would be improved only if that total relationship was improved«. Hence the shift, as in the Bangladeshi study, to a broader community development objective.

For all that, the seven studies do present some quite specific attempts to measure both costs and outcomes — on an aggregate, per capita and comparative basis —

and also to suggest the nature or level of hidden contribution in some cases. Thus Stacy drew upon WHO indices of infant mortality and morbidity, linking results with government health records. Comparisons were made via hospital and other records with other Aboriginal communities elsewhere in the Centre. Thus evaluation was mainly of what people had acted on rather than principally of what they had retained; the disjunction took the researcher into a quite different, anthropological, mode in an attempt to understand and so evaluate more comprehensively.

For the Tototo Kilemba project, as Clark explains »ongoing evaluation was deemed of critical importance to all concerned« and was a central consideration for each party. Statistical tools were deployed to measure the significance of changes in knowledge, attitude and especially behaviour, including for instance participation in community affairs as well as diet and other health-related behaviours. Indicators ranged from income to confidence. Controls and comparisons were attempted but proved »a somewhat risky business«; »in small, closely-knit villages like those on the Kenyan coast... in a sense there is no such thing as a nonparticipant«.

Further south, in Swaziland, Nxumalo's account is less sophisticated in terms of outcome measures, and is based on discussion with the various kinds of participants, and on project documents. It conveys the same »spillover« effect through the word of mouth of extension officers and others. Nxumalo lists a number of very specific results, mainly in terms of vocational training and the products of the individuals and groups trained, but refers also to broader purposes: promoting self-reliance and strengthening local capabilities.

Dighe writes about the problems of evaluating SEWA and its cost- effectiveness, in a context where »emergent needs and demands of its members have consistently determined priorities and the course of action«. Not only are inputs diverse and sometimes invisible; it is also »not possible to determine the economic value of eliminating the middleman, or assign a cash value to the psychological gain achieved through increased self-confidence and a sense of self-worth«. Some quantitative data were available but these missed the »important yet somewhat intangible gains«. »A purely quantitative assessment would however present a very incomplete and unbalanced picture.« This said, Dighe then proceeds to give quantitative measures for the SEWA Union, Banking Services, Economic Programme and other services, but returns to the perceptible, yet inscrutable, change in the status of women, in respect of which considerable success was claimed.

In the project in adjacent Rajasthan, Seva Mandir workers have specific measures of literacy attainment (15,000 men and 3,500 women) and functional knowledge learned and applied (over 500 families). The Shrivastavas however chose not to evaluate in this way, but in terms of the effect of the individuals and communities involved both in the villages and in Seva Mandir. »We all became stronger, more aware of our strength individually and collectively.« »We have seen individuals take hold of their lives, growing in self-confidence and feelings of self-worth«, women shifting their perception of their own importance vis-a-vis men — as Rajkumari bears witness in her testimony appended to the study. Note that survey measures were used in an attempt to guage the gains in this elusive area. As to cost effectiveness, the Seva Mandir workers produce compelling evidence, using international functional literacy as well as national school cost comparisons, of the efficiency of their work in terms of literacy gains.

Rezaul Haque, a qualified doctor, partly echoes the approach to evaluation in a health-centred programme of Stacy, a qualified nurse. His indicators include infant and overall mortality rates (with very significant differences) and impressive statistics for the efficiency and effectiveness of para-medics' performance via operations, outpatient services, bed occupancy rates, adoption of family planning practices, and so on. Haque also gives numbers for children in the experimental primary school, and for loans for agriculture via cooperative groups. A per capita calculation of GK's medical expenditure at 11.02 taka is compared with the national expenditure of 26.89 taka. Haque however gives no less importance to the liberation of women to ride bicycles, and the disappearance of burkas among the female patients.

In the final study, Felix Sugirtharaj largely ignores the subject of quantifiable performance indicators, making clear that the values, purposes and ideology that drove the ARP workers were of a different order than most education, literacy or health education programmes would seek to operationalise via performance measures. It is in a context of gross exploitation and poor understanding by the peasant of his own existence »that I talk about creating and strengthening an awareness of social change among the voiceless through a pedagogical approach to conscientisation«. Sugirtharaj does however tabulate a number of very specific attainments (and targets at that stage yet to be reached), establishing a claim for significant gains in estimated economic value for very low visible cash inputs. Reading his account of work in Tamilnadu and across the border, it is evident that neither lifestyle nor priorities lend themselves to the kind of measurement of outcomes now favoured for instance by managers of the formal education system in Britain. More More generally, though, this consideration of »how to measure it« should ring alarm bells with many readers. There is no excuse for retreating into abstractions when asked about value for money. But there is surely a danger that the more ambitious and more important purposes of adult educators at least within social movements will be squeezed out if there is insistence upon quantification of all outcomes.

The Main Achievements

Each reader may make a different judgement on which of these projects succeeded or failed, and to what extent. The individuality, and subjectivity, of each worker-contributor emerge through the accounts, to mesh with the judgements and feelings of each reader, as the latter draw on their own sense of values and priorities, their different experiences of their own society and their own work.

In a superficial sense the first account is a story of failure. Stacy shows how Pitjantjatjara participants in the Institute of Aboriginal Development's programmes did learn »the facts« of nutrition, but failed to alter their behaviour. Behind this she uncovers a fundamental difference of perception on the part of black and white players as to what the game was about. Aborigines sought a means for relating to Sandra Stacy and others, whereas the Institute sought to improve health among the Pitjantjatjara, directly or, later, via a broader community development approach. There were no identifiable gains according to the providers' performance measures, though there may have been important spin-off in terms of white society's gradual learning that, and how, Aboriginal people were different.

The NCCK-WEI project in Kenya was much more successful. It helped the providing partners — the National Christian Council of Kenya and World Education — to learn how to implement and evaluate certain kinds of nonformal education programmes. It also brought direct and tangible benefits to most of the village communities and groups involved. Noreen Clark is able to show quite clearly areas of gain in diet and other health matters as well as in knowledge, awareness and confidence, while identifying some other areas where there were no significant changes, such as owning latrines and boiling water. Income, and income-generating potential, showed clear and measurable gains. Evidently the gains were not limited to the individuals who took the role of student or learner, but spilled over into their immediate groups, and beyond that through emulation and contagion to others in their own villages and beyond. Not surprisingly, Clark herself therefore places much stress upon the group-building and participatory aspects of the project as major positive outcomes. She concludes with a discussion why such programmes are so rare, given the undoubted success.

The next two studies, from Swaziland and Ahmedabad, both present a number of economic and social gains. Each had very lofty ambitions. In Swaziland »by improving conditions here it was hoped to reduce migration to urban areas«, thus reducing the social damage caused to Swazi families and communities by the economic migration of men seeking work in South Africa. Perhaps this sensitivity to dependency reflected in the concern not to allow the (successful) Revolving Loan Fund to become more than a short-term bridge to conventional financial resources. Nxumalo finds quite specific and tangible gains in skills and their economic application, and reports that the project was quickly introduced into the other provinces of the country. On the other hand, »although the project was a success, in that those who took part earned income, politically it has not given women much awareness of their problems«; »it was unsuccessful in reaching the real target group« of the poorest people; and »it failed to involve the community during both the planning and the project selection stages«.

SEWA, an earlier established project, also recorded very specific gains in a number of economic areas, but the account conveys a much more encompassing sense of movement, with political, social and cultural dimensions containing and giving larger meaning to the specific material successes. SEWA effected a »cultural revolution in economic and gender relations«. The work of the Association included education and training in fairly traditional senses, as well as the overnight crash course in literacy so that a group of women could sign their names without error for a bank account. Dighe is also able to log specific successes in many other areas: Union membership numbers and attainments; banking services for women and the escape which these afforded from money lenders, middlemen and exploitative traders; maternal protection with dramatic reductions in maternal mortality; cooperative economic enterprises through which women felt empowered as well as becoming a little less poor; and perceptible improvement in women's status, with a tangible local impact, and beneficial influence well beyond the city of Ahmedabad.

The next two studies also read very positively in terms of what was achieved. The Seva Mandir account, like that of GK, stresses the organisation's own learning and growth in understanding, but always in an outward-looking rather than indulgent, self-preoccupied way. Thus, referring to changes following training sessions to the institutional structure, »workers became to a greater degree partners in decision-making. Our new strategy meant working with the neighbourhood groups.... we spent a lot of time organising village meetings before organising a programme«. Of particular interest in the Seva Mandir appraisal is less the specific attainments — mobile library scheme, wells dug, credit unions established, village health workers trained — than the conclusion that »adult education was still the best way to open up an area for further development work«. The Shrivastavas clearly placed particular value on the ongoing results of Seva Mandir's interventions in terms of the mobilisation of groups and individuals to pursue community development addressed at poverty and exploitation.

Gonoshasthaya Kendra, too, »sided with the culture of the poor«. Haque presents systematically and carefully the achievements of GK on a number of health and other indicators of development but there is no mistaking the large and integrative vision which continued to inspire GK workers: of social transformation of the immediate region and ultimately of the whole society of Bangladesh. The original focus of GK was on the basic health care needs of particular rural communities. Haque does not back away from measuring achievements by this criterion, but his own evaluation also reflects the shift to focussing on poverty as »the root of the causes pertinent to underdevelopment«, and so on its eradication. Success was not complete. Some specific issues of a local kind were unresolved, like the murder of Nizam. More broadly »the Savar project demonstrated an eminently sensible approach to bringing basic health care and family planning services to rural people in a poor country«. Yet »its broader impact depends upon political will and national policy«; finding solutions here was beyond the capacity of GK.

The final study is couched much more explicitly in terms of politics, ideology and the exercise of power. »This case study explains the people's movement in terms of social and political transformation. More should be done to organise the unorganised rural masses before it is too late.« Sugirtharaj, as »a pragmatist with vision«, writes of »a mass class consciousness... to increase their struggles and intensify their commitment to total change«. The spirit of this is well captured in the key-phrases and key sentences in his account. Achievements are measured in terms of groups trained and able to continue the struggle against exploitation after the animators have moved on; and secondly in terms of specific gains, for instance via organised strikes, in release from bondage, raising of wages, winning of land, and so forth.

Some Generalisations

How do we summarise the achievements documented through these seven accounts? It would be misleading to order them on a single scale from low to high success. This review has demonstrated the diversity of criteria employed by the different project leaders and members. The rueful learning of the Aboriginal account contrasts with the measured confidence of that from Kenya, but both can point to gains at one level or another; and none of the accounts claims to be an unqualified success. Haque's story is as open and self-aware as Stacy's. Despite a formidable basis for claiming quite remarkable success through many health care and other indicators, he concludes on a note of reservation concerning the limitations of a small-scale nongovernmental operation in less than favourable political circumstances. The ARP team in Southern India was in a sense too busy to worry with the kinds of measures used by Clark, Stacy and Haque. Their achievements must remain unmeasurable and unknowable. The further one moves away from specific behavioural outcomes of clearly marked off educational programmes, the harder does evaluation become.

One way of reworking the studies from this perspective is to create a framework for review. This might distinguish immediate, short-term, and tangible, probably also measurable, aims and achievements, from long-term, indirect, largely immeasurable and unprovable, aspirations and outcomes. The values and purposes infusing the work of all the groups described here have the effect of locating much of their attention towards the latter, larger, end: community development if not full-blown social transformation. This is not to deny a commitment to the individuals immediately involved, or a thoroughly professional preoccupation with the nuts and bolts of participatory methods of teaching and organising, as several of the accounts clearly show.

Running across this time dimension for review we might lay a second axis. This has to do with the range of objectives insofar as they pertain to the strictly educational, or attend rather to broader development objectives. The former might be expected to tend to cluster towards the more immediate end of the time-line, while larger development objectives couched in terms of the reduction and eradication of poverty, disease and exploitation would tend to sit at the other end.

There is not in fact a close correlation in this set of studies, in this sense, for several display a commitment to very specific and immediate »non-educational« changes — behavioural changes to do with income-generation or healthy diet and practices, for example. Conversely, there are indications in several of the projects of hopes and expectations for quite long-term, indirect and immeasurable educational gains which will in turn trigger off gains in the wider development sense. Several of the accounts are thus effectively essays on the theme of continuing, lifelong, individual, group and community learning, measured indirectly in terms of social, economic and political action rather than say by literacy rates. In this sense the dimension »education- development« begins to look less like a polarity, more like a loop or spiral.

Reviewing the set of studies in comparison with the earlier set of large-scale programmes brought together as *National Development Strategies*, it is self-evident that their geographical scope and impact is generally more limited. This represents a problem over which several project leaders, as well as authors of these accounts, worry: how to accelerate the replication and dissemination of local successes; and why is it that local successes are not more quickly taken up, or linked up with other grassroots activities, to accelerate the assault on poverty and exploitation? Of the seven projects presented here, five appear to have reached the most needy, »the poorest of the poor«, and to have achieved some clear gains. Though none is presented as an unqualified success, the majority appear to establish a firm claim to have directly addressed the problems of poverty and exploitation and to have made a direct and identifiable improvement among the key »target group«. The exceptions are the Australian example, and also the Swazi study, in that the latter did not on the whole reach the poorest people, for whom it was especially intended, though it brought about specific improvements among those whom it did reach.

Offsetting the limited numerical reach of these micro-projects is the greater depth and intensity of impact where the energies were thus locally concentrated. The governmental programmes which reached many people in the main achieved little for them, given the relative conservatism of such government-controlled initiatives (with the exception of that of the Nicaraguan Sandinistas). Each account in this volume betrays at the least a commitment to wide-reaching community development. Even the relatively apolitical studies with which the set begins acknowledge issues of political will and interest, and Clark sees resistance to changing the economic status quo as a major block to programmes like Tototo-Kilemba. The story told by Simanga Nxumalo is rather different, being quasi-governmental. Here the more intransigent political and economic reality concerned the country's powerful neighbour, South Africa. Within the tiny country of Swaziland the project was in fact taken up for extension to the other three provinces.

The remaining accounts are all quite frankly and progressively »political«, and radical, though their attitude and tactics to local and national political power varies. Sugirtharaj describes uncompromising confrontation — conscientisation and empowerment through action. Haque describes the careful balancing act performed by GK where »confrontation tactics have been skilfully deployed« along with selective cooperation, such that the Bangladeshi Government itself used some of the services of GK. Thus the conscientisation which dropped away from the original purposes of the Indian National Adult Education Programme (NAEP), for example, remained central to the work of these small, radical NGOs. The results for those involved and affected as teachers, organisers or »target group« members were often transformational. We may conclude with confidence that the effects ran much deeper than those of the large-scale governmental programmes where they were directly felt. What remains uncertain is how far the indirect influences may have spread. Stacy refers to some possible influence on the development of other programmes. Clark and Haque conclude that the efforts they describe could in principle be replicable and economical nation-wide. Sugirtharaj discusses how to link up and energise different isolated micro- projects so that the process of change can be accelerated. How to amplify the impact of minimally resourced voluntary efforts often of an antigovernmental kind — whatever the formal harmony with national development aims — remains a puzzle and a challenge.

By What Means?

Values and Commitment

Common to most of these accounts is a sense of commitment, often of dedication and self-sacrifice, on the part of the project workers. At times this took the form of sharing the lifestyle, hardships and risks of those with whom they were working — the women standing alongside the street traders who suffered harassment, the doctors who could have chosen the comfort of a city practice in Bangladesh, the animators who went out into the remote areas from Madras and lived simply with Harijans and other villagers. With Sugirtharaj this commitment takes on a clearly religious quality, and in other instances too, most notably GK, there is a conscious attempt at congruence between project workers' lifestyle and the causes promoted through their work — a form of communality and sharing that some who thought to work there could not stomach, and which had in part to be compromised. This sense of citizenship, ranging from self-sacrifice and guts to dedicated and sustained professionalism in often hard and unrewarding circumstances above all distinguishes these mainly nongovernmental efforts from the programmes of governments. Not surprisingly the large-scale project having the most similar flavour among those described in the earlier companion volume is of the Buddhist and Gandhian-inspired nongovernmental Sarvodaya Movement in Sri Lanka.

Strategies and Planning

Most of the studies reveal a sharp strategic sense and a capacity for strategic planning. Maybe the paucity of resources combined with the enormity of the task called forth this quality; maybe the sort of people attracted to such work tend to possess this kind of practical intelligence as well as sense of commitment. Whatever the explanation, one cannot but be struck by the awareness which the accounts suggest of strategic choices, and of the possible consequences of taking different paths, eg. in respect of working with government, or accepting overseas aid. Most accounts display a strong sense of the interconnectedness of policies and activities. This is reflected in awareness of the problems of what Clark calls categorical approaches to development: thinking and working in compartments. Generally the accounts display a keen sense of the interconnectedness and interactivity between different initiatives to help the poor or alleviate poverty: see for instance the note on literacy with which Sugirtharaj concludes his study. Along with this appeared to go a higher than usual level of self-consciousness of the role of the agency, its mission and evolving sense of purposes and priorities. Admittedly the very process of addressing these issues for the purpose of this research project may have exaggerated the phenomenon; but it does read as a distinctive and largely common feature.

Education in Context

The several accounts share a frequently unstated assumption that education belongs in its social, economic, cultural and political context. While there are distinguishable moments when the »clientele« are being educated or trained — sitting in some kind of classroom situation — all of the educational endeavour is presented as arising out of and responding to some felt, »non- educational«, need. (Stacy's is a fascinating account in which the »students« attended and studied but the effort »failed« in the sense that the need that was met was not that which the IAD had identified and set as its objective.)

Some adult educator readers of these stories may have asked themselves from time to time whether these are accounts of adult education at all. Some stories, like Stacy's, Haque's and the Shrivastavas', set out the pedagogy and supporting arrangements for teaching, or fostering learning. One can visualise classroom scenes, lamplit on rush matting, interwoven with teacher- animator training, as illustrated by keyword, case study, role- play and other recognisable methods. Dighe and Sugirtharaj on the other hand tell a tale of social, cultural, political and economic action in which the educational effort is woven into and often hidden by the organising, striking and so forth, although from to time a particular training or education event stands out. For these workers the whole programme or campaign is educational, and the whole of education is also political. Villagers and street traders moved in and out of more formal learning situations when a need presented itself for this.

Where there was a problem as between the felt needs of the poor and the purposes of the educator animators it may have been from the more political, or professional, aspirations of the latter. Stacy reveals this most clearly, but Sugirthiraj remarks that among reasons for moving out from the slums of Madras to the most backward rural areas was that »most of the slum-dwellers were more interested in solving day-to-day problems such as getting water pipes, street lights and latrines for their slums, than in transforming their powerlessness into fruitful action to build people's power«. In the rural areas, it seems, an easier marriage was struck between working for empowerment and winning some immediate gains to sustain hope and commitment among the poor. These exceptions should not hide from us the more salient fact that most of this nonformal education took place »in context«, in response to the clearly identified and felt needs of the poor. It was a means, not an alternative, to action. The contrast with much Western adult education which seeks to tempt and persuade »hobby-type« students into taking more sustained and serious courses could not be clearer. The »register mentality« is conspicuous by its absence.

Indigenous Resources

Another common theme is the recognition of indigenous wisdom, knowledge and ability, and the attempt to build on this in the different development efforts. It takes the form, most commonly, of an account of the way middle class animators learnt from village people, and were forced to re-examine their own assumptions and prejudices. for example about family planning. In the Savar project GK built on the traditional knowledge and standing of dais to reduce mortality at and around childbirth (as well as trusting formally little educated youngsters to become highly successful para-medicals on barefoot doctor lines). Noreen Clark shows how the **harambee** spirit was tapped in the NCCK-WEI project, recalling the »problem of success« of adult education for women in Kenya described in the companion volume to this one. Sugirtharaj, looking at the same point from a different direction, attacks the »visitors in a zoo« phenomenon when (middle class) students come to look at villagers whom they are meant. but are ill-equipped, to learn to help.

Stacy shows how the Institute in Alice Springs sought to build on the »information, feelings, interests and beliefs« of Aboriginal people. The Tototo-Kilemba project tried to start with existing groups, and to ensure that those selected for training were chosen by the people themselves, and not selected from above. The workers at Savar did likewise. Writing about Appropriate Technology, Nxumalo shows the importance of designing in accord with traditional ways of cooking, and reports how local chiefs were used to facilitate adoption of change. She, like Clark, holds that failure to bring about change is a failure not of the people but of the adult educators and the project. Dighe, echoing Nxumalo, tells how organisers found the use of traditional cultural gatherings a more effective entry point than formal meetings. The combination of this culturally sensitive approach with real valuing and practice of participatory methods, at all stages from identification of needs and participants through to programmes of education-and-action, appears to be an important factor in the success of these grassroots efforts. As was suggested in the earlier companion to this volume »perception of and respect for indigenous knowledge appears a litmus test for the potency of adult education for development...«

Organisation and Management

It was suggested above that workers in these micro-projects displayed considerable strategic sense, and also a high level of self-awareness about their own organisational arrangements, and about the learning and development of their generally small nongovernmental organisations. In the first study Stacy shows how interdepartmental tensions about priorities crept into IAD as it grew. Haque relates the successive reorganisations which GK planned and underwent in an effort to remain responsive and effective. Reorganisation sits alongside reconsideration of objectives and priorities; or rather, frequently does, or should, flow from it. Several of the studies document major reappraisal, leading to a shift in style or direction; Seva Mandir is a good example, as well as GK and, in terms of the decision to shift from the slums to the remote countryside, the ARP workers of Tamilnadu. Reference has been made already to the quality of »congruence«, trying to practise what one preaches, notably in the stories told by Haque and Sugirtharaj. This together with the capacity to redesign and redirect the organisation and its activities emerges as one of the strengths of these micro-projects, when set alongside larger governmental projects which are often so heavily departmentalised, compartmentalised, and hard to turn around.

Relating to Government

Nongovernmental organisations committed to adult education for development commonly experience delicate and strained relations with government, especially where their language runs to people's movements, conscientisation, organisation and so on. Sometimes those leading adult education movements find themselves to be not only radical in their attitude to the status quo but revolutionary in the implications of their position for the socio-economic and political structure. An obvious example was the experience in Brazil of Paulo Freire, doyen of many adult educators in the South. On the other hand most NGOs acknowledge the power and resources of the State, and the desirability of giving people access to their rights as citizens.

Less dramatic than confrontation and imprisonment, there is the problem of departmentalism or sectoralism which tends to characterise large formal organisations. Even small NGOs wrestle with the problem of segmentation of effort and perhaps rivalry between different sections and groups, as Stacy and Haque in their different ways suggest. Generally however these accounts are characterised by an integrative, relatively wholistic, approach to development, and frequently by capacity for shift of effort as new needs and understandings emerge. Thus working with government can be problematic even for the relatively apolitical, as Clark's and Nxumalo's studies reveal.

None the less, taken as a set the stories suggest that NGOs can achieve much by working with government while retaining their distinct identity and freedom of action. The tightrope is best illustrated here by Haque's account of the ways that GK did collaborate for instance in some areas of training, while retaining a strong identity, freedom and sense of purpose. The Centre was recognised and honoured by the Government while its members deliberated on the alternatives for radical or revolutionary reform of the State and society, recognising for their part, as Haque points out, that the causes of poverty lay in the structure of society. The same issues appear and are acted out in several of the studies at the local level. Particularly in a large country and administrative system like India, the maybe radical and imaginative policies for development at the centre may be thwarted at regional or very local levels, where officials may be lazy, corrupt, incompetent, or simply conservative. Dighe and Sugirtharaj, for example, illustrate how organisation as a form of adult education can assist citizens to know and to claim their rights.

Aid and Resources

It may seem odd to leave to the end the matter of resources. Yet this accurately reflects what most of these studies suggest: that for the workers in these small, minimally resourced projects, money was not a major consideration — contrast for example the contemporary story of adult education in Britain. The efforts of socially committed voluntary workers, and similar dedication and effort by modestly paid workers as at GK, clearly represented a massive hidden resource. This in turn mobilised community effort among the poor in their roles as learners and as agents in their own enhanced self-reliance and development. Where case study authors are able to put together figures of visible costs, income from all sources is modest and output generally quite remarkable, looked at in comparative per capita terms. If only, it is said or implied, government would support this kind of work nation-wide, development would accelerate dramatically and poverty and ill-health be reduced at costs which even the very poor nations — like Swaziland and Bangladesh — could afford.

Several of these micro-projects attracted national government funds by one means or another: direct grants in the case of the Swazi study, indirectly for contracted work in Bangladesh. Most of them were also beneficiaries of overseas aid, whether from governmental sources or from nongovernmental aid agencies. In Swaziland the funding sources were mainly governmental and relatively speaking quite substantial. The Kenyan study is itself an account of partnership between a US-based NGO (WEI) and a national NGO, the NCCK. The SEWA, GK and Seva Mandir projects all benefitted from overseas aid as well as moral support. They share however a commitment to self-reliance, a wish not to become dependent on charity and in turn to foster dependency in the people they work with. According to Dighe there was initial union and philanthropic support of various kinds »but by and large most funds were self-generated. The operating principle was that while the seed capital might be provided by an outside agency or agencies, it is participation of the members which provides the necessary impetus... to make it self-sustaining.« Similarly the Revolving Fund in Swaziland was for short-term loans only, for fear of causing dependency.

In the Savar project Haque stresses that »contributions from individuals for health care removed the stigma of charity and created an awareness of the value of health in the mind of the beneficiaries.« Haque shows proportions of recurrent expenditure recovered through service charges to poor recipients — concepts and proportions which would gladden the heart of a British cabinet minister or institutional head! Sugirtharaj is yet more explicit on dependency and aid matters. Note that the ARP workers felt they had left some areas too soon, so concerned were they not to create dependency on outside agents. Subsequently they created a visiting animator support system »to encourage people to stand firm and continue the struggle for their lost rights«. He goes on to say that ARP used donations from friends in India and abroad, but »now the labourers are asked to manage with their subscriptions only«. He wonders where they will manage all that is needed in a self-sustaining way without financial support. »It is however only a dream to think that people's movements would grow only with foreign funds. We have the right to use the resources in our own country; why should we not encourage these movements to do so?« This spirit of sturdy counterdependency surely constitutes a daunting challenge to those in British adult education, even allowing for the differences of tradition and circumstance.

Some Recurring Issues

We may now briefly recap upon several themes which are common to most of these grassroots »micro-projects«.

Many share a claim to have made a quite deep and significant but very local impact. The problem of replication and diffusion therefore presents itself. The different, part-governmental, character of the project in the anyway very small country of Swaziland sets it apart. Clark and Haque each allude to the latent viability of the respective approaches nationally or still more widely, while recognising likely political reservations about going this way. The different Indian studies make reference to national networks, support and dissemination within the NGO sector. One gains an impression of an invisible college of grassroots workers maybe influencing and permeating national thought and practice in the Gandhian tradition, though on the face of it the scale of the country, its bureaucracy and its development problems is totally daunting. Sugirtharaj's study is particularly interesting in this respect, for he considers at some length the need for and the problems bedevilling any attempt at linking up these diverse, often highly suspicious, microgroups. He is scathing about national intellectual leaders, academics and politicians, including those working for overseas aid agencies. Each in their different ways lacks credibility. Yet other micro-groups are looked upon with jealousy as possibly seeking to take over. This account sharpens the differences between micro- and official, national development, projects: the commitment, dedication and effectiveness of the former to achieve powerful results, but the fragmentation which, unless something like Sri Lanka's Sarvodaya can draw them together, appears to be a condition of life.

The relationship with authority and the power of the State is another recurring theme, as we have already seen, both in respect of the tendency of the State to fragment development efforts in ways which do not accord with the needs and realities experienced by the poor, and in terms of a »fear of infection«. Voluntary workers value their autonomy and separate identity, and are often very hostile to the corruption or mismanagement which they discern in government, especially perhaps at the local level. They are therefore loathe to be identified and confused with agents of the State — an identification which might prove fatal to any attempt to work with the more exploited and marginalised. On the other hand the State deploys resources needed for development, and which belong to citizens, including the marginalised, as a right. Many running such projects, in countries of the West as well as the South, have to learn to sup with a long spoon, and to balance cooperation and confrontation in their dealings with officialdom at whatever level. Sugirtharaj again provides a particular additional note, with his discussion of the issues at stake in considering joining a (radical) political party; for the suspiciousness of the State as actually experienced at local level runs equally through the experience with politicians generally. In Britain, of course, adult education is an occupation rather than an organisation, although it shares some characteristics also of a »movement«. The question therefore really only arises in certain sectors such as the Workers' Educational Association, or different of its branches.

Another theme identified above is that of dependency: whether on the State, on overseas or other voluntary or charitable aid; or on the educator/animator who is so often an intruder, invader or insurgent into a dispossessed community — which is often, and uncomfortably, called in the West a »target group«. There are good reasons for concern. It is not unusual for strong, radical, maybe indigenous, voluntary groups and organisations to come to rely on the State grants which they win in times of relatively liberal government, then to become partly paralysed as acquired dependency makes them vulnerable to official bullying and blackmail. Grants may shrink; become project-specific; be tied to stringent audit requirements; and paid retrospectively. NGOs may come to depend on drip-feeding which is conditional on compliance. The experience of Aboriginal Health and Legal Aid Services in Australia illustrates the difficulties and dangers. In Britain reliance upon short-term »pump-priming« and similar forms of aid is loosely similar.

In Britain, with the »rolling back of the State«, including the Welfare State, a debate has developed about the proper role of charity and aid. This is not the place to consider the role of international aid and development agencies, particularly bodies like the IMF and the World Bank, beyond asking who benefits and who pays in the long run from these international and intergovernmental arrangements. Nor will we consider as such the role and impact of voluntary international aid on a mass, pop-folk basis, led notably by Bob Geldorf, interesting and maybe significant as it is in the »selfish eighties«. The charity debate turns on what it is necessary and proper for the State to undertake, and what complementary role the voluntary sector and charitable efforts might play. A liberal concern in Britain is that voluntary citizen efforts, particularly in the way of charitable giving and voluntary welfare effort, are coming to fill a space illegitimately left by the contracting State rather than complementing, filling out and innovating around a core of State support which is seen as a fundamental human and citizen right. The witnesses for radical adult education in the South in this book use charitable aid with caution, and look rather more to individuals paying their way than to State support as protection again dependency. Is there a moral for adult educators and kindred voluntary sector workers in Britain? Should the fight to retain proper welfare support in the public sector be wedded to a more sturdy attempt to re-anchor at least radical adult education, education for change and development, in private and voluntary effort?

A fourth recurring issue is the style and values of a voluntary organisation — often the basis of its strength and distinctive character. This encompasses a capacity to reconsider objectives, priorities, structures and means, by reference to the essential values and purposes of the association or group. This book is full of examples of flexibility and adaptability; of the centrality of values, commitment and a sense of mission, and of the willingness to reconsider and change the means in the light of experience. Associations like Seva Mandir, IAD, GK and SEWA are patently »learning organisations«. Within them personal growth, learning and change appears almost a condition of survival.

Alongside this there is a sensitivity to what might be called authenticity and congruence: practising what one preaches; living a lifestyle congruent with the purpose of alleviating poverty and confronting inequality. As Rezaul Haque, for example, explains, participative democracy is practised in the management of the organisation alongside participatory methods in the training and teaching of GK. Noreen Clark suggests that congruence and integrity are virtually preconditions for success, in identifying where among the village projects leadership selection was manipulated — and where the project was least successful. Allied to the subject of participation in that of learner motivation. Most of these studies reveal a high level of consultation, needs identification, and indeed personal identification with the oppressed, on the part of the educator-animators. Read together, and well illustrated for example by Clark and Nxumalo, they suggest that success correlated highly with amount and quality of »client« participation at all stages of the work. This needs-led and participatory approach meant that health or education projects were not presented or experienced thus; health and other educational activities came and went within a multifaceted community development project as they proved relevant and necessary. The »bums on seats« register mentality, and the constraints this imposes on both providers and learners, well known to British workers, seldom features in these accounts. An exception is where Seva Mandir worked within the NAEP framework but had to go it alone in the more remote and needy areas. Here government requirements could not be met. Registers and audit requirements proved incompatible with remote hamlet living.

Another recurrent theme was referred to in the opening chapter of this book as the middle class dilemma, something which has been discerned as a weakness, or at least a paradox within his position, by some critics of Paulo Freire. It is evident that the workers described in these studies are mostly well educated, loosely speaking middle class, generally »self-appointed«, change agents or catalysts intervening in the lives of socially, economically and culturally very different, impoverished others. The stories echo with more or less explicit reference to the learning, sensitising processes undergone by these socially committed middle class workers; to the confrontation with their own prejudices and assumptions, the continuous reminding and relearning which was involved. In turn they echo this same theme from several of the large-scale studies in the earlier volume — notably from the Republic of Korea, Nicaragua and Sri Lanka, where »the remaking of the middle classes« was in evidence. With few exceptions (perhaps for example the period of Red Guard ascendancy in China) this circumstance of »middle class« leadership within society, including conscientisation and mobilisation for social, cultural and political change, appears unavoidable: some from among the already empowered assume part of the task of fostering the empowerment of others.

Is this a problem? It may be, on the one hand, if such activists become paralysed by self-doubt about their legitimacy, or undermined on these grounds by those with an interest in resisting change. More obviously it can be a serious problem if it disables and continues to disempower the marginalised within their »culture of silence«. The case studies in this volume however point to ways of avoiding these dangers: valuing and building on indigenous wisdom; taking steps not to create dependency; and supporting local leadership chosen by and for local communities.

Finally, many of these studies call attention to the crucial role of women in development in different countries of the South. Often this coincides or intersects with health care and health education programmes. In terms of distinctive women's roles this has to do with childbirth and early infant as well as maternal mortality, as in the GK and Seva Mandir projects. More broadly it concerns matters of diet, child welfare and health care of young children, for instance to deal with diarrhoea. More broadly still it concerns preventive health and hygiene practices affecting whole families and communities. Since women tend to be the carriers of water and firewood as well as the feeders and nurturers of families, they are directly involved in several senses. Thus we read here of boring tubewells, constructing more efficient cooking stoves, learning about a balanced diet, consuming more eggs and chickens.

Such a list, if completed there, should outrage adult educators — perhaps now men as well as women — in the South as well as the West, who object to women's education being restricted to women's domestic roles as functionaries of the social order for child- bearing, child-rearing and family nurturance. The studies in this volume generally run much further. Several describe training to equip women with vocational or income-generating skills. Often these are explicitly intended to enhance their economic independence and self-reliance, individually or as members of a group or village community. In some instances there is the explicit purpose of raising women's status and bargaining power vis-a-vis men, especially their own husbands, as Haque makes clear: »at the root of the weak position of women in village society is their dependence on father or husband for their daily food. A degree of economic independence would greatly improve their lot... By providing village women with a money-earning skill, GK aimed to strengthen their position at home, give them some respite from exploitation, and enable them to enlarge their spiritual as well as economic contribution to the community.« Education for women's empowerment also distinguished the work of SEWA in Ahmedabad, where women were helped to organise for economic and other ends by a wide range of means. For Seva Mandir the central purpose of the activities described here appeared to be the empowerment, especially of women, for broad-based political and social action via groups: Rajkumari's autobiographical account tells it all.

What Are The Implications?

For The South

The causes of poverty lie in the structure of society. At its sharpest and most radical, grassroots adult education for development means supporting people's movements for social and political transformation. This is a role nongovernmental organisations uniquely, if sometimes hazardously, can and do play. As *National Development Strategies* showed, it is very unusual for governments to be willing and able to adopt such a role, or even willingly to tolerate it in the voluntary sector. Movement-type programmes like some of those described here can play a very significant part, by way of developing models, attempting innovation, serving as resource centres, goading and persuading those running the larger governmental programmes to take some risks, as well as directly conscientising, mobilising and partly empowering communities at a local level. In Tamilnadu ARP workers provide internship training for theological students; in Savar GK did the same for medical students. Thus can there be some linkage and spillover into the formal educational, government-supported, sector as well as, for instance, by running experimental primary schools on new lines which government may choose to emulate.

Clearly adult education alone is not enough. However, defined and treated as it is in some of these examples, it is not necessarily just the dependent variable of Western sociological texts. The Shrivastavas conclude that it is in fact the best intervention or start-up point for locality-based development efforts. All of these studies reveal a mature awareness of the connectedness necessary for development programmes to succeed; and of the separatist departmentalism which bedevils and disables so many government-led development efforts. Adult education may thus be a sharp tool for development, wielded by grassroots organisations, but whatever the definitional boundaries it can be only one tool among several in a larger kit.

If integration is a keyword, so are some other well-worn terms like participation, conscientisation or consciousness-raising, organising, mobilising, and empowering. Recognising and valuing local indigenous knowledge and experience, listening to the community and following its lead, as in the choice of local leaders for animator training, proves essential. Imported models from abroad are unlikely to flourish, but this may also be true of models imported from elsewhere in the same country, across cultural, ethnic or other social divides. Interventions and attempted programmes not anchored in people's felt needs are unlikely to last long. Education and training as such succeed most powerfully when they are sought for a purpose: like Dighe's women in Ahmedabad who sat up all night to be able to sign for a bank account in the morning. As International Literacy Year approaches in 1990, there is a danger that the big battalions at national and international level, tempted by the international versions of register and league table mentalities, will (again) decide what literacy is good for whom and (again) ignore the lessons of the SEWAs and ARPs.

We have noted the salience of »integration« if adult education is to work as part of a development strategy; and noted too a tendency in the voluntary committed sector as represented in these studies to work strategically, flexibly and wholistically rather than in watertight compartments. Connect this with the theme of global interdependency in Chapter One. Until recently ecological concerns have tended to be defined in the South as a luxury of the North. More recently still disasters like that at Bhopal, and the 1988 floods in Bangladesh linked with deforestation, as well as dumping of toxic wastes in poor countries of the South, have brought home to South and North the interdependency of the global community. It seems probable that adult educators in the South, who have already in India for instance supported the women's tree-hugging campaign, and sought compensation for Bhopal victims through international collaboration, will take a lead in promoting a global ecological perspective for intelligent development, both through classes and courses and by more direct action.

For The West

It was suggested in the earlier set of studies of adult education and the reduction of poverty (p.6) that »the bell tolls no less for the West than for the South«. There was reference to the emergence of a new unemployed underclass in post-industrial societies. Gelpi, Gaventa, Jackson, Lovett and others have addressed aspects of this. The Croom Helm Radical Forum on Adult Education testifies to growing interest and concern in these issues, as does the International Series to the growing internationalism in adult education; see for example Tom Lovett et.al., *Adult Education and Community Action*, published in this Forum in 1983, which concludes, apropos Northern Ireland, with the »urgent need to create such an alternative adult education system or institution, committed to the twin processes of uniting the working class and resolving the deep social, economic and political inequalities and injustices inherent in this society, through collective action...«

The post-industrial West is of course vastly different from the countries represented in this book, Australia apart, but lessons as well as comparisons can still be drawn. The more radically inclined adult educators in Britain tend to live uneasily on the fringes of regular educational institutions, or to move outside them. Unease with the »register mentality« is sharpened by the grip of the »iron eighties« on performance of adult education sub-systems within the regular structures of university and local authority education. Quantitative measures and budget constraints wedded to the experience, threat or rumour of curriculum interference have tended to erode the fact or sense of free space, the cracks and crevices within which innovative and »non- hegemonic« work can be carried on. Within departments and centres cautious managers may look more closely at their own radical fringes. Those who wish to play safe have additional arguments to cut back the more politicised work, which might attract unwelcome political attention. Self-censorship may make formal censorship unnecessary.

The predicament of »adult education for a change« in Britain thus appears delicate. A centralising State which uses power quite openly in the interest of those who are propertied and more affluent, and is determined, while exercising close control and accountability, to reduce public expenditure, has little time for the »liberal tradition«, at least at the taxpayer's expense, and less for radical adult education which alerts the dispossessed to the causes of their disadvantage and organises them to redress it. On the other hand development, understood as economic development, is more acceptable. Phrased as self-reliance, local economic development or enterprise, linked perhaps to small and medium enterprises (SME), technological innovation in backward sectors, or as the regeneration of the inner cities, it can unlock funds from many government sources in England and increasingly also in Brussels.

One lesson from the South is to cast out some of the sterile and paralysing dichotomies still found in the baggage of the liberal tradition. Notable among these, reflecting the light from these several case studies of adult education confronting great need and adversity, are the dichotomy between the »liberal« and the »vocational«, that between »education« and »training«, and that between »education« and »action«. The workers portrayed in this book would have little patience with such distinctions, since their work is characteristically needs-driven as well as anchored in a set of values which tend to straddle and synthesise each of these polarities.

Adult education in Britain has increasingly »migrated in« towards the mainstream of educational provision. It has also won a new salience with the demography of the late eighties and early nineties: falling numbers of young people coming out of the school system into higher education and onto the labour market, with resulting under-supply in both these sectors. Suddenly the twin but often contrasted educational purposes of equity and economic growth appear to come together. The keyword is Access.

Formal, and increasingly formalised, adult education is thus winning a place in the sun: warmed by the promotion of equity through access to post-secondary education for adults as well as by government favour for helping to meet employers' needs. Looked at »from the South«, this appears both good and bad. Good because at last the unhealthy, subtly class-conscious division between vocational (useful) and liberal (decorative) education is beginning to dissolve. Bad because the whole effort of publicly funded adult education may be sucked into a monolithic growth- oriented system of provision which does little or nothing about structural inequality, little or nothing for the impoverished and marginalised. Nothing, that is, unless the tatters of »trickle-down theory« can be patched together. The evidence for this in contemporary Britain is unconvincing.

An alternative approach for grassroots development-oriented adult education in the West is to look to social movements as adult education, and to ask how the educative dimensions of learning- through-action in the Women's, Peace, Green and other areas of community purpose and action may be enhanced. Adult education through these forces is unlikely to attract public subsidy, and may be denied the name of education by those in formal adult education. However the education for development which undoubtedly occurred in the stories told above seldom attracted direct State support; nor did its activists agonise long about whether it should be called education (or training). They did however undoubtedly cause to occur a lot of (immediately applicable) adult learning. Looked at thus, the »liberal dilemma« begins to look more like whether to remain within the formal system, and promote access within the older, more individualistic, paradigm, or to move out »into the cold« and work for »transformational collectivities« of the kind found in these micro-projects of the South.

For Internationalism in Adult Education

The evidence of the seven stories in this book is that internationalism can be a significant force to support local, radical efforts. At the same time several of the accounts reveal far- sighted concern not to become dependent especially on overseas aid. If the sample here is any evidence it seems unlikely that grassroots workers in such projects will follow their governments into that international indebtedness and dependency which has become a critical problem for South and North alike. Different authors are understandably proud of the recognition that the work of their small agencies has won abroad, as well as elsewhere within their own countries. Several refer to visits to the project, international recognition, or visits out of the country by their own project workers. Some link with local universities, specifically for internship-type training but also thus into the international world of scholarly and professional exchanges. The Kenya project was an example of international partnership. International aid was crucial to the partly governmental project in Swaziland. GK arose out of aid from expatriates in the war of liberation and like the Indian projects came to rely upon help from friends abroad in the form of agencies like Oxfam, but sought always to set a limit and term to aid from outside. None of the accounts suggests that alien models or assumptions were imported (the special case of the Pitjantjatjara nation excepted), although the ideas and spirit of Freire, in particular, respect no frontiers.

As the world becomes aware of barely comprehensible problems like the damaged ozone layer and the »greenhouse effect«, the destruction of and threat to the unexplored natural laboratories and reservoirs of tropical forest, polar region and deep ocean, this intelligent internationalism provides a heartening note with which to end a set of stories of local struggle in the face of apparently insuperable problems. The spirit of purpose and optimism which pervades most of these accounts tends also to characterise the international meetings of ICAE, Unesco and others referred to in Chapter One. The cost, and distraction, of »globe-trotting« and conference-going deserves the closer scrutiny which it now appears to attract. But these studies also suggest that if local communities are to be empowered in this new »global village« (paradoxical term indeed) very effective international collaboration is essential, for adult education as more obviously for environmental groups. They also suggest that the West can learn from the South as the pendulum in the West swings back somewhat from the individual towards the collective end of the spectrum of educational endeavour.

ADULT EDUCATION AND DEVELOPMENT

would like to invite its readers to become authors of the journal. Possible themes of future issues are:

- culture and communication
- international cooperation, partnership and professionalism
- evaluation and research
- orality, literacy, print and electronic media
- technology: innovations, transfer and alternatives
- global and local concerns: environment and peace
- teaching, training and learning
- informal and traditional sector
- production and income generating activities in and through education
- non-governmental agencies in adult education and development
- government: recognition of and responsibilities for adult education
- health and nutrition
- innovations: concepts, strategies and projects
- case studies and country reports
- university adult education
- agricultural extension and rural development

and material for our regular Literacy Corner and North-South-Forum.

For further communication, please contact the editor at the address on the inside front cover.

For Product Safety Concerns and Information please contact our EU
representative GPSR@taylorandfrancis.com
Taylor & Francis Verlag GmbH, Kaufingerstraße 24, 80331 München, Germany